PRAISE FOR
The Mass Psychology of Addiction

"Dr Johnson offers a most welcome contribution to the field of addiction. While describing basic information and explanations for the topic, Dr. Johnson attempts an integrative approach based on neuropsychoanalysis. His scholarly and personal accounts enrich the awareness needed to address such a challenging topic. Suitable and friendly for all types of interested audiences; the reader will find this a unique account."

—Daniela Mosri-Flores, PhD, professor of psychology, Universidad International, Mexico City; editor, *Neuropsychoanalysis*

"Dr. Brian Johnson's *The Mass Psychology of Addiction* is a groundbreaking and timely examination of one of society's most urgent public health crises. This book offers a transformative exploration of addiction, delving deep into its psychological, societal, and structural roots. Johnson's innovative integration of neuropsychoanalytic treatment is nothing short of revolutionary, bridging the often-overlooked gap between mental health and neurobiology. His approach provides a holistic framework that reshapes how we understand and treat addiction—both in clinical practice and beyond.

"What sets this book apart is Johnson's focus on trauma and intergenerational abuse as central drivers of substance use. He reveals how untreated psychological wounds fuel addictive behavior, compellingly illustrated through real-life patient stories. These case studies are more than just examples—they offer profound insights into the intricate relationship between personal history and addiction, empowering clinicians to develop trauma-informed, empathetic care strategies. Johnson's writing makes it clear that to truly treat addiction, we must address the underlying psychological pain, not just the symptoms.

"From a research perspective, *The Mass Psychology of Addiction* opens entirely new avenues for exploration. Johnson brilliantly merges individual psychological frameworks with broader public health perspectives, urging scholars to view addiction through both lenses. His sharp critique of industries and government complicity in perpetuating addiction makes a bold call for systemic reform, not just individual treatment. Johnson's advocacy for a public health approach to addiction is not only innovative but crucial. His blending of personal narratives with societal critique offers fertile ground for new interdisciplinary research.

"But Johnson doesn't stop there. His visionary ideas for public policy are nothing short of radical. His proposal for an 'Alcohol Purchase License' and State Addictive Drug Centers (SAD Centers) seeks to dismantle the underground drug industry and shift public consciousness toward greater accountability. These pragmatic harm-reduction strategies offer bold solutions to reduce addiction's grip on society. Perhaps most provocatively,

Johnson challenges us to confront the economic and political systems that profit from addiction. His call for personal responsibility alongside systemic reform is a powerful wake-up call to both policymakers and the public. Being passive, he warns, only perpetuates harm.

"*The Mass Psychology of Addiction* is a masterful, multilayered analysis that combines compelling personal stories with a scathing critique of societal complicity in addiction. It offers fresh perspectives for clinical practice, research, and public policy, and it will undoubtedly change the way you think about addictive disorders. Dr. Johnson's work is poised to make a profound impact, not just in the treatment of addiction but in how we, as a society, confront it. This book is a must-read for anyone committed to addressing the addiction crisis at its core."

—Stephen Faraone PhD, distinguished professor of psychiatry, State University of New York Upstate Medical University, Harvard Medical School

"There are many good books that teach and excite you but few that change your thinking. *The Mass Psychology of Addiction* by Dr. Brian Johnson, a psychiatrist and neuropsychoanalyst, is one of them. It deals with addiction in everyday life—from nicotine to pain pills and heroin. The science is wide-ranging, from the latest in biology to new understandings from neuropsychoanalysis. These deep, well-integrated insights are presented in a jargon-free style, making the message resonate with sophisticated clinicians as well as laypersons. Each major theme is brought to life with powerful, sometimes raw, real-life stories (including very personal vignettes), and all of this is beautifully wrapped in layers of science and humanism. The villains who destroy so many lives are the exception: They are called out in stark, unsparing detail. This is a must-read for anyone interested in the power of addiction and how to break free."

—Mantosh Dewan, MD, president, State University of New York Upstate Medical University, SUNY distinguished service professor

"In his book, *The Mass Psychology of Addiction*, Dr. Brian Johnson draws on his many years of experience as a board-certified addiction psychiatrist, scientist, and analyst [to present] a compelling model of the psychology, neuroscience, and interpersonal/cultural aspects of addiction. Dr. Johnson has been a pioneer in the field of addictions, with extensive scholarly work and research. He was the first to have a published report on the psychoanalysis of a man with active alcoholism. He has also researched new ways of understanding the neuroscience of addiction and pain and was the first to link abnormalities in the opioid receptor system with difficulties of fibromyalgia and autism.

"As a very busy clinician working with addicted patients from the lower economic strata, Dr. Johnson has personal insight into the consequences of addictive illness. Indeed, the most shocking aspects of this book are the devastating personal and societal [effects] of addiction that Dr. Johnson elaborates in stark and blunt terms while adding numerous case studies from his rich experience to drive these points home. More controversial and yet fascinating is his argument of how the denial system of addictions permeates beyond the suffering of individuals to the larger society, shaping societal values, attitudes, and language that support the denial system. He goes on to argue that a combination of denial and the profit motive have created an unconscious system of collective collusion among medical professions, government, and corporations to perpetuate certain drugs such as tobacco, alcohol, cannabis, and controlled prescription substances.

"I recommend this book to anyone who wants to learn more about addictions from someone who has unparalleled experience and expertise in their field. Whether you agree with all of Dr. Johnson's arguments or not, this book is guaranteed to challenge what you thought you knew about addiction."

>—**Robert Gregory, MD, professor and former chair of psychiatry, State University of New York Upstate Medical University; chair of the College of Research Fellows, American Psychoanalytic Association**

"Gratitude to this tenured professor of addiction psychiatry for sharing his decades of experience in terms we all can understand. In *The Mass Psychology of Addiction*, Professor Johnson has courageously addressed topics often considered controversial in academia. The book offers provocative discussions such as Dr. Johnson might have with his many medical students, encouraging them to think critically about addiction and its impact on patients and society."

—**Terrance M. Bedient, FACHE, director, Committee for Physician Health; vice president, Medical Society of the State of New York; former chair of Alcoholics Anonymous**

"Dr. Brian Johnson's book analysis of addiction is as foundational as Sigmund Freud's *Interpretation of Dreams*. It is both practical and inspirational for those in the helping professions and those who are helping themselves to become free from addiction and denial."

—**Harold Bursztajn, MD, cofounder of Program for Psychiatry in the Law, Harvard Medical School**

The Mass Psychology of Addiction
by Brian Johnson, MD

© Copyright 2024 Brian Johnson, MD

ISBN 979-8-88824-548-4

All rights reserved. No part of this publication may be reproduced, stored in a retrieval system, or transmitted in any form or by any means—electronic, mechanical, photocopy, recording, or any other—except for brief quotations in printed reviews, without the prior written permission of the author.

Published by

3705 Shore Drive
Virginia Beach, VA 23455
800-435-4811
www.koehlerbooks.com

The Mass Psychology of Addiction

BRIAN JOHNSON, MD

VIRGINIA BEACH
CAPE CHARLES

Table of Contents

Introduction 1

PART 1: THE ADDICTIVE DRUG INDUSTRY 7

Chapter 1: Killers in Bedroom Communities, Street Dealers across the United States 8

Chapter 2: Tobacco—A Key to Understanding America's Addictive Psychology 21

Chapter 3: How the Industry Takes Advantage of the Two Reasons for Addiction—Psychological and Due to Brain Changes Caused by Drugs 32

Chapter 4 Defining Addiction 50

PART 2: HOW ADDICTION WORKS 57

Chapter 5: The PANIC System and Abusive Relationships 58

Chapter 6: Opioids as a Replacement for People 67

Chapter 7: Opioids 101 72

Chapter 8: Autism and Fibromyalgia as Disorders of the Endogenous Opioid Hormonal System 82

Chapter 9: Ignoring the Function of Opioids to Regulate Closeness, Pharmaceutical Dealers, The Right to Pain Treatment Movement 94

Chapter 10: Benzos and SSRIs 118

PART 3: TREATMENT 127

Chapter 11: Tricks and Tips for Counselors, Sensitive Treatment May Get You in Trouble 128

Chapter 12: Neuropsychoanalytic Treatment of Addiction, Upstate Medical University Addiction Medicine 193

Chapter 13: What Are the Outcomes of Neuropsychoanalytic Treatment of Addiction? 197

Chapter 14: Conventional Treatment of Addiction 203

Chapter 15: One Physician's Experience of Attempting to Provide Principled Leadership 213

PART 4: PUBLIC HEALTH SOLUTIONS 221

Chapter 16: Alcohol Purchase License 224

Chapter 17: Government Distribution of Drugs: SAD Centers 232

PART 5: MASS PSYCHOLOGY 235

Chapter 18: The Awful Reality of Addiction 236

Chapter 19: Choosing a Different Path 245

Chapter 20: Up Against the System That Sells Drugs 259

Epilogue: Recovering from Denial Requires Courage, From Internal Change to Action 261

REFERENCES 264

Notes for Chapter 13 275

Introduction

May is an elegant sixty-year-old woman. She had been a highly respected history professor at an Ivy League school for over three decades. She wore dignified, stylish clothing and had strong opinions that she was not shy to express in the classroom or during friendly debates with her colleagues. She went to conferences and spent several semesters abroad. She had a clean, beautiful house. She published papers in top journals.

Most of her colleagues did not suspect May's secret. She was an alcoholic. May often went home after teaching and downed a pint of vodka. She hid her empty bottles in the bottom of her trash cans. Occasionally, she drank just before she hopped into her car to drive to work. When she was having a particularly difficult day, she slipped into bathroom stalls at the university and snuck swigs of booze from a flask she carried in her purse.

If you were connected to May and learned of her addiction, what would you think? What would your first reaction to her alcoholism be? Would you assume she lacked moral fortitude? Would you think she was weak, had no self-control, or was disgusting? Would you shame her?

Even if you consider yourself evolved enough to understand that alcoholism is a disease and expressed compassion for May, would some of your negative associations with her drinking also be lurking around in your unconscious? Our cultural norm is to shame people with addiction issues, to judge them harshly, and to believe those who don't have these issues are somehow superior.

Odds are, if you live anywhere in the United States, you have one or two degrees of separation from a family member, neighbor, friend, or colleague who struggles with addiction. On any given day in mostly every small town, suburb, and city, multiple Alcoholics Anonymous and Narcotics Anonymous meetings take place. There are currently 69,812 AA groups and 27,677 NA meetings in the United States.

AA is the most effective intervention for alcoholism.[1] But most people with addiction don't go to meetings. Something drives them away from experts in recovery. May would go at times but not sincerely engage. She harbored a never-spoken sense of superiority. She hosted an AA meeting at the university. But she never had an AA sponsor.

Alcohol kills 4 percent of the US population.[2] May's addiction, as is the case with most addicted individuals I have worked with over a half century, is rooted in problems that are inherent in our society, history, families, and communities. There is a deep-seated reason people use substances and keep from engaging, but it is not conscious.

When May started working with me to get sober, she didn't know why she drank so often and so much. After several months of transference-focused psychotherapy twice a week where the only rule was, "Say what comes to mind," one day, May said, "Oh, I don't only have to talk about addiction."

She then began to talk about being raped starting at age three. Her grandfather would take her hand, lead her away from a large family gathering, and bring her into the basement. More free association and dream analysis revealed that she had been blocking from her awareness a deeper wound, the fact that her mother and grandmother/rapist's wife knew about the abuse and did nothing to stop it. Her mother was washing her bloody underwear. About twenty adults knew that her grandfather was taking her into the basement to rape her.

Why did this happen? A common response to overwhelming trauma is to perpetrate it on another helpless victim. We see intergenerational chains of addiction in families such as May's.

Intergenerational trauma is common to many addicted patients, regardless of whether they are addicted to booze they buy at the local store or heroin they buy on the street that has been smuggled in by a cartel. May speculated that her mother had been raped by the same man, her mother's father.

Over the years, I've heard countless stories of child physical and sexual abuse and neglect. As with May, abuse and neglect are always present together. Most of our patients started using drugs or drinking (alcohol in large quantities is just another drug) as a way of avoiding feelings that are connected to memories of terror—drugs get rid of feelings.

May's brain was irreversibly changed by her drinking. Her neurobiology was altered in a completely explicable way common to most addicted individuals. We are born with a brain pathway—SEEKING—that energizes our pursuit of the necessities to stay alive and procreate: food, water, sleep, sex, and relationships. Addictive drugs take over SEEKING permanently, making May's pursuit of alcohol more important than any natural needs. This is why alcoholism is a lifelong disease.

When I worked with May, I could relate to her. My father was a blackout drunk who would come home from the bar where he day-drank, down a fifth of Johnnie Walker Red every night, and then pass out. When I went to school, the television would still be on in front of him, and he sat in the living room, empty bottles next to his reclining chair.

My brother was addicted to drugs. I don't know which addiction killed him because he had said, "I'm going to come up to Boston and cut your throat." I stopped talking to him for safety reasons. I was informed that he died by my sister. She said that the neighbors smelled his decomposing body and called the police. I don't know how he died.

I identified with May's tenacity in escaping her family trauma by going away to college and making a life for herself, separate from the toxicity and trauma in her family. I had done the same thing.

I also related to her secrecy. I didn't tell many colleagues about my past. For a long time, I wasn't even consciously aware that my profession was in any way related to my upbringing.

Unconsciously, I had been using my history to relate to my patients. The key to getting along with anyone who has been hurt is to use your own experience to identify with them. We can all do this. Many of us have grown up in environments where addiction has been prevalent. Growing up without having been hurt is impossible.

Addiction is commonplace in our society. I likely didn't recognize any addicted individual, especially my patients, as living in a reality that was foreign to me. If we examine our society and communities closely enough, we will likely recognize addicted individuals all around us.

May's story may seem unpalatable, but perhaps many people who have suffered a blackout or hangover in their lives can stomach how drinking can get out of control. What about drug addiction? Who are these people? Why would they use drugs?

Raina spent twenty years in a fog because she got hooked on OxyContin, which doctors prescribed to alleviate pain following a knee operation in 2000. The dose had been steadily getting larger. Opioids are commonly prescribed for chronic pain.

Raina had been given clonazepam (Klonopin) for the anxiety generated by the social isolation caused by OxyContin. Anxiety is the natural signal we all get when we become disconnected from people. More clonazepam made her more unrelated and more anxious, resulting in her asking her doctor for more. More pain, more OxyContin. More anxiety, more Klonopin. Without her daughter's alert recognition that Raina's treatment was all wrong, and her daughter bringing Raina to our service, Raina might have died from an accidental oxycodone/clonazepam overdose. Although this did not happen with Raina, 80 percent of people addicted to heroin started with prescribed painkillers. Doctors kill their patients.

It is easy to blame these individuals, but it is truly not their fault. Some of us have a genetic predisposition to becoming addicted to alcohol or drugs. Additional factors must bring out the genetic predisposition. No one is responsible for their genes. No one is responsible for their addiction.

Addiction is complicated. It takes root in a mosaic of modifiable social factors. Primary among these is money. Drug dealers exploit the psychological and neurobiological underpinnings of addiction. There is a wide range of drug dealers feeding from the money trough, from government-taxed tobacco and alcohol producers and advertisers to pharmaceutical companies, drug kingpins, and street dealers. They promote products that feed addiction and contribute to long-term harm from using drugs.

Brutal systems are headed up by brutal individuals who often operate by force, not caring who dies as a casualty of their products, operating covert campaigns to influence the medical industry, and many enforcing their power at some level of their chain of operations through outright murder.

Let's take a look at how this happens.

PART 1

THE ADDICTIVE DRUG INDUSTRY

CHAPTER ONE

Killers in Bedroom Communities
Street Dealers across the United States

I sat in my office in Syracuse listening to Reuben describe how drug dealers in his neighborhood sent him a graphic video of the rape, torture, and murder of his wife and their five-year-old son. But that is not how the treatment started. Reuben spent the first two treatment hours after his intake saying not one word. Ben Milczarsky, MD, an upstate psychiatry resident, spent fifty minutes, and me twenty, honoring Reuben's wish to use his time in silence. Then, he let us know what he struggled with. Murder. He detailed how the drug dealers had held his family for a week. They had videoed repeated rapes of his wife. They cut off all four limbs, then gouged out her eyes, but they allowed her to keep her tongue so she could say goodbye. They drowned his son in a bathtub.

Having not drunk or used drugs before the video, Reuben spiraled into alcoholism to quash his emotions. Alcoholic drinking resulted in him being hospitalized for recurrent pancreatitis. The doctors prescribed opioids. Reuben developed addiction to painkillers. He started injecting heroin. The University Hospital (UH) doctors referred Reuben to our neuropsychoanalytic addiction treatment service.

Part of me was relieved to hear Reuben's confession. At least he was talking. The fact that he trusted me with what happened to him was a win. He was articulate. I remember sitting there, witnessing, trying to simply be present.

The other part of me was full of dread. I was horrified by the things he was telling me. Who wouldn't be? But Reuben's history didn't shock me, not entirely.

Reuben was entangled in a complicated system of drug-related murder and street violence that plague thousands of communities across the world. Drugs kill. So do drug dealers. Often. Although horrifying and complicated, Reuben's story is not exceptional. I'd heard countless stories of people attacked by drug dealers.

When I worked as a resident, then a teacher of addiction medicine, at Harvard University in Cambridge and Boston, I heard patients recounting their exposure to the Italian Mafia, whose ancestors come from Italy where they often still know relatives, and the Irish mafia, similarly still with connections in Ireland. Families descended from immigrants from both countries are part of the townie population in Boston. Academics have almost always moved into Boston from other parts of the United States or are from other countries.

Sitting with my residents one day, I innocently asked Marta, a woman on our inpatient service, to tell me her first memory.

"I was five years old. I went into the garage to find a man [her Mafia father had] chained by his arms, legs, and neck, begging me for help."

Another patient, Maria, said she turned to heroin to dissociate from the horrific things that she saw, such as a gang of men in the Mafia led by her father, breaking her boyfriend's hands in front of her to "teach" him not to hurt her. We will find out what happened to Marta and Maria later.

Many people are surprised that 22 percent of Americans die from drug addiction every year. How could this be reality?

Twenty-two percent includes deaths from legal government-sanctioned and taxed drugs such as nicotine and alcohol, prescription medications, and to a smaller extent, illegal drugs like heroin and fentanyl. Not included in this number is murder.

I was reading an interview in the *New York Times Magazine* in 2013 in which Boston Mayor Menino explained how *The Departed* was accurate in depicting the Massachusetts of the past but that people like that didn't exist anymore.

I shook my head, disbelieving. The statement simply wasn't true. Martin Scorsese, the director of *The Departed*, created a beautiful artistic representation of the world we live in. Over the years, I'd heard patients revealing horrific stories that sounded right out of *The Departed*.

I had learned that the ideal way to carry out a murder is to fly the killers in from Dublin. The local Irish Mafia contact tours the killers around the neighborhood. The trio, killers, and concierge drink, do lines of cocaine, and plan out the hit. The victim is killed. The killers fly home.

One of my patients was living with the local Irish Mafia contact when I left Boston in 2008. My psychoanalytic colleague Jerry (real name withheld for safety) was able to help her figure out how to disengage while staying sober—and alive.

But brutality is not specific to mob bosses. When I worked at the Dimock Health Center in the economically depressed African American Roxbury section of Boston, we were faced with running groups where some of the patients had addictions, and others were drug-selling psychopaths who had been advised by their lawyers to plead for drug treatment over prison. The drug dealers would go to group and laugh at the addicted patients as chumps they planned to sell to.

The formulation we came up with to address this group therapy problem was "money addiction." Teenagers are recruited to sell drugs in school. For a while, they feel elated that they have gone from being impoverished to having guns, women, and cars. They gradually become aware that they are likely to be killed or incarcerated. But they are in too deep. A common response to the terror is to start using the drugs they have been selling. Things get worse from there. As I carried out treatments to help patients be sober, in my private office or on academic treatment services, my patients told me bone-chilling stories of what happened when they tried to leave their relationship with drug dealers.

Syracuse, where I moved in 2008, is a college town set along the Erie Canal, famous for hosting the State Fair and being the snowiest city in New York. It is infested with drug dealers. All the surrounding towns have their own set of drug dealers.

Barry had been a small-town drug dealer. By twenty, he was styling, with guns, an attractive girlfriend, and $100,000 in the bank. But living life as a drug dealer is dangerous.

One night, Barry was lured downtown to sell to a customer. A dozen men jumped out of nearby trees and started to beat him. He was able to escape. Later, he got caught by the police for selling drugs and was put on probation.

Barry decided he had to get out of the business. The bigger dealers, who delivered his drugs, told him that the price for getting out of the business was $100,000. He went from being prosperous and successful to having no skills to make any money and living on public assistance.

Marijuana shows up on probation urine drug screens. Barry smoked synthetic cannabis, spike, so that urine drug screens would not be positive. Spike is a wastebasket term for many different synthetic drugs that are sent here through the US mail. No one knows what spike is because it is manufactured in China. I have joked with my patients that they are allowing their bodies to be used for Chinese drug dealer market research to see which of their invented intoxicating drugs will sell the best.

Intoxicated on spike, Barry collapsed in his shower and woke up blind. Blind, he lost his ability to drive to treatment. His girlfriend left him. This is the course of money addiction.

Cultural norms can complicate treatment. We met Malik at UH. He had become drunk, violent, and disorganized and was hospitalized for diabetic ketoacidosis. He was using alcohol because he couldn't use drugs any longer because urine drug screens were conducted by his probation officer.

Malik got sober on our outpatient service. Until his psychotherapy with us, he had been completely disregarding his type 1 diabetes. With treatment, he had started checking his blood sugars and using insulin. He was near discharge.

Malik's cousin finished a few years in prison where the cousin's main activity had been weightlifting. The cousin confidently beat up the heroin dealer on their street and told the man that he, Malik's cousin, was now the local drug dealer. The drug dealer came back with a gun and shot the cousin to death.

The treatment became daily psychotherapy to discuss whether Malik was honor bound to kill the drug dealer. Every day, we agreed that for that day, Malik would not go to the street and kill the dealer. After ten days, the dealer was arrested for the murder by the police, and the crisis was over.

If you are born into a poor community overrun by drug dealers, sometimes there is no way out. Those who become entrenched in that environment often find it impossible to leave. Those who are brutalized by this brand of street violence often internalize it and act out within the confines of that world in dangerous ways—whether through self-harm or by perpetuating violence on the streets.

Why is there no way out? Isn't this a free country where anyone can do anything they want? That ideology is not true to the nature of humans. I've heard one story after another where the adult patient told me that she/he was a child who hoped for help. When it became clear that there was no one, they turned to drugs and violence.

Jesse dreaded the sound of the blue truck. It meant that his drunk father was coming home. One day, his father didn't like what Jesse had to say, which Jesse realized when his father picked up a heavy pan from the dinner table and smacked him across the face. Jesse had a scar running from his eye, across his nose, and onto his cheek. His mother just sat there. She didn't say a word.

One day, his mother took Jesse's little brother to the movies. Jesse begged to go. She left him home. He heard the blue truck. His father tried to kill him. Jesse ran all over the house, dodging and hiding. His mother came home. Nothing was said.

But Jesse had extraordinary ability as a baseball player. He imagined pitching for the Red Sox. Jesse still had his coach.

One day at practice, he heard his coach give the roster of who was going to the regional playoffs. Jesse's name wasn't on the list. Jesse felt he was left off despite his talent because he was regarded as a troublemaker. It was also evident from Jesse's stories that neither of his parents went to his games. Jesse believed that the coach's son made the travel team because his father made the decision about the team roster. Jesse knew he was a better ballplayer than the son. The coach had been his last hope for a caring adult.

Jesse remembered hopping the fence at the back of the ball field and going down to the railroad tracks to drink. It was the start of alcoholic drinking, drug dealing, and violence.

Jesse was only eighteen when I started treating him. He was on Social Security Disability with good Medicare insurance. After a year of psychotherapy, I proposed that he come four days per week for more intensive treatment.

Jesse's first analytic hour featured a dream where four clowns were trying to kill him. He ran through a carnival, terrified. A car came along. The driver offered to rescue him. Jessie got in. Then, he realized that the four clowns were in the car.

I interpreted the dream as the four clowns representing the four days a week of psychoanalysis. Jesse was describing my help as a way to counter the fear of being killed. But there was danger everywhere.

I felt wonderful as he left. He had been able to bring up his fear about starting psychoanalysis immediately. Jessie was a good case.

I next heard from him three years later when a prison nurse called to verify that I had prescribed bupropion to treat his ADHD. In retrospect, the terror of seeing me four times a week intensified a transference that was not analyzable. I was probably represented in the dream as Jesse's silent mother, who had never protected him from his father, driving a car/truck full of danger. Jesse came back to treatment when he got out of prison. But the years of having no one to protect him, when he feared that his father would murder him, had traumatized him so deeply that the damage was difficult to heal. Jesse did get sober when he got out of prison, with the combination of psychotherapy and Alcoholics Anonymous.

I want to contrast Jesse's story with something I ran across as part of my political activism. It comes from an interview with an elected judge in the sports section of our local paper here in Syracuse+:

> I ran for a group called the Striders. I don't know how I got started. Maybe because of my brother. But the coach was this guy named Richie. Richie was this young white guy with blond hair and blue eyes. And why he chose to work with a bunch of black kids, I have no idea. But he was good because he cared about us.
>
> "I wasn't the fastest, I wasn't the best. But Richie did something nice for me: He gave me a sweatsuit, a bag to put it in, some cleats and he said, essentially, 'I'm doing this for you, Vanessa, because you try. You try, and I need the rest of the girls to see this.'"
>
> I used to have asthma when I was a kid. The way they dealt with us was I was in a health class. Which means I didn't do a lot of learning. I did a lot of lying on a cot. And I think that running helped me to get out of that health class, get mainstreamed. I don't have asthma anymore. So, he saved my life. He helped me create good health habits.
>
> Running is a beautiful thing. In terms of what it does for your overall health and your mind. If you read anything about me, you know that I was in multiple elections, and I lost. How do you say: Keep going? How do you say: Try again? Because I didn't win every race. But ultimately, what you find when you're running track is the person you're running against is yourself. And so, can you hang in there, can you do it?
>
> If I hadn't had the ability to run track and engage in

athletics, would I be here today? I don't know. Because I don't know where else I would have picked up the skills to try and try and try. To keep working on something. Not in a math class. Not in an English class, necessarily.

But certainly, once you get into the arena and you actually start competing, it's no longer, "I can do it." It's: "How good can I be? Can I come back from a loss?" All those other things.

Vanessa had that one person who cared. She also had the capacity to let her coach help her. These are the two things needed to get out. Jesse had no one growing up, and he lacked the ability to let me help. Now Vanessa is a judge and Jesse is struggling.

People born into more affluent communities, who never lost loved ones to street drugs, may find it easy to dismiss my stories as movie scripts foreign to their own realities. They may look down on people who become involved in these systems, dismiss them as being morally weak or having a lack of self-control—a mythology and system of denial our culture has adopted.

When we look deeper, we find that judgments about moral weakness and lack of self-control have nothing to do with reality. Jesse's trauma and Reuben's trauma are rooted in the same ground as May's. Jesse's and Reuben's addiction to drugs were a secondary injury that occurred after the child abuse that is the commonplace history of the vast majority of our patients. Drugs get rid of feelings that go with memories of terror that may not be conscious.

Intergenerational transmission of trauma is a psychological injury also present in the houses of parents who have been exposed to wars, torture, killing, and abuse. The parents who suffered these psychological injuries often don't get help to deal with their pain; they may not even admit it. They are silent and distant. They reenact their psychological wounds on their children through physical, sexual, and emotional abuse and neglect. The children live out a version of their parent's trauma that they have absorbed on an unconscious level.

Reuben's parents hadn't processed their own wartime trauma, fleeing Chile in order to not be killed by Pinochet's police. They had reason to be afraid. Reuben's uncle had been thrown out of a helicopter. The effects of this trauma continued after the family moved to the US. His father often physically abused Reuben as a little boy, making him kneel toward the wall for hours. Neither the older children nor his mother protected him.

Despite, and partially due to, these difficulties, Reuben excelled in academics. He wanted to be acclaimed. He was a teenager with a slight build. At five foot five and 130 pounds, he made the starting lineup on his high school basketball team. He was the Athenian ideal, excelling intellectually and physically. But his parents never supported his accomplishments.

Reuben went to college and graduated. He was bicultural and fluent in the Spanish his parents spoke at home. He returned to Chile, where he met his wife, a local woman, and they had a child.

Living in Chile, he started to observe that the police and drug dealers were working together. Taking matters into their own hands, he and his friends started capturing and then releasing drug dealers after they had burned the drugs.

This is where Reuben's history gets tricky. Growing up impoverished in Syracuse took its toll. Reuben was still bound to those streets. When excelling in the classroom and on the basketball court didn't provide him with the validation he needed, didn't fulfill his need to replace the absence of love he never was able to experience as a child, he obtained love by using the fantasy that he was like Batman, confronting villains that the police couldn't contain. Looking down on the police and deciding that he could do a better job was a grandiose approach. This plan, of course, eventually backfired when his wife and son were killed.

Reuben returned to Syracuse a widower. He began murdering drug dealers, especially targeting heads of organizations. This vigilantism was not completely outrageous in Reuben's cultural context. If you come from a circumscribed neighborhood with Wild West rules laid out by dealers, you may believe a perfectly reasonable response would be to take matters into your own hands through violence.

I also learned over the years how drug dealers seize communities and turn them into their personal fortresses. In most places where dealers have a substantial foothold, they also have a few police officers on their payroll. Patients from poor communities tell me that they are afraid to call the police, afraid that a policeman on the drug dealer payroll will report the complaint, and the result of their complaint that selling drugs is going on in their neighborhood will be their murder.

The most spectacular example of this occurred when Jesse went back to prison in the middle of being sober, going to AA, and working with me in psychotherapy. He was not a pacifist. When confronted on the street by a group of teenagers who wanted to rob him, he fought back, injuring a few. The teenagers got together and made a complaint that Jesse had attacked them.

Jesse felt so confident that he was innocent that he asked for a jury trial. I asked if he wanted a letter for the court saying he was sober, in AA, and in treatment with me. Jesse grandiosely refused, sure that he didn't need it. Because he had a long criminal record, he was convicted and went back to prison.

Months later, in a state prison in Massachusetts, Jesse was talking with a friend. His friend was suddenly hit in the face and knocked down by a member of the Latin Kings. Jesse heard the sound of his friend's skull hitting the cement floor. The attack caused his friend permanent brain damage.

Corrections officers at the prison asked Jesse to make an official statement about who had attacked his friend. Jesse refused. In prison, reporting who has committed a crime is referred to as "snitching." The "snitch" is usually punished, and sometimes killed, by gang members.

The corrections officers worked on Jesse. They appealed to his sense of justice. They said that if no one ever reports crimes in prison, prisons will always be violent places. They said that a member of the Latin

Kings should not be allowed to go free after nearly killing Jesse's friend.

Jesse had gone from being violent himself to understanding that we all need to work together to help each other. The corrections officers promised that his report would be completely confidential. It would be used to punish the gang member for his attack, but the name of the person who filed the report would be one-hundred-percent secret.

Jesse filed a sworn statement saying that he had seen his friend hurt by the gang member. The next day, Jesse received a phone call from one of his friends who was incarcerated at *another* prison. His friend said that everyone at the *other* prison was talking about what would happen to Jesse on account of his testimony against the Latin Kings.

How could something like this happen? Chances are that Jesse was interrogated by several honest, caring corrections officers—and one who was on the payroll of the Latin Kings. The Latin Kings, a gang notorious for drug dealing, are also good at terror. Everyone in the prison knew that Jesse would pay for being a snitch.

Late that night, three men appeared in Jesse's cell and started to beat him to death. He had been on his guard, he woke up, and he was a good fighter. He didn't die. The men disappeared from his cell.

I heard this story when Jesse was released from prison several months later. He had been held in protective custody for the rest of his prison stay. He had post-traumatic stress disorder (PTSD), a feeling that he was about to be killed any minute, even though there was no longer an apparent danger. He had panic attacks: episodes of fear that struck him suddenly, went on for a few minutes, and then left.

One day soon after his release, Jesse was driving down the street when someone threw a huge rock through his windshield. This made him think that the Latin Kings were still after him. It added to his terror.

Optimal recovery requires doing something aggressive about what was done to you as a child. In its wisdom, AA has built this into its program. Step twelve of AA involves saving lives by carrying the message of recovery to those who need help.

Jesse's attempt to punish the Latin King almost killed him. His vulnerability was his grandiosity combined with the danger once he landed back in prison. Jesse was unable to ask for help when he needed it to stay out of prison. Once there, his illness continued to progress. He did not ask anyone in prison for their input about signing the complaint against his friend's assailant.

For Reuben, it was the same: his vulnerability was his grandiosity. Back in Syracuse, he started murdering drug dealers. It is a miracle he is still alive. Humility is necessary for recovery. You can only survive under difficult circumstances if you recognize that none of us wins alone.

As May mastered her terror, she recognized that alcoholic drinking is submitting to yet another, transmogrified, form of abuse. The women's AA meetings at which she sought help had discussions about sexual violence. Almost every woman in AA has been a victim.

May remembered being taken to a pediatrician who examined her vagina and told her parents, "She is not intact." She considered why there was no child protective services report. The pediatrician was honoring the secrecy of incest.

May realized that the alcoholism and suicide in her community were a response to terror. She realized that what was done to her is common. May is investigating Mormon communities in Utah, the religion and state she grew up in, where thousands (this is not a misprint) of children are being raped and murdered.

May is not working alone. She has a network of activists. Incest is prevented by making community members aware. Adults can rape children only if there are many accomplices. May alerts child protective services to victims she knows of personally. By writing, May invites others to join her in protesting about the complicity of physicians who don't report physical findings of sexual abuse and Mormon leaders who participate in abuse under the cover of being church elders. Like Jesse and Reuben, she is risking her life. Unlike Jesse's and Reuben's responses, which were aggressive but grandiosely solo, this is an endeavor that has a chance of succeeding. May has told others what was done to her and is working with others who care to do something about this ongoing atrocity.

We have considered smaller enterprises that are limited in size because of a lack of government collaboration. Criminals buying police and using guns are not effective ways to run a business. It is more effective for corporations to sell drugs out in the open. We need to see what we know about legal businesses that traffic addictive drugs.

CHAPTER TWO

Tobacco—A Key to Understanding America's Addictive Psychology

Tobacco accelerates arterial disease, worsening atherosclerosis in the brain, heart, and legs, while the nicotine stiffens the walls of arteries by causing chronic constriction.

Using the lung to get nicotine to the brain gradually plugs up bronchioles while destroying the exchange space membrane where oxygen goes into the blood and carbon dioxide comes out—euphemistically called chronic obstructive lung disease, COPD.

COPD caused by cigarettes ought to be called "cigarette lung." Why isn't it? Coal miners suffer from "black lung." "Black" refers to coal dust that they can't avoid while working in the mines. I am not going to answer this question now, but I want the reader to think, *Gee, I never thought to ask that question. Why isn't damage to the lung caused by inhaling burning tobacco leaves called "cigarette lung?" Aren't physicians hiding the cause of the disease from their patients?*

Wouldn't the term *cigarette lung* help patients and their physicians address the addiction that leads to increasing efforts to breathe, carrying oxygen tanks around, a demanding effort to breathe, as if running an endless marathon, and finally, after years of feeling like one is about to suffocate, giving up and suffocating?

We know that people who become addicted to smoking cigarettes are putting their lives in danger every time they inhale. Why do patients keep inhaling cigarettes when they know it is killing them?

Adults still feel the guilt and shame they used to replace the helplessness they experienced as victims of childhood abuse and neglect. Better the only sinner in heaven than the only good person in hell. Children can't tolerate the reality that they live with abusive and uncaring parents.

How Smoking Became Fashionable

Once upon a time, cigarettes were fashionable. Women wearing cloche hats and men in fedoras sat in dark smoky bars, flicking their ashes into glass ashtrays.

Cigarettes were given to soldiers during World War I by our government, which is an important partner of the industry. Soldiers learned to treat their PTSD with nicotine. During World War II, Camel placed ads encouraging people to buy cigarettes to send to American troops overseas.

Women who stayed home and started working in factories, on the heels of popular cultural figures like Rosie the Riveter, were encouraged to indulge in a toke occasionally, with campaign slogans such as "free women smoke." Cigarettes were advertised for women as "torches of freedom," a version of Orwell's "slavery is freedom."

Governments have often worked internationally to promote the selling of addictive drugs.[3] The British had an insoluble balance of trade with China because while the British were crazy about Chinese tea, the Chinese people did not want anything that the British had to sell. The Chinese government protected their citizens by refusing to let British merchants sell opium from the British colony of India. The "Opium Wars" of the nineteenth century were Britain's two invasions of China to solve Britain's balance of payments problem. By addicting millions of Chinese citizens, they had a way to pay for "all the tea in China." Chinese citizens were killed directly by the British army, and then by opium. Drug dealers kill for a living.

In a similar way, needing some way to balance America's appetite for Japanese cars against our inability to interest the Japanese in American products, President Ronald Reagan effectively bargained with the Japanese in the 1980s to allow American cigarettes into Japan, mandating that if they weren't allowed, he would invoke tariffs against Hondas and Toyotas being shipped to the United States.[4] The Japanese government resisted for the same public health reasons that the Chinese government had a century before: addiction kills. President Reagan was able to have the Japanese government allow some of their citizens to be killed by American tobacco companies.

Trusting the government to always do the right thing is an important aspect of the mass psychology of addiction. The American government and almost every government in the world works with tobacco dealers. The exception is Nepal.

Idealization

Cigarette companies pushed their product to audiences by paying glamorous actors over the decades to smoke on screen. Lucille Ball, John Wayne, Clint Eastwood, James Dean, John Travolta, Arnold

Schwarzenegger, Charlize Theron, and a thousand other actors show that the toughest heroes use cigarettes.

Cigarettes were marketed as if they made women slim and sexy rather than sick and dead.

Doctor cover has been an unconscionable yet common strategy for advertisers to develop strong customer bases for their products, from cigarettes to prescription drugs to marijuana to vaping. The glamorous image of smoking was endorsed by people in the medical industry over the decades. Cigarette companies hired doctors in the 1940s to participate in campaigns such as "More doctors smoke Camels than any other brand," perpetuating the illusion that smoking is good for you. The message was that doctors are prosperous, health-conscious, and want you to use tobacco.

Every American subpopulation was targeted with advertisements that were invented to use idealization. In the 1950s, formidable tobacco company Phillip Morris sought out and created relationships with African American organizations and their leaders, like the United Negro College Fund, the National Urban League, and the National Association for the Advancement of Colored People. These connections were used to sway African American smokers toward addiction, and also for political purposes, when tobacco cessation and control bills were on the agendas of state and federal legislatures.

Starting with Red Man chewing tobacco in 1904, American tobacco companies have targeted vulnerable, poor, and oppressed Native American communities. In 2017, American Tobacco invented "Real, simple, different" Natural American Spirit cigarettes to appeal to ethnic pride, blurring the difference between religious use of tobacco in ceremonies and addiction.

Notice the theme of idealization. Cigarettes support valiant soldiers. Cigarettes make women slim, sexy, and free. Cigarettes are inhaled by handsome and beautiful actors who perform as lifesaving heroes in movies. Cigarettes are endorsed by health-conscious physicians, by enemies of racism, by spiritual Native Americans.

Tobacco giants such as Phillip Morris and RJ Reynolds have repeated tactics that have been in place since the industry started, which has been referred to as a playbook, to steer people toward their products and encourage their reliance on them. These include the perpetuation of junk science, becoming involved in sleazy policymaking practices through political contributions, and "health washing," i.e., "More doctors smoke Camels than any other brand." They deny corporate responsibility for encouraging individuals to slowly poison their bodies with tobacco products.

Technological Innovation

American cigarettes lead the addictive drug industry in technological innovations. An invention of the late nineteenth century was the cigarette machine. Before that, tobacco was awkward to use: pipes, snuff, buying papers, and rolling cigarettes oneself. Now cigarettes are well packaged and easy to use.

Scientists working for tobacco companies genetically modified plants to produce low-nicotine brands for teenagers, mixed with other chemicals to make those brands acidic and the toxic nicotine relatively poorly absorbed, to aid in the process of starting addictive use despite the dizziness, respiratory pain, and nausea that initially accompanies inhaling cigarettes. Plants were genetically modified to produce high-nicotine brands, mixed with high pH/basic chemicals, to make the high blood nicotine levels hard to live without for brands marketed to lifelong smokers.

A recent innovation is the vaping device. Tobacco nicotine is heated by an electric coil, vaporized, and inhaled.

Profits

Altria/Phillip Morris sells about half of the cigarettes in the United States.[5] Their net revenues for 2022 were about $81 billion, with profits of $9 billion. If one considers that that company's cigarettes killed half of the 480,000 Americans who died from tobacco in 2022,

Altria is making $337,000 per death in revenue. Their profit margin is 11 percent of sales, so their profit per death is $37,000. In contrast, the average profit margin of a grocery store is 1 percent. The money mainly goes to rich stockholders who can use tobacco profits to buy a third vacation home or sports car. Another way to describe profits is that every year, cigarette sales are $173 billion, and the cost to Americans is $600 billion (CDC, accessed 12/13/23).

Thirty-two percent of Americans who make less than $20,000 per year and 12 percent who make more than $100,000 inhale tobacco. The American Lung Association says cigarettes cost the average smoker $2,190 per year. Cigarettes increase the income gap in the United States. The American Cancer Association notes the following (a summary): The tobacco industry has a long and well-documented history of targeting people with limited incomes with discounts and promotions of its deadly and addictive products dating back over sixty years. Previously secret tobacco industry documents confirm the companies have utilized a variety of tactics to target people with limited incomes. Historically, the tobacco industry has engaged in the following tactics to target people with limited incomes:

- Handed out free cigarettes to children in housing projects, particularly targeting Black children from households with limited incomes.
- Provided tobacco coupons with food stamps by enclosing coupons for $0.25 off a pack of cigarettes in the envelope with food stamps. This program was targeted at Black and Hispanic families living in inner-city neighborhoods with limited incomes.
- Targeted coupons at women with limited incomes.
- Gave away gas cash cards and other rewards debit cards targeted at women with limited incomes.

When Smoking Became Unfashionable

There is an unseen battle going on between the tobacco companies and activists who know the companies are mass murderers. In the twentieth century, 100 million people were killed by tobacco. In the twenty-first century, it is likely to be a billion.[4] Activists work to influence legislators and governments, just like the tobacco company executives. The goals are different. The activists want to save lives, and the tobacco companies are like all drug dealers: they kill people for a living.

In 1999, the United States Department of Justice filed lawsuits against Phillip Morris and several of the largest tobacco companies in the United States for racketeering. In 2006, Judge Gladys Kessler issued an opinion of several thousand pages holding these companies liable for violating the Racketeer Influenced and Corrupt Organizations Act because they had spent several decades defrauding the public about the addictive nature and health consequences of smoking.

On May 22, 2009, the US Court of Appeals for the DC Circuit largely affirmed the district court opinion and these remedies. In June 2009, the Tobacco Control Act (TCA or Act) was signed into law, granting the Food and Drug Administration (FDA) comprehensive regulatory authority over the marketing, manufacture, and distribution of cigarettes, cigarette tobacco, roll-your-own tobacco, smokeless tobacco, and any other tobacco products the FDA deems to be subject to the Act's requirements. The TCA imposed restrictions on the conduct of manufacturers, including limiting marketing, prohibiting false or misleading labeling, restricting claims of modified risk, and requiring warning labels.

Smoking cigarettes went the other way, becoming unfashionable. Smoking was outlawed in bars and restaurants, offices, and even in parks and on certain public streets. Those who were addicted to cigarettes were often treated like pariahs. One of my patients said, "When we inject heroin, at least we go into the bathroom. Those people smoke their cigarettes right out on the street!"

The TCA caused a spike in the cost of cigarettes and a polite and inconspicuous two-line warning about the hazards of smoking on the sides or back ends of cigarette packs. One can wonder if the TCA was a step toward combating the cigarette industry or a way to show that the American government was doing "something." Deaths continued at the same rate.

In countries like Australia, manufacturers' warnings include cigarette packs displaying graphic pictures of the diseases caused by smoking.

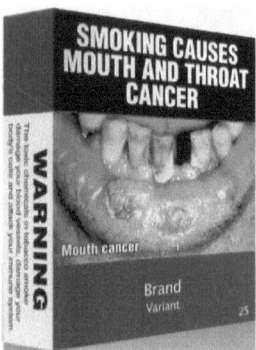

For the FDA to require a written warning but not do anything to change a half million per year death rate perpetuates the denial of the American people that the government is doing "something" about addiction. If the FDA were not collaborating with tobacco companies to kill Americans, millions of lives would be saved.

According to the World Health Organization (WHO), tobacco kills about 8 million people per year. Over 7 million are killed directly, and another 1.3 million are killed by inhaling the smoke from relatives and friends: "secondhand smoke" (WHO, 12/13/23).

When people addicted to cigarettes kill with secondhand smoke, is it done consciously? Does it matter? Before you read it here, were you aware that we are likely to see a billion deaths from tobacco in this century worldwide? Does it matter if you are aware of it or not? These questions have complicated answers; we need more information about addiction to resolve them.

How Tobacco Use Started

While examining any of the addictive substances that underpin many of the problems in our society, it is important that we also look at the collective traumas and injustices they are rooted in. People may start using as a way of repressing difficult emotions associated with the trauma perpetuated by, and often suffered by, their families. But the collective trauma connected to cigarettes also has an impact. Every time we pick up a cigarette, we are contributing to an industry that is rooted in some of our country's worst practices, including slavery and racism.

Tobacco in and of itself is not bad. It is a plant. Tobacco plants make nicotine as a natural insecticide. It is an evolutionary adaptation to predator insects who would otherwise eat the plant's leaves. Nicotine is good for tobacco plants.

Native Americans harvested tobacco themselves. They smoked it in pipes and burned it in sacred ceremonies. In Virginia, they introduced it to European colonists.

Let's start the next phase of our investigation with a simple history lesson—one never taught in school. The United States was founded by drug dealers. European immigrants murdered many of the Virginia Tidewater natives. They scattered the survivors to the west away from the river bottomland soil so good for growing tobacco, seventeenth-century ethnic cleansing. The predecessors of Presidents Washington and Jefferson started importing traumatized Africans to produce the most lethal drug of all—nicotine.

Slavery and drug dealing formed the basis for the economic center of what became the foremost colony of the American Revolution. By 1670, half the men in England were addicted to the drug.[4] Our founding fathers knew that addictive drugs sell. George Washington, Thomas Jefferson, and many signatories of the Declaration of Independence were drug dealers. Between the two of them, Washington and Jefferson owned more than 500 slaves who produced tobacco on their farms for sale to the British.[5]

Of course, drug dealers created American slavery! The drug dealers' problem was that they couldn't get European immigrants to work with such a toxic plant. Importing Africans who could be marked as property because of their skin color solved the problem. This is from the Kentucky Poison Control Center:

> Nicotine, the addictive ingredient in tobacco, is not safe—whether it is eaten, touched or inhaled. Symptoms of mild nicotine poisoning include stomach problems like nausea, vomiting and diarrhea. More severe cases can include dizziness, sweating, headache, hyperactivity or restlessness. Changes in blood pressure and heart rate can occur, followed by difficulty breathing. In rare cases, nicotine poisoning can result in seizures, coma, and even death. Children are especially at risk for this poisoning due to their small size; even a small amount can be dangerous.

Nicotine poisoning contracted during harvesting is called green tobacco sickness. If forced to pick leaves off the plants all day, as the Virginia slaves were, the workers would be sick continually. So would the workers who hung the green leaves up in drying sheds or those who took the leaves down for bundling and transport to England.

Tobacco was widely sold in 1789 and has been legal since. Members of our government, starting with the president and Congress, collaborate in killing. Without tobacco money to win reelection among a complacent and ignorant set of voters, politicians would be vulnerable to losing their jobs.

This kind of behavior is what drug dealers do. If we don't come to feel this in our bones—that drug dealing is the economic engine that drives the disease of addiction—we will continue to be paralyzed, swim in ambivalence, and be an American populace of victims.

Americans continue to inhale tobacco legally and die.

CHAPTER THREE

How the Industry Takes Advantage of the Two Reasons for Addiction—Psychological and Due to Brain Changes Caused by Drugs

While the use of cigarettes may be psychologically rooted in childhood trauma or even collective trauma, such as professional work as a soldier, fireman, or policeman, continuing to smoke is more complicated. As is the case with all addictions, harm is worsened by a series of brain changes. We can examine the progression from psychological to physical addiction by considering the use of tobacco.

Many patients I have worked with are able to get sober from deeply ingrained drug and alcohol use successfully, but they still cling to their cigarettes. Patients will stop injecting heroin, then say that nicotine was their first drug, the hardest drug to stop. Addicted persons need to live out childhood abuse as an action rather than a conscious memory. The function of maintaining at least one addiction is to use nicotine consumption as a behavior that both hides and enacts abuse. The success of psychotherapy with addictions is, in part, because talking is the opposite of behaving. As soon as patients fully grasp that addictive behaviors enact and extend childhood abuse and neglect, they can stop the addictive behaviors and continue to explore the childhood experiences that the addiction is based on.

Unfortunately, the experience of abuse and neglect can enter the transference relationship, resulting in avoiding the treater and the treatment. Resolution of childhood abuse requires reexperiencing the distress with the therapist while also being able to observe that the feeling is based on previous relationships. They experience inchoate distress coming to their treatment hours. If the bad feelings are not verbalized, patients can drop out of treatment.

Think about what happens if physicians don't repeatedly bring up that their patients are committing slow suicide with tobacco. Neither the patient nor the physician is conscious that the physician is enacting the role of an unprotecting parent. Won't patients move to another primary-care physician if the doctor brings up their concern about active tobacco addiction at every visit?

Most primary-care physicians have too many patients, too many referrals. There is no reason that they would mind losing a few patients whose lives they tried to save by addressing tobacco use. Not doing everything one can do to save patients' lives and having to watch helplessly while they die from addiction seems worse than risking that the patient will abandon the relationship. Primary-care physicians who aggressively bring up cigarette use as potentially lethal save lives and avoid watching patients who quit over this issue get sick, sicker, and die.

In fact, one way to understand primary-care physicians avoiding the topic of tobacco addiction is that it is a symptom of PTSD, a disease caused by watching people die. Calling the gradual suffocation caused by using the lung to get nicotine into the brain COPD rather than cigarette lung could have the same avoidance function. The doctor doesn't have to think consciously, *If this patient doesn't stop, I will have to watch them die.*

I have a flashbulb memory of being on call one night and watching a patient using every ounce of effort to keep breathing, followed by hearing the next morning that she had died. It was an awful experience. Focusing on bronchodilators and steroids to ease dyspnea rather than on addiction to tobacco would represent an unconscious countertransference. Like any behavior that enacts a problem while keeping it unconscious, avoidance of addressing tobacco addiction would cause a "return of the repressed" horrifying experience of watching patients die. It keeps happening to physicians who are trying not to think about it.

Cigarette-addicted persons have lived in this society where smoking is no longer socially acceptable. They have come to understand how dangerous tobacco is. They have seen the commercial of the man who speaks through a computerized microphone he holds to an open hole on his neck—because throat cancer caused him to lose his ability to speak. They have seen the commercial where a man coughs up blood and then cries when he is telling his family he has cancer. "Quitting smoking is hard. Telling your family that you have lung cancer is harder," the commercial says. This may not be true. For some people, talking about quitting smoking is harder than talking about dying from cancer.

Behavior often conflicts with the knowledge that a substance is harmful, as is evidenced in May's, Reuben's, and Jessie's stories. They found it easier to use drugs until we were able to highlight the enactment of childhood abandonment. One sees over and over that as frightening as it is to die from the use of addictive drugs as an adult, it is even more frightening to be afraid of dying, or being abandoned, as a child.

The fear of being abandoned as a child is called "annihilation anxiety." It is the worst kind of fear there is. Addicted adults feel the annihilation anxiety consciously but repress the ideas/memories that go along with the feeling. They will say that inhaling cigarettes relaxes them. Partly, this is because of temporary relief from nicotine withdrawal. But a second unconscious mechanism seems to be simultaneously evading conscious memories of abuse and living them out. May's, Reuben's, and Jessie's mothers chose to stay with the abusers, functionally abandoning their children.

Real death was less frightening than the feeling of annihilation anxiety combined with the conscious memory of where it came from. This defense is called repression; the feeling is present, but the memory is repressed. This is why inhaling a cigarette produces "relief." It symbolizes ongoing submission to abuse.

I don't make this model. I just service it. This is the way humans are.

Getting Addicted

I have heard many stories about becoming addicted to nicotine. The child is among smoking children, often in the context that their parents are addicted. The child tries inhaling the smoke. They cough. They feel nauseous, the body's defense against a poison.

Why nausea? Evolutionarily, we are not built to defend against inhaling drugs. Humans started doing this in the seventeenth century. No other animal inhales drugs, so there is not a history of evolutionary protection. Animals are designed to get nauseous and vomit up accidentally ingested dangerous materials. Dogs vomit when they eat something bad. Nicotine is poison.

Inhaling cigarettes hurts the throat. Only by persisting until tolerance to the noxious drug, alteration of nicotinic receptors in the brain and gut, and craving based on the changes to the SEEKING pathway set in is it relaxing to escape the discomfort of nicotine withdrawal. This is unconscious submission to abuse. Who would use a drug that causes discomfort multiple times a day?

The hurdle that it takes effort to become addicted is cemented into the denial system. As you now know, all addictive drugs are idealized. "I was able to tolerate the pain, dizziness, and nausea of learning to smoke" is a source of pride. That's what people tell me. Their childhood memory of mastering the distress caused by inhaling burning tobacco leaves made them the equal of the older children that they looked up to.

Subtle cognitive impairment makes the victim less able to use human relationships to address this life-threatening situation. The ability to engage in human relationships, a complex cognitive endeavor, is necessary to become abstinent. Commonly, partners, children, and friends say something like, "I am so worried about your smoking."

The addicted person disengages. "I am not ready to think about smoking now. Let's just have a nice evening. I am under so much stress!" Relating requires effort. Avoiding is effortless. And eventually, the smoker becomes too cognitively impaired to use the help of those around them.

Cognitive impairment is a consequence of tobacco use, even in teenagers. But the saddest thing we see is in older people. The tobacco closes off small arteries in the brain as a consequence. The medical term for this is "multi-infarct dementia." Having done several thousand modified mini-mental status (3MS) cognitive exams, I have learned that cognitive symptoms of multi-infarct dementia start around age sixty.

The most sensitive item in the 3MS is naming ten four-legged animals in thirty seconds. Early on, when they get only seven, the patient can take in the information that they are having a medical consequence of inhaling tobacco. But insight is a cognitive function. As the impairment progresses, the victim loses their ability to understand what is being done to them. By the time the thirty seconds elapse, after "Dog, cat, uh—bird," patients express denial. "That is a ridiculous test." Having no capacity to see that something is horribly wrong, they are not able to use our help and go right on inhaling tobacco.

Tobacco is the most successful addictive drug. Tobacco companies have their victims each contribute a few dollars a day to their income for decades. The company continues to profit while each cigarette increases the chance of the customer dying from the drug. Drugs that cause more obvious damage are less successful. Better a leech than a tiger. People see tigers and are immediately fearful.

People don't see or feel leeches and don't notice the slow, cumulative damage from cigarettes. The result is the occasional patient who prides themselves on getting sober from heroin or alcohol but whose denial system for cigarettes we can't interpret before they die from cancer or have a life-altering stroke.

I have a flashbulb memory of screening an older patient for tuberculosis so I could send him from the hospital to an inpatient alcohol rehab. His chest X-ray looked like he had a golf ball in his lung. It was obviously cancer, doubtless caused by the many cigarettes he had inhaled. I had to refer him immediately for cancer treatment instead of rehab. I was sure he would be dead soon, and in my intuition, I'm sure that he knew it too.

SEEKING—The Pathway Nicotine Takes Over
Loss of will was understood by American genius Bill Wilson and his early collaborators, who made the concept implicit in the first three steps of Alcoholics Anonymous, especially step three: "We turned our will over to god as we understand him." Bill Wilson understood the loss of will to alcoholic drinking and the need to substitute the thinking of a group of drunks (god) to make any decision that had to do with whether to drink. Let's understand how the will is taken over by addictive drugs. It has to do with how drugs change SEEKING.

Neuropsychoanalysts use Jaak Panksepp's brain research-derived models as part of our core concepts. Dr. Panksepp thought about going to medical school but decided instead to find out about emotions in animals as his life's work. This goal put him in opposition to the field of cognitive neuroscience since discussing emotions in animals is dismissed as "anthropomorphizing." The main tool Jaak used was systematic observations of how animals behaved when he put electrodes in various parts of their brains and how drug administration changed their behavior. He was able to trace neural pathways.

Dr. Panksepp found a warm home among the neuropsychoanalysts, starring at every Congress from 2000 until his death in 2017. He originated the convention of capitalizing the brain's drive and instinctual pathways to differentiate them from the emotions that they subserve.

SEEKING is like Frodo Baggins' ring of power. It is supreme. It controls the other six powerful drive and instinctual systems whose neural pathways Dr. Panksepp also discovered.

The dopaminergic neurons of SEEKING originate in the ventral tegmental area of the midbrain. From there, they have axons running through the hypothalamus, where various inputs tune this "goad without a goal."[7] SEEKING motivates animals to sleep, drink, eat, have sex, and look for relationships when the SEEKING pathway is tuned to that goal by hormones that cross the blood-brain barrier. For example, ghrelin from the stomach turns on the wish to eat. If one has not had sex recently, hypothalamic tuning with estradiol will help scan the environment for attractive potential partners. [8]

SEEKING is the source of the energy to move in the brain. The method of reproduction for plants is to shed 1,000 seeds to have one land in a place where a new plant can grow. Animals must move through their environment to find resources to stay alive and procreate.

To make this clear, when I use the audience response system during presentations, I ask, "Why don't plants have brains?"
  A. They are too stupid.
  B. Their reproductive strategy requires no brain.
  C. Chlorophyll is neurotoxic.
  D. Who needs a brain to vegetate?

Here is Jaak Panksepp's diffusion tensor imaging picture of the SEEKING pathway in green, with the brown PANIC pathway lying directly on top of it, as if the depressive symptoms that cancel drives like sleep, sex, and eating are meant to be shut down by PANIC signaling SEEKING. PANIC is turned on by abandonment.

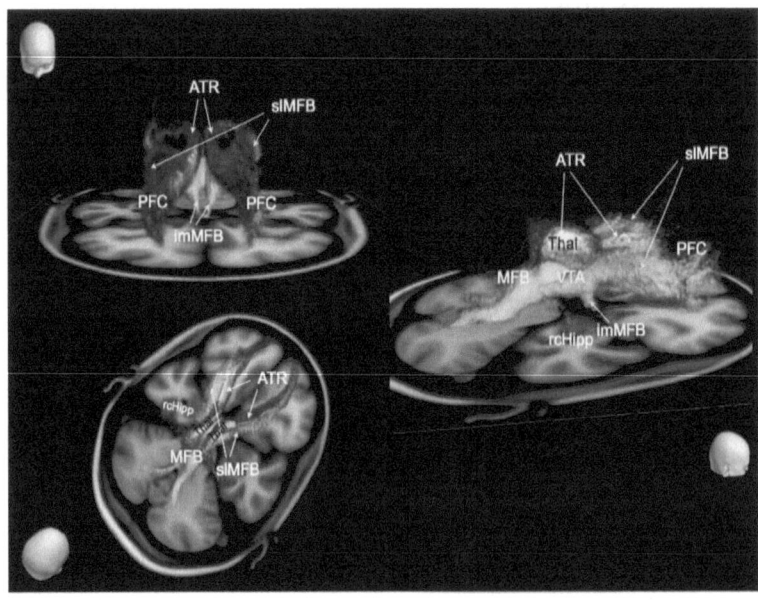

The hallmark of SEEKING pathway change is drug dreams. Neuropsychoanalyst Mark Solms discovered that the SEEKING and dreaming pathways are identical. When my patients are reliably off cigarettes, they still report dreams of smoking, often accompanied by a panicked feeling on awakening because they have relapsed. The instant of panic remits when they realize that it was just a dream.

The addiction treatment community has erroneously named the SEEKING pathway "the reward system." This comes from neuroscientists of the twentieth century using behavioral psychology studies of animals where stimulating the SEEKING pathway resulted in goal-directed behaviors such as eating and drinking, animal goals for survival. Animals can't tell you what they feel. Calling the change in SEEKING "the reward system" stigmatizes drug use, as if people using drugs were preferring pleasure over good judgment.

This is cultural denial, passed on by scientists to our citizens as if it were the truth. Active addiction is awful. There is nothing rewarding about it. With repeated use, every time a cigarette-addicted person lights up, their brain compensates for revved-up nicotine signals by reducing the number of nicotinic acetylcholine receptors. This means while the brain is being stimulated, overwhelmed with too much signal, it is being depleted of receptors at the same time, a brain response pattern that causes tolerance. This is what happens to the brain with repeated use of all addictive drugs. No "reward" is necessary. The smoker is just trying to get back to normal function despite changes to SEEKING.

Pleasure is the least powerful driver of behavior. It is the cessation of the unpleasure of the urgent need for a cigarette that makes the nicotine-addicted person feel good. Nicotine provides "relief." The addicted person associates taking a drag with feeling less unpleasure.

Unless drug use is combined with denial, there is no addiction. Denial has nothing to do with reality or other persons. It is reflective of the combination of psychological causes to enact abuse and biological changes, most importantly to the SEEKING pathway, causing drug craving.

I have seen dubious rationalizations, but patients really believe them. They have convinced themselves these excuses are logical. For example, a heroin-addicted patient may tell me that it is the right time for them to stop injecting heroin into their veins, but it is not the right time to stop inhaling burning tobacco leaves. "You can't do more than one thing at a time," they say.

This is an odd justification to keep using one drug while trying to stop another. It is completely illogical. It gives an internal explanation of the enactment of abuse.

My favorite rationalization of all time is being told, "I have to do this." The patient pantomimes moving a cigarette from a distance to their mouth and back down again.

I have also noticed patients crave the familiarity and comfort of smoking with other people who are outcasts, whether it is outside an AA meeting or on the street with other men while waiting for a drug dealer to pull up. There is a kind of rebellion and false intimacy associated with smoking. The apex of idealization of drug use is calling it "enjoying a cigarette with a friend" rather than "actively addicted persons feel better with other actively addicted persons, safe from having the odd behavior of using the lung to get drugs into the brain." Joining others in life-threatening behaviors is nothing a friend would do.

Research by Elizabeth Stuyt[10] showed that abstinence from tobacco during treatment for other substance use improves outcomes. She found that subjects who did not inhale tobacco completed a year sober from alcohol or heroin after a month in her inpatient rehab at 50 percent, subjects who continued to inhale tobacco at 12 percent, and subjects who stopped tobacco at 100 percent. There is only one SEEKING pathway in the brain. Turning on craving with one drug turns on craving for other drugs.

Using tobacco after successfully kicking an addiction to a different drug can be dangerous. Cigarettes can be a marker for a return to the addictive use of opioids or alcohol. Patients have often told me, "I wanted to go back to heroin, but I smoked a cigarette instead."

The interpretation is this: "The cigarette is a marker of craving heroin, and inhaling it makes injecting more likely. There is one craving center in the brain." Patients report that they chain-smoke after injecting. They are aware that heroin use causes cigarette use but not conscious that cigarette use causes heroin use.

Tobacco Anchors Drug Use in General

In the 1990s, cigarette companies were using slimy tactics to hook children on cigarettes, including those that specifically targeted children with a cartoon character, "Joe Camel." Advertisements in convenience stores, grocery stores, and gas stations were often deliberately put down low so they were visible to children. Tobacco companies understand idealization of dangerous substances.

The child who walked into the convenience store in the 1990s and was face-to-face with a cartoon sticker of Joe Camel at eye level may have come to smoke cigarettes as a rite of passage as a teenager, and after becoming addicted to nicotine, a "gateway" drug, they are more likely to accumulate addictions to drugs like booze, pot, and cocaine. Children who start using tobacco before the age of fifteen are eighty times more likely to use illicit drugs.[11] Tobacco is the "heaviest" drug, more addictive, more lethal than alcohol, and while probably causing no more craving than the other plant-based insecticide cocaine, it causes an order of magnitude more deaths.

Cigarettes are important to dealers of illicit drugs since they are the primo gateway drug. Cigarettes are a foundation of the entire addictive drug industry, like a big department store may anchor smaller vendors at a mall. Get children started doing the illegal act of obtaining cigarettes before they are twenty-one, change their brains to facilitate more addictive drugs chaining the SEEKING pathway, and they are set up for purveyors of other drugs.

It is perhaps the epitome of proof that companies pushing tobacco products are in fact drug dealers: they have always targeted children. Despite all the evidence of the horrendous health consequences of smoking, they continue to do so to this day. This is most obvious when we look at vaping.

Vaping

Cigarette manufacturers are constantly trying to improve the cigarette pack, sort of like car companies constantly trying to improve the appeal of their gas-fueled cars, also an old technology. But the recent innovation, the nicotine addiction equivalent of the electric car, is vaping. Cigarette use among children has been gradually declining. The technology to vaporize nicotine, to appeal to children with candy flavors of nicotine, has enabled the tobacco industry to slow the rate of decline of addiction among children.

Enter 2020. Vaping became fashionable. Tobacco nicotine was laced with fruit flavors: grape, watermelon, sherbet, etc., to draw attention away from its addictive qualities and to appeal to younger generations, especially teenagers.

What a wonderful way to get children addicted! The device uses an electric heater to vaporize a nicotine-containing liquid. The machine is cleverly designed so that the device is visually bewitching.

Why don't children vape once in a while? Children like ice cream, but they don't eat it every day. Children love the mall, but they don't go every day. Pleasure, as we have seen, has nothing to do with addiction. The driver of addiction is that a drug that changes the SEEKING pathway takes over the will.

There is a brilliantly explored animal model of how drugs take over the will, the single-cell organism toxoplasma gondii. Toxoplasma lives in cats' guts without causing disease. The cats are happy. The toxoplasma are happy. But how to get to the next cat? Rats are evolutionarily adapted to their predator. The minute they smell a cat, they run in terror.

The cat poops out toxoplasma. A rat brushes by the cat poop. Some of the poop adheres to their fur. The rat licks their fur. The toxoplasma enters the rat digestive system. The toxoplasma penetrates the gut and is pumped through the blood, seeding rat tissues. The toxoplasma is attacked by the rat's immune system, transforming it into its cyst phase of the life cycle. Cysts make tyrosine hydroxylase, a rate-limiting enzyme in dopamine production from the tyrosine in food. The rat is flooded with dopamine.

There is one place in the brain, the amygdala, where the FEAR and LUST instinctual pathways (more of Panksepp-discovered capitalized behavior-determining pathways) run so close that the dopamine seems to jump neural tracks, transforming FEAR into LUST. Now when infected rats smell cats, they are drawn to the most handsome or beautiful sex partner imaginable. These are now rat zombies of the toxoplasma.

Infected rats walk up to cats. The cats eat the rats. Toxoplasma have completed their life cycle. They are back in the gut of a cat.

This is how drug addiction works. The SEEKING pathway is the seat of will.[12] It motivates us to do things that we want to do.

Like zombie rats, zombie children are controlled by cigarette companies. Rats are not happy to be eaten, and cigarette smokers are not happy to be killed. A drug that can change the SEEKING pathway can make the victim behave in ways that make life unpleasant.

This is a second, decisive concept—a drug cannot be addictive unless it has the capacity to take over the brain of the customer. Addiction involves mind control. The drug user experiences a wish for the drug without being aware that their brain has been reorganized by the drug. Saying that one "enjoys" smoking is an expression of mind control.

In an exchange with a world-famous colleague when we had both just published a paper about the concept of will, I suggested he had had his will taken over by a tobacco company. He replied that although many friends and colleagues had expressed concern about his smoking, he enjoyed it. He experienced a wish for the drug without being aware that his brain had been reorganized by the drug.

Once addicted to vaping nicotine, children will see cigarettes as not dangerous—just as zombie rats experience cats as no longer dangerous. They try one cigarette, the nicotine delivered to the now tolerant child is what they were vaping, and snap, the jaws of the trap shut. The brain that had been reorganized to urgently want nicotine now causes these children to inhale tobacco. Twenty-four percent of high school students were users of tobacco in 2020.[13]

A denial system "explains" to the victim why inhaling dirt, carcinogen, and nicotine is all right "for now." This defense is called "displacement." The victim does not do today what they need to do. The action is deferred to tomorrow. The next day, they still plan to quit "tomorrow." Tomorrow never comes. One day at a time is the key to recovery. "Do the next right thing"—today.

The age of kids vaping ranges from eleven to eighteen. In 2021, the National Youth Tobacco Survey found that approximately two million middle and high school students in the United States used vapes/e-cigarettes, with eight out of ten using the flavored kind. Among those children inhaling nicotine, about a third also inhale pot, resulting in many children graduating from high school already addicted to two drugs.

Adults buy into the hype too. Vaping is purported to be safer, less caustic to your lungs and organs, even nonaddictive. It is marketed as a "healthier," and often even harmless, alternative to smoking cigarettes. Doctors participate in this idea by suggesting that vaping is a way to stop inhaling nicotine by inhaling nicotine, a twenty-first century equivalent of "More doctors smoke Camels."

Now the distinct plasticine scent of vapes can be smelled in almost every public location, including the streets. Part of the reason is that vaping is more socially acceptable than smoking cigarettes because it is believed to be somehow related to stopping cigarette use.

This is not true. Some studies show that for every twenty people who try vaping for tobacco cessation, one succeeds, providing cover for the millions who start or continue nicotine addiction by vaping. Although vape smoke probably does contain less than the 7,000 chemicals you inhale in a cigarette, the chemical components in e-cigarettes are largely unknown. In 2022, the CDC reported nearly 3,000 cases of vaping-associated pulmonary injury (EVALI) and 64 deaths that were associated with it. More data links vaping to asthma, chronic lung disease, and heart disease. As was the case with smoking a century ago, enough research hasn't been done yet to determine the health risks associated with vaping because the devices are still new.

SEEKING and Cocaine

Cocaine, methamphetamine, and nicotine are the upper drug group that turns on dopamine directly. Cocaine and nicotine are naturally produced insecticides that give a survival advantage to plants that have evolved to produce them. They are poisons.

SEEKING is engaged by cocaine. I am not surprised that its use is not pleasant once the dopamine system has been degraded. When one listens to users of amphetamines, cocaine, or nicotine, they are not looking for pleasure; they are looking for the sense that SEEKING is fully engaged. Most of us experience this when we are focused on a task: playing basketball, giving a talk, watching an adventure movie, or reading a novel where one urgently wants to know what is going to happen next. All the latter activities require effort.

Smoking a cigarette or using a crack pipe is a passive experience. SEEKING is turned on by the drug without any effort. In fact, some users of crack cocaine report that after a hit, they become unable to move—because the flood of acetylcholine caused by poisoning of the monoamine reuptake transporter protein puts their muscles into spasm.

A cleverly done experiment was carried out with macaque monkeys. They were raised in solitary confinement. This seems to make macaques as miserable as humans would be if raised alone. Their dopamine systems were imaged and found to be uniformly small and low functioning.

Then, they were put together. Like humans, macaques form social hierarchies. The dopamine systems were imaged again. Now the dominant macaques had robust dopamine systems while the subordinate monkeys continued to have small and low-functioning dopamine systems.

Cocaine was introduced into the colony. Low status, low dopamine macaques used compulsively. High status, robust SEEKING monkeys tried the cocaine, but they did not use it much.[14]

My anthropomorphized version of this is based on listening to patients, and a formerly cocaine-addicted physician colleague, describe the effect of cocaine. It makes one feel healthy, engaged, energized—exactly what the SEEKING pathway does.

This would make cocaine an ideal drug for disengaged and bored people. High status, busy persons are already high in SEEKING. They would not have the time to experiment. If they tried cocaine, they would be likely to find it a minor experience.

My physician friend was addicted before he went to medical school. He would say that Alcoholics Anonymous saved his life and gave him the spiritual mission to become a physician addiction specialist. I am suggesting again that adopting an addiction is not a random event. Some people are vulnerable to addiction, and some are not.

Do We Want What We Like?

Wanting and liking are based on two different neural systems. The feeling of wanting is created by SEEKING. Liking is not a pathway but rather a state in the brain caused by a widespread upsurge of endogenous morphine, which we will be considering later.

Therefore, when people with addiction say, "I like to drink," we can translate this into "I want to drink. It is an uncontrollable compulsion. I am going to say, 'I like to drink' to avoid consciously recognizing the horror that my life has become when I drink alcohol."

As long as one can drink, pass out, drink again, pass out again—you are all set. The huge issue is the unpleasure of not drinking. If you can get a drink, the unpleasure goes away. If you are out of money or throw up with every drink because you have alcoholic gastritis, you are miserable.

Or—you get off a plane after not smoking for hours on the flight. You urgently want a cigarette. Or—you have been in prison for years without being able to inject heroin. You have your drug dealer pick you up at the prison gates. Or—your government payment arrives by direct deposit at midnight, you haven't used cocaine since the last payment, and your drug dealer is at your door with cocaine at midnight because he knows when your check arrives. All of these are real stories. When you get to an environment where you can use, craving is extreme, and it disappears temporarily when you take the drug.

The driver of using is not the pleasure of the drug but rather the unpleasure of unrequited craving. Craving is not steady. Withdrawal, being stuck on a plane, then getting off, being in prison, then getting out, having no money, then getting your government payment—these "drug cues" turn on craving.

What exactly is the function of the 'liking' system? It helps one choose between alternatives. If you have $20, and you are a teenager at the mall, do you go for pizza, go to the movies, or buy that cool T-shirt you saw in the window? None of these experiences is driven. The next day, you may forget much about the choices involved.

Liking is not a drive pathway; it is a distributed system. Did you like the movie? Did you buy the red T-shirt or the blue one? Which pizza place did you go to? It doesn't make much difference. Drugs that engage SEEKING make one urgently want them, ahead of any pleasure. Choices don't make much difference and are marked by the experience of pleasure. Addicted persons urgently and unreasonably want drugs no matter what the horror.

Pleasant experiences are less remembered. What was the name of that movie we saw last year at the mall? Should we watch it again on TV?

Note another aspect of the dysfunction of the neuroscience term "the reward system." Using this term confuses neuroscientists interested in addiction. They are thinking about the behaviorist concept of "reward" as something that motivates animals, say the motive of a chicken to peck a key to obtain a kernel of corn. This is anthropomorphized into "The chicken enjoys the corn, and persons addicted to cocaine must enjoy the cocaine." Not understanding how addiction works gets in the way of brain research into cocaine addiction, in addition to creating stigma in our culture.

The Base of This System Is Greed, Lack of Accountability, and Lack of Awareness

Our government supports the sale of drugs by not holding legal addictive drug sellers responsible for the harm caused by their drugs. If you are a well-meaning inventor of a toy for children, and two children choke to death while playing with your toy, you must pay damages. If you produce an addictive drug that you know will injure and kill users, often you have no responsibility. We don't subsidize the toy industry. But by paying for the health costs of tobacco, alcohol, and marijuana, we make it lucrative to sell drugs that cause sickness and death.

Do drug dealers understand craving, the lack of pleasure in drug use, the way their drugs change the brain? Yes, they do. Drug dealers start to put fentanyl into other drugs to increase cravings for their product. We had a patient, who just thought she was smoking crack, go through opioid withdrawal. We had a patient, who just thought he was buying marijuana, die from a fentanyl overdose.

What exactly is an addiction? Caffeine is a drug. People go into caffeine withdrawal. Does this mean that coffee is addictive?

CHAPTER FOUR

Defining Addiction

No one seems to know what addiction is. The four-word definition is "Repeated harm from use." If one inhales sticks of dirt, carcinogen, and nicotine, every stick creates harm. There is no such thing as "social" cigarette use.

On the other hand, alcohol is more variable. One can drink every day, more a Mediterranean tradition than American, and live to an old age. Some people smoke marijuana every night, and it does no harm. Marijuana, like alcohol, is a drug that affects people adversely when they start using it first thing in the morning.

Another slightly longer way to say the same thing is this: "The addicted person urgently wants the drug even though they know it is harming them."

"Repeated harm from use." When I give talks, I start with this definition and then ask all the people in the audience who are "addicted" to coffee to raise their hands or click on the audience response system. Those who raised their hands didn't get the definition. Coffee protects your liver from cirrhosis and cancer, your brain from Alzheimer's disease, multiple sclerosis, and Parkinson's disease, your heart from infarction, your skin from melanoma, your colon from cancer, your joints from gout, your endocrine system from type 2 diabetes, and your mental health from depression and suicide.[15]

Is coffee addictive? No. There is no harm. There is a withdrawal syndrome featuring headache and exhaustion. If you are taking a cross-country plane ride, you can use the withdrawal syndrome to your advantage by skipping your morning coffee. All the way from coast to coast, you can't wake up. You have a coffee when you get to San Francisco or New York. There is a physical withdrawal syndrome from caffeine, but it is not an addictive drug. It does not harm.

Addiction requires harm. One aspect of the mass psychology of addiction is misuse of the term "addiction" for things that people like to do, like drink coffee. To see your friends, family members, or maybe yourself die from drug addiction is too much to bear. We turn to fantasy to imagine that the coffee we drink or the television we watch are addictions. Therefore, the world is full of good and bad that we take together cheerfully.

A denial system must be present for addiction to run its course. Addicted persons want to use their drugs and have a pleasant life. They don't want to consciously and intentionally harm themselves. Therefore, the harm created must be unconsciously experienced.

One example I gave in a paper[16] was Michael, whose girlfriend insisted he come for an evaluation with me because he was drinking twelve beers per day. He drank coffee and smoked cigarettes all morning. He drank beer and smoked cigarettes all afternoon and evening. Michael made good money, had lots of friends, and had a loving girlfriend. Initially, we could not find one bit of harm from drinking.

I screened Michael for alcoholic hepatitis. We found mild elevation of his liver enzymes. He immediately shifted to six alcoholic beers per day and six nonalcoholic beers per day. His liver was fine when he reduced his alcohol intake.

Michael then told me that his real addiction was to cigarettes, and I helped him stop. In his five-year follow-up, he was smoking zero cigarettes per day and drinking about four beers per day. Michael and his girlfriend had instituted a "cleanse" month each January when they completely abstained.

Michael was not addicted to alcohol because there was no denial system. The minute I demonstrated harm to him from his drinking, he modified his behavior in a way that eliminated the harm.

Finally, addictions, whether to drug use or activities such as shopping or gambling, involve loss of control of previously pleasant behaviors. It is the compulsive activity that causes harm. Addiction psychoanalyst Lance Dodes, MD,[17] identified the unconscious hostility contained within addictive behaviors.

Recreational Behavior	Compulsive Behavior	12-Step Recovery Group
Drinking alcohol	Alcoholism	Alcoholics Anonymous
Drinking coffee	Using stimulants such as nicotine, cocaine, or methamphetamine	Narcotics Anonymous
Gambling	Gambling with consequences	Gamblers Anonymous
Shopping	Shopping with consequences	Debtors Anonymous
Making love	Sex with consequences	Sex and Love Addicts Anonymous
Eating	Harm caused by eating	Overeaters Anonymous
Loving people with addiction	Codependently facilitating addiction in a loved one	Al-anon

Compulsions are symptoms that ward off consciousness of a wish to hurt others by taking action to protect them. This defense is called undoing. Checking that the gas stove is off is classic. The person checks carefully that the knobs on the stove are off and goes to bed. Five minutes later, they have to get up and check again. The stove is safe. Five minutes later, they have to get out of bed and check again.

When asked why the person would keep checking, a compulsive justification is "This is a life-and-death matter! If I were to go to sleep without all the care I pour into checking, the house could fill with gas, and a spark could ignite it. My whole family would be killed!"

When asked if there could be feelings of wanting to murder the family, most of us would say, "Of course I want to kill my husband/wife/children/parents sometimes." My mentor for Upstate medical politics, George Blakeslee, relished saying, "Certain people are alive only because it is illegal to kill them."

The person with the compulsion blandly assures, "I love my family. Doctor, the idea that I have urges to kill them is crazy."

When the compulsion is enacted to keep the hostility unconscious, an inside problem about unconscious hostile impulses becomes an outside problem about the knobs on the stove. Since the urge to kill is there no matter how many times one "protects" via undoing that urge, the compulsion goes on until the compulsion is analyzed enough that the wish to kill can be consciously endured. The intent expressed by the compulsive behavior has to be put into words before the undoing behavior is no longer required.

When Freud analyzed the "Rat Man" and discovered the basis for compulsions, he wrote on the first page of his report[18] that sometimes neurotic patients like the rat man can use psychoanalysis to identify the childhood and adult situations that underlay the reluctance to experience the wish to hurt others, but some patients will never tolerate the exploration needed. Freud suggested that eventually medications would be invented that would be needed for sicker patients who were not analyzable. Medications are used now to treat compulsions.

In a way, we are going to have to say the same thing about opioid addiction later. Some patients can tolerate an investigative form of treatment for opioid use disorder, while sicker patients may need medications such as buprenorphine maintenance.

Dr. Dodes's insight was that, in addiction, the compulsion expresses the unconscious hostility by displacement of the wish to injure those close to the person. One way to deal with interpersonal conflict is to talk about it. "My darling, would you please put your dirty dishes directly into the dishwasher instead of leaving them in the sink for me?" The anger produced by finding your wife's dishes in the sink is addressed interpersonally with words. Well-related couples bring up issues that provoke anger often to resolve the issues immediately.

If a husband is drinking alcoholically, it may be because he can't tolerate angry feelings. The words that might express alcoholic drinking could be, "Dishes in the sink again. Won't she be sorry when she comes home and finds me drunk." This is called "the return of the repressed." The wish to punish the wife is evident to the wife but not to the husband. The job of the therapist is to help the husband be conscious of the anger.

Patients may say, "Oh, I didn't know I was drinking because I was angry." Experiencing anger may come into focus as something that the patient was afraid of when growing up. One common example is a parent expressing anger. The little boy became afraid to express angry feelings. When faced with another close relationship, in this case with his wife, the childhood experience is remembered, but not consciously. The wife causes the traumatic memory to be reexperienced, but not consciously. The anger is repressed, then returns as alcoholic drinking.

This brings up a commonly used term in analyzing addictions: "intentional but not conscious." Is the husband, who punished his wife for leaving her dishes in the sink by getting drunk instead of talking to her, responsible for his intentional but not conscious hostile behavior? Yes. Taking responsibility is a healthy way to live. It makes us more powerful actors in our human environment. Can he change his behavior without understanding that drinking alcoholically is "about something"? In psychoanalytic treatment, no. Psychoanalysts need to help our patients be conscious of intentional but not conscious behaviors.

While we help patients uncover unconscious motives for dysfunctional behavior, this same issue is addressed by Alcoholics Anonymous in steps four to ten: take a "fearless moral inventory," then discuss one's failings with a confidant, and eventually, continue "to take a personal inventory and when we were wrong promptly admit it." Does the man need to trace the origin of his difficulty tolerating angry feelings back to childhood abuse? No. AA doesn't require its members to understand or fix childhood experiences. Whatever method is useful to allow good functioning in the present is a fine way to address problems.

Actively addicted people are not nice people. Not seeing the hateful wish to injure others that is expressed by addictive behaviors is cultural or mass denial.

We will consider medical providers later. But we can foreshadow a problem now. Doctors and nurses are expected to be polite, helpful, and caring toward their patients. If they are consciously aware that addiction is a disease that requires hostile behaviors not to be part of their patients' awareness, it leads to successful management of hateful patients. If the provider is not able to allow themselves to be aware that the disease is producing hostility, a commonly used defense is "reaction formation." The patient behaves hostilely, for example, by demanding drugs that they are addicted to. The doctor prescribes the medication. The angrier the provider becomes, the "nicer" they are to the patient. This defense costs us millions of dollars in medical care that is not effective.

For example, I have seen many patients who wish to be admitted to the psychiatric ward for shelter. I have often joked that part of orientation at the Rescue Mission must be "If you get tired of staying here and want to have a hot shower in a safe place, go to the Upstate Emergency Department and tell the psychiatrist that you are suicidal."

I listened and advised, "Come see us outpatient. We will treat you," and discharged the patient. This sometimes resulted in the patient averring, "I am not here for psychiatric treatment. I need to be admitted!"

One patient said, "If I run in front of a car on Adams Street, can I come back?"

I responded, "Sure, come on back when you get run over."

The goal of threatening suicide is hostile but not conscious. It costs $3,000 per day to hospitalize these patients, and their street behavior sometimes injures other patients and our staff. Looking back at previous psychiatric admissions, notes usually said that the patient refused to go to groups and refused addiction aftercare. The "depression" was gone in a day or two. They got a hot shower in a safe place.

In this chapter, we started with a basic definition of addiction—"Repeated harm from use"—and went through some of the underlying psychological dynamics. We discussed why addictive drug use has a compulsive quality that keeps the person from knowing that they are behaving in a hostile way.

This in no way negates the biological nature of addictive drug use changing the SEEKING pathway. We saw that there is a change in thinking caused by the brain change, the denial system. I can only ask the reader to allow two explanations for the same addictive behavior. We do in psychoanalysis, calling it "the principle of multiple function."[19] We understand that behaviors can have multiple causes and motives.

PART 2

HOW ADDICTION WORKS

CHAPTER 5

The PANIC System and Abusive Relationships

We all develop appetites for particular things. When SEEKING is operating within us, it gets tuned to things in the environment.

I hate seaweed. I avoid Japanese restaurants. But I am sure that if I grew up in Japan, I would love seaweed, know many kinds, and fondly look forward to getting some homestyle cooking at the Tokyo Restaurant. Exposure to things influenced by SEEKING early in life creates our interests. For food, it can be seaweed.

For relationships, it is particular types of people. Many people know the idea "We all try to marry our mother or father." This is because we are raised by parents who become the model for who we want to be with because childhood SEEKING is being connected with how each parent feels, smells, talks, interacts, etc.

If one is blessed with kind, attentive parents, you won't think too much about it as a teenager. Your goal at fifteen or twenty-two will be to separate from your parents. But the relationships you form will be based on the kindness, the warmth, of your childhood SEEKING pathway being tuned to wonderful people.

Mostly, you will not be consciously aware of who you are SEEKING. If you shop around, if you have an unconscious agenda about parent-like qualities, you will eventually fall in love—urgently want someone wonderful. This person will resemble your parents in many ways. Wanting and liking will be congruent.

What if you didn't like your parents? What if you grew up neglected and mistreated? Won't you correct this when you grow up and choose a great partner in a way that you could not when you were born to the parents you had?

Unfortunately, this is not how we are built. You will urgently want, the wanting system, someone you don't like, the liking system. What a neurotic conflict! Two neural systems, but only one is in control. SEEKING is the pathway that rules all others. It produces a feeling of urgency. You dated some nice people, but when you were with them, you weren't turned on. They were not what you were looking for, what you wanted.

This is a "We don't make this model, we just service it," moment.

Addicted persons complain about their romantic partners. Not uncommonly, our patient was abused, either overtly or in subtle emotional ways that propitiate relapse, by a partner. Having one's partner be actively addicted usually gives the other "codependent" partner maximum control—until they need treatment again.

We see this when we ask for the drug dealer's name, address, and phone number to send to the Syracuse District Attorney's Office. We run into a conflict between loyalty and conscience that goes far beyond refusing to "snitch." Addicted persons who were abused as children make a tight relationship with their drug dealers.

"I love my drug dealer" is not an uncommon statement on our service. When we go over the facts, the idea that the drug dealer may kill the patient comes out consciously. But the feeling of attachment is unaffected. The patient may be sympathetic to ideas like "He is like a serial rapist. If you don't help us get him arrested, if he doesn't kill you, there will be other victims." But we can't abrogate the feelings of desire, of attachment. Turning in the drug dealer just feels wrong to many of our patients.

Feeling loyalty to abusive partners is a common problem for addicted patients. Jeremy told us that he had a wonderful experience with our outpatient alcohol detox. We loaded him on 2,000 mg of valproic acid, gave him 700 mg of chlordiazepoxide over a few hours, and sent him home in remission from withdrawal after taking 500 mg of disulfiram (Antabuse) given by his girlfriend in front of us.

Jeremy slept great, came back for psychotherapy hours the next two days, then disappeared for eighteen months. When he returned, we asked, "What happened? If you had a good experience with us, why didn't you come back?"

Jeremy explained that after detoxing, his girlfriend refused to give him a ride back for appointments, and he had no other way to get to us.

We also found notes from his cancer doctor in our shared electronic record that he had complained bitterly about being mistreated by me. We had diagnosed borderline personality disorder. Apparently, splitting had ensued. He hated me and maintained his wish to be with his girlfriend despite the fact that she had destroyed his treatment.

Jeremy explained that he had recognized during his 280 days sober that his girlfriend was abusive and a "relapse trigger." He also had a "reservation" that if he was diagnosed with cancer, he would drink again. He was diagnosed with cancer. He drank again.

Jeremy was hospitalized for five days for alcohol withdrawal, describing the experience as "sweating, shaking, insomnia, dangerously high blood pressure," followed by inpatient rehab, a halfway house, and returning "To find out why I drink," with warm feelings toward me. On his return after substantial treatment and solid engagement in AA, he no longer met the criteria for borderline personality.

Part of Jeremy's psychotherapy involved remembering and working through childhood abuse. This may be an example of a wanting/liking conflict, that Jeremy had an intense bond with someone who mistreated him and not much investment in a kind doctor who treated him well.

Often, our patients have "personality disorders," a condition where poor interpersonal functioning makes good relationships at work or with partners impossible. The patient with a personality disorder can be appealing, especially if one is on the good side of the defense of splitting. The patient appears intelligent and yet behaves in ways that are oddly dysfunctional.

When drugs are used to get rid of anxiety generated by not being able to tolerate closeness, addiction has supervened. Work, love, and self-care, the main goals of living, are disrupted by character issues. It is common that a personality disorder is the main psychopathology driving refractory addiction.

If the patient gets engaged with us, they bring expected relationships: internal models of how people act toward them. If we are not abusive, they may disengage. They find their experience with our young, appealing trainees "boring." Alternatively, they may insist that we are abusive.

PANIC was a beautiful discovery of Dr. Panksepp's. FEAR is the neural instinctual pathway that looks outward for anything that can hurt you physically. One can be afraid of a partner or a tiger. PANIC is the instinctual system that measures how close others are. If one is dangerously alone, anxiety warns to get closer. If partners are dangerous, if they inspire fear, and one keeps a distance, one is in a constant panic.

It also hurts to be with people who are not emotionally available. In a description of the function of unconscious fantasy, Anne Erreich[20] wrote, "Avoidantly attached children have had innumerable experiences of having their neediness rejected by their mother, and so, despite signs of physiologic signs of distress, they rebuff or ignore their mother when frightened, denying their neediness and/or doing to their mothers what has been done to them. Especially given what is known about the sophisticated cognitive abilities of even very young infants, it is hard to imagine a mindless infant or toddler who doesn't initially register *consciously* of its mother's rebuff. More likely the early accumulation of this type of experience turns initial awareness into an out-of-awareness prediction or expectation, resulting in a defensive inhibition of the subjective awareness of neediness, as well as need-seeking behavior. This dynamic eventually evolves into a characterological style of relating to self and others. As Paley (2007) puts it, 'Since predictions incorporate past experience and learning, the past biases current experience. In a sense we learn to predict what to expect from the future and then live the future that we expect.'"

The unconscious fantasy of many of our addicted patients "predicts" that the person one depends on will ignore one's need for closeness. This fantasy is applied to current relationships. Therefore, even the most attentive psychoanalyst can't meet the needs of some avoidantly attached patients.

For these patients, closeness causes intolerable anxiety. We try to be close to our patients, and they pull away. If we are unaware of this transference, and the patient is only registering that coming to see us makes them anxious, patients may drop out of treatment because of an uninterpreted transference and post on physician reviews, "If you see Johnson, run."

These concepts can now be added into our understanding of how drugs work. People do not randomly get addicted. Avoidantly attached persons are vulnerable to addiction. Drug dealers approach the general population but capture the subset of persons who have intolerable feelings, including those vulnerable because they are avoidantly attached.

Repetition of Sexual Abuse

When the drive for food is turned on by ghrelin from the stomach, the infant behaves in a way that conveys their hunger, and the parents feed the child. When the child is tired and the drive for sleep is turned on, the parent tunes in and puts the child to bed. If one is a healthy child in this kind of propitious environment, one is constantly played with and cared for, and your lust system is tactfully ignored by adults.

LUST, the neural pathway Dr. Panksepp identified that motivates sexual behavior in animals such as us, is optimally developed in a peer environment[21] starting in adolescence. As you reach puberty, you notice a new drive that moves you to gradually become involved with peers in a sexual way.

Adults are strictly avoided. They are *not* who you are interested in. Adults do not teach children about sex. Children teach each other—in a healthy environment. The exception is childhood sexual abuse.

If one grows up in a benign environment, there is no intense urge to be with good people. They are always there. It is like having food around when you are not particularly hungry. There is not a strong desire to eat. If you are approached by a predator, you move away. Liking generates a wish to be with pleasant people.

If you grow up with abuse and neglect, you are chronically starved for love. A lonely child is approached by an adult predator. An unfortunate aspect of the sexual abuse is that it transforms the loneliness into a sense of a "special" relationship with the predator. The predator is welcomed despite the sexual abuse because of the intense attention.

Abusive adult relationships arise in a context of loneliness created by unconsciously living out neglect. This experience creates a hunger for closeness in the adult, who was a victimized child, for abuse, whether from partners or drug dealers.

Not being able to acknowledge that one lives in a hostile environment, the child takes responsibility for the abuse, creating a sense of shame to replace helplessness. Unfortunately, when adults, the shame can be projected into benign treaters, making them unattractive to patients who SEEK abuse unconsciously.

"You think I'm nothing but a drug addict!" some patients will protest. We are working on an addiction and pain service with empathy for our patients. But the patient's feelings are projected into us, replicating in us the patient's experience of childhood helplessness against a hostile adult. Projection protects at the expense of making the person all alone.

Many abused persons actively disengage from good relationships in this way, then complain that everyone they know is abusive. The sexually abused person assumes that they want what they like, recreating abusive relationships because they want partners who they know unconsciously will hurt them. They find they don't like one partner after another. They disengage unconsciously by using projection and then are lonely.

As you see on the diffusion tensor imaging picture (on page 38), PANIC lies directly on top of SEEKING, as if to turn off basic SEEKING functions to pursue food, water, sex, sleep, and closeness. Addicted persons are usually depressed. Loneliness and isolation are the drivers of their depression.

How Common Is Child Abuse?

We have seen that we can't just ask people if they were abused as children because many of them have repressed their memories of abuse. Intoxicated people are some of the people who we would want to interview, but drug use would make their answers unreliable. Therefore, I am going to focus on the perpetrators.

A finding from the National Epidemiologic Study of Alcoholism and Related Conditions is that when the antisocial personality disorder prevalence was combined with adult antisocial behavioral syndrome, persons only meeting the adult antisocial criteria, it was 25 percent of the population: 32 percent of men and 18 percent of women.[22] Antisocial personality disorder diagnosis requires that before the age of fifteen, the person was aggressive toward people and animals, such as using weapons to harm another, torturing animals, forcing sex on others, destruction of property, deceitfulness or theft, or serious violations of rules, such as being truant from school. Adult antisocial personality behavioral syndrome does not require that the childhood criteria for antisocial personality disorder be met, but it requires at least three of the following behaviors:

- Failure to conform to social norms, repeatedly performing acts that are grounds for arrest.
- Deceitfulness, as indicated by repeated lying, use of aliases, or conning others for personal profit or pleasure.
- Impulsivity or failure to plan ahead.

- Irritability and aggressiveness, as indicated by repeated physical fights or assaults.
- Reckless disregard for safety of self or others.
- Consistent irresponsibility, as indicated by repeated failure to sustain consistent work behavior or honor financial obligations.
- Lack of remorse, as indicated by being indifferent to or rationalizing having hurt, mistreated, or stolen from another.

Peeling away the fantasy that our general human environment is benign is necessary for safer living in the world full of perpetrators. One learns by listening to addicted persons that predators have a special ability to see potential victims.

I first learned this when the archdiocese of Boston settled its priest abuse cases. The predator priests chose their victims carefully. Financial remuneration required a forensic report by a psychiatrist. I heard one story after another of a boy whose priest had carefully evaluated him for potential exploitation. These men all had "après-coup" psychopathology, where reaching puberty after sexual abuse left them aware of heterosexual urges and yet terrified that the priests' sexual activity with them meant that they were homosexual, deepening the trauma. Drug use in this nonclinical middle-aged population was ubiquitous. Drugs were used to get rid of enduring distress. I am sure that the millions of dollars of Catholic Church settlement fueled a boom among the liquor stores and drug dealers of Boston.

When we are calmly accepting of the patient's statements, the technique is called "witnessing," a way to validate and make more real the patient's memories.[23] Our anger is a tolerated countertransference shared in supervision.

Predators' ability to see potential victims in their environment means that victims need to be warned that they communicate vulnerability. Rape victims get recurrently raped. One common therapeutic response to being raped that is discussed on our service is acquiring the ability to kill a man. When a predator steps forward to attack, they expect victims will reflexively step back in fear. By aggressively stepping forward and leading with one's elbow, one can strike the anterior neck, crushing his larynx.

Victims take responsibility for being attacked—a defense against feeling helpless. We don't blame victims for being hurt. We make them aware that in a dangerous human environment, recovery of rage and aggressiveness is necessary to avoid further harm. Predators can sense the fear of rape victims. When helplessness is replaced by aggression, predators look for more vulnerable victims.

The instinctual systems RAGE, FEAR, and PANIC are awful to experience. When Dr. Panksepp put his animals in a box where embedded electrodes turned on in half the box, the animals wanted their electrodes activated when implanted in the LUST, CARE, and PLAY pathways and migrated away from stimulation when electrodes were implanted in the RAGE, FEAR, and PANIC pathways.

The real-world concomitant is probably that in families where children are enjoyed and engaged, childhood is excellent. In families where the unpleasant feelings of RAGE, FEAR, and PANIC are constant, teenagers look for drugs that turn off inescapable misery. Adolescents are the hardest addicted population to engage because they have just learned how to suffer less, they idealize their drug experience, and they do all they can to escape a treatment that they fear will turn RAGE, FEAR, and PANIC back on.

About 25 percent of parents are abusive. Twenty-two percent of Americans die from drug addiction. Correlation does not imply causation, but there must be some relationship between these two realities.

CHAPTER 6

Opioids as a Replacement for People

I am going to increase the complexity of our endeavor by describing the unusual nature of opioid addiction. My plea is that if addiction weren't a complicated bio-psycho-social phenomenon, it would be less recalcitrant to treatment. My assumption is that a good explanation of addiction will lead to a clearer path forward.

Scientific work is done in two ways: idiographic and nomothetic. The classic ideographic example is Charles Darwin's description of the nature of evolution. Darwin sailed around the world with an important stop at the Galapagos Islands. He thought for years and formulated gradual selective genetic changes to adapt to environmental conditions as the engine of speciation.

Although there was some skepticism about his idiographic theory, researchers using nomothetic science, using tools such as statistical analysis of genetic datasets, were able to prove and extend Darwin's concepts. Generally, ideographic science has to precede nomothetic science, observations before numerical analysis, or one ends up with a meaningless collection of unrelated facts—nothing to build treatments on for a life-and-death illness like addiction.

I am reporting in this case report about Guillermo, a systematic observation followed by a neuroscience-backed explanation about a novel finding. He had psychological and physical addiction to opioids, but not to alcohol or marijuana, despite continued use.[24] This is evidence that there is something unique about opioids. Guillermo did not need to give up all addictive drugs to be well.

Guillermo was forty when he initially presented to me with a twenty-four-year history of injecting heroin. He had been to every modality of treatment, inpatient and outpatient. Nothing had worked for more than a few weeks.

He wanted once a week treatment, which is what I provided. Initially, he would arrive at his morning hour with the pinpoint pupils of recently injected heroin. Over my objection, he went on methadone maintenance. He tapered over six months.

Guillermo accurately intuited that the jump from 5 mg per day to zero was unreasonable. Being rich, he flew to a country where a physician could prescribe 5 mg methadone pills. He tapered by breaking the pills into quarters over the next three months. During his final three months of treatment, off opioids, he felt sure he was stably sober. He broke up with his partner, who wanted to continue to inject heroin. We terminated.

I saw him three years later, when his new girlfriend said that he was depressed and should consult me. I found no depression. He had used heroin once when someone on the street offered to sell it to him.

A year later, he was "chipping," using on weekends. He asked to see me once a week. I refused, saying that he had failed once a week treatment. I invited him to come four times per week and lie on my couch. The reply was a more profane version of "You are out of your mind."

He tried twice more for once a week treatment, then came four times per week for psychoanalysis. The initial few months of treatment involved his wish to use heroin and have a good life. We discussed his minor withdrawal every Monday.

We watched his use expand from Saturday to Friday/Saturday to Thursday/Friday/Saturday/Sunday. His Hamilton Depression Rating Scale was 20—moderate. He flew to Cancun to spend two weeks on the beach getting the drug out of his system. Now we were in big trouble.

Annihilation anxiety entered the transference. Guillermo dreaded coming to see me, and I hated seeing him because his annihilation anxiety inhabited me. This countertransference was used to inform the treatment, but it was never spoken about by me.

Guillermo often had nothing to say. I interpreted that the annihilation anxiety needed to be connected with memories. The defense, feelings without ideas, was repression. He started to tell his story by association.

He had teenage parents. His mother probably had borderline personality with recurrent suicide attempts and hospitalizations. When his parents separated soon after his birth, his father was awarded custody but had no interest. Guillermo went with his mother.

During his analysis, Guillermo recovered memories from his first two years of life, memories being alone in an apartment, playing with dirty newspapers. He remembered a boyfriend trying to choke him to death in his crib, only to be pulled off him by his mother.

These memories are called "flashbulb memories." Sometimes, we remember intensely because of heightened anxiety. If the events are even more frightening, they are repressed. Dreams and free association allow them to resurface consciously. It was the distress of the transference—provoked annihilation anxiety that facilitated remembering.

His father checked in with his mother every few months, ending with the mother telling the father, "I dropped him at the orphanage."

Hearing this, his father walked into the orphanage and asked the nuns if he could hold his son. The father walked out the front door and took Guillermo to his parents in the mountains above Bogotá. Guillermo had fond memories of life with his grandmother, who was warm and loving, and his grandfather, who took Guillermo all over town and into the mountains.

This period ended abruptly when Guillermo was twelve. His father, who he hardly knew, walked in the door and announced, "Guillermo, you have a mother and two sisters in Bogotá. I have come to take you home!"

Guillermo excelled at sports and in the academic area that became the base for his business. He was the Cinderella of the house—clearly inferior to his sisters and assigned a number of tasks that he experienced as designed to show him that he was required to submit to his father's authority. There was a crescendo of rebellion and punishment, followed by more rebellion and more punishment, that ended with his father dropping him in downtown Bogotá at age sixteen, saying, "Good luck. You are on your own."

As a charismatic sixteen-year-old, he landed on his feet with a group of artists who injected heroin. He built the concepts that would make him rich and moved to the United States to get away from heroin. He started his business and resumed injecting heroin.

I had no idea how the annihilation anxiety was going to resolve. We had developed the scaffolding on which his difficulty resided, but we were both still exceedingly miserable when we were together. My interpretations were mostly clarifications, along with transference interpretations, that we were experiencing the feelings that went with his childhood memories within our relationship.

Guillermo stuck with the treatment despite his distress when seeing me, which is what we see with neurotic-level patients who start treatment with more ability to tolerate anxiety than borderline patients. He could make the leap of faith that his addiction was about something, and as two smart, well-meaning people, we could get to that something.

Guillermo resolved his anxiety with two actions that surprised me. The first was to find his mother, who, by now, had moved to Venezuela and had a family. He flew down and spent some time getting to know her and her family. He came back with the notion that he had a mother who he had a warm relationship with. The second action was that he insisted on changing the frequency of our meetings to twice a week.

The terror about having relationships had been managed with heroin that granted Guillermo the chemical feeling that he was with someone who loved him while simultaneously avoiding real relatedness. This was his chance to figure out how to regulate closeness in his relationship with me. I had refused the distance of renewing once a week supportive psychotherapy and insisted on four days a week psychoanalysis. Guillermo decided to regulate his closeness to me by changing to twice a week. I recognized that this was the way Guillermo had decided to work out the problem underlying his heroin addiction: recreate the annihilation anxiety in our relationship, then take command of regulating closeness, enforcing his will on me, and demanding to come twice a week. We met twice a week from then on.

Having mastered this with me, Guillermo also managed his relationship with his girlfriend by flying elsewhere to see good friends when he experienced being uncomfortably close with her.

We terminated his treatment after three years. He seemed reliably off heroin.

Nine years after we concluded our work together, I found Guillermo on Facebook. We had a relaxing hour-talk by phone.

He said he had taken one oxycodone pill. "It was stupid!" He said he drank and smoked marijuana sometimes. "I am an old guy. I can't drink like I used to." He had broken up with his last girlfriend because he decided she had alcoholism. He had his first child with his current partner. I sent the 2010 paper's manuscript for his approval.

When he called to approve publication, he said, "My girlfriend said you nailed me."

He meant that how close they were continued to be an issue that was frequently discussed. I understood this to mean that closeness still provoked anxiety, but that Guillermo had the insight to tolerate his anxiety and keep the issue under discussion with his partner. He no longer needed heroin to enact/block the annihilation terror.

Endogenous opioids regulate closeness. This is why Guillermo was able to use alcohol and marijuana. There was no psychological function that made them addictive. The specific function of opioid use to create the feeling of closeness was replaced by his ability to use human interactions, rendering opioids no longer needed.

We will discuss disorders that have to do with opioid function. But first, we need to be sure you know the basics about opioids.

CHAPTER 7

Opioids 101

Solomon Snyder was a pioneer in the field of neuroscience who realized that morphine must have natural receptors to work its magic. He found them and the natural molecule that is produced to fit those receptors in the 1970s.

Unfortunately, he did two other things that work against our use of his discoveries. Initially, he called the molecule "endogenous morphine." This was great. Unfortunately, he contracted "endogenous morphine" to "endorphin." This is an example of switching from English to Greek, the linguistic convention when we want to name something new in science. But the word *endorphin* sounds odd and obscure.

The second mistake was to label endogenous opioids a "neuropeptide." A neuropeptide is a protein that regulates neurotransmission in the brain. One also often finds endogenous opioids described as a "neurotransmitter," a small molecule that creates an immediate effect on whether a synapse fires or not.

An alternative moniker for the types of endogenous opioids that the brain makes is "hormone." A hormone circulates through the blood and has receptors all over the body. An example of a hormone is insulin. It is secreted by the pancreas and responsible for a number of functions, including putting glucose into fat cells.

Here is a table from a 2014 paper about where endogenous opioids have receptors:

TARGETS OF THE ENDOGENOUS OPIOID HORMONAL SYSTEM

- Gut
- Blood: monocytes, B-lymphocytes, T-lymphocytes, mast cells
- Keratinocytes (skin cells)
- Synovium (lining of joints)
- Peripheral nervous system: peripheral fibers, dorsal root ganglia
- Central nervous system: periaqueductal gray, medial thalamus, hippocampus, striatum, locus coeruleus, substantia gelatinosa of the spinal cord, substantia gelatinosa of the brainstem

Why do people in opioid withdrawal have vomiting, diarrhea, gut cramps, and abdominal pain? It is because opioids have inhibitory receptors in the gut. Acetylcholine stimulates the smooth muscle of the intestines, producing peristalsis, the contraction of the gut to churn food though to the rectum, where the digested remnants of food are expelled into the toilet as poop.

Everything in the body is regulated by a series of biological drivers and brakes. While acetylcholine is driving peristalsis, endogenous opioids are slowing the intestinal contraction. Patients who use nicotine and cocaine, drugs that intensify acetylcholine driving to the gut, often report that the first thing they do after using cigarettes or crack is poop. Upper drugs turn on the gut driver. When doctors put patients on opioids, the patients get constipated. Giving exogenous hormone intensifies the brake.

When opioid medications brake the gut, the acetylcholine driver up-regulates. In opioid withdrawal, with a strengthened driver and a weakened brake, peristalsis is overactive, producing the vomiting, diarrhea, gut cramps, and abdominal pain of opioid withdrawal.

We are, unfortunately, saddled with the twentieth-century term "detoxification." Short-acting opioid medications disappear in a day. The toxin is out. But in the gut, endogenous morphine and its receptors, and acetylcholine and its receptors, must rebalance, restoring normal gut function. "Restoration of homeostasis" is a more accurate term than detoxification. This can take a week. It may also be that the homeostasis does not fully return. We will consider this problem later when we discuss the cold pressor test.

The Origin of Opioid Medications

If derived from the poppy plant, opioid medications are called "opiates." Poppy plants have been used for thousands of years because they contain morphine, called on some TV shows about ancient times "milk of the poppy."

Morphine and diacetylmorphine (heroin) are opiates. Heroin was invented by the Bayer pharmaceutical company in 1898 by slightly modifying the morphine molecule. It was oddly chosen, among all the opioid medications, to be made illegal in 1924. Synthetic drugs like fentanyl or methadone stimulate the same receptor system. Anything that does this is an "opioid," including all opiates. Making heroin illegal functioned as a fig leaf over the reality that the whole class of opioid drugs is dangerously addictive. Although one would think that the fig leaf has been removed by the opioid crisis, opioid medication prescribing has not gone down much recently.

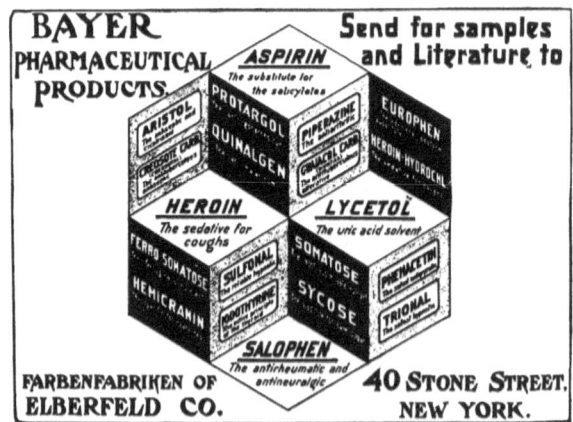

The main differences in opioid medications involve potency and duration of action. An alcohol equivalent regarding potency is beer, wine, whiskey, and vodka. They are different beverages, but all contain alcohol. Whiskey and vodka have high potency because they have more alcohol per volume than beer or wine. Fentanyl and heroin activate opioid receptors. They are called "pure agonists." Fentanyl is one hundred times more powerful than morphine; heroin is three times more potent.

Buprenorphine, most commonly referred to by its original commercial name, Suboxone, is a "mixed agonist—antagonist." The more fentanyl or heroin you take, the more likely you will stop breathing: an overdose. The more buprenorphine you take, the less likely you will stop breathing because the higher the dose, the more the antagonist effect is active at the receptor.

The third class of drugs are pure blockers. Naloxone is only active by nasal insufflation, intramuscular or intravenous administration. Naloxone is marketed as Narcan for accidental overdoses. The other common blocking drug is naltrexone. It can be given orally or by intramuscular injection.

Can you get "high" with buprenorphine or methadone? Before we can answer, we have to ask, "What does 'high' mean?" My best understanding from my patients is that what they mean is high functioning.

The opioid system in animals has a function to reward relatedness. If you see a friend or hold your baby or lover, it feels good. This is because your endogenous opioid system is stimulated by the contact. This function of opioids was first discovered by Jaak Panksepp in 1981.[25] Being able to relate is a sign of high functioning.

The Goldilocks Nature of Opioid Tone

Goldilocks entered the three bears' house and found three bowls of porridge. She hungrily tasted the first and said, "This porridge is too hot!"

Tasting the second, she said, "This porridge is too cold!"

The third was "just right," and she ate it all.

Tone refers to how much opioid receptors are activated by opioids. People enjoy an opioid tone that is "just right," but they feel uncomfortable when it is too high or too low.

Human contact increases opioid tone. When alone, we feel an appetite to make contact. This feels good because our opioid tone goes up toward its optimal point. As our appetite lessens, so does the interest in more contact. After too much contact, it starts to hurt.

OPIOID TONE AND RELATEDNESS

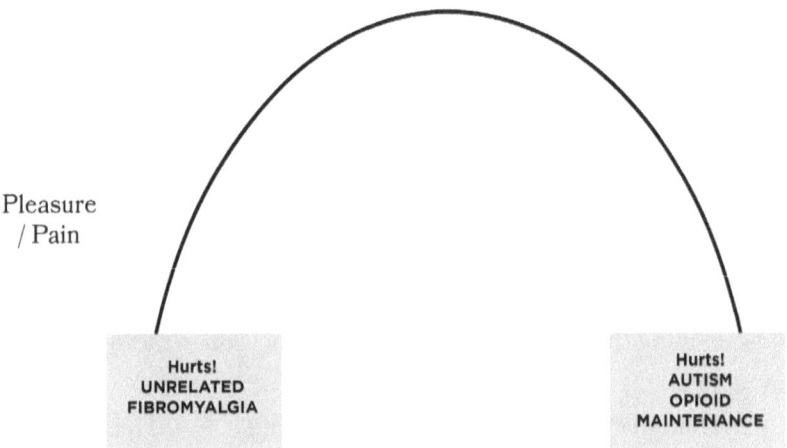

Central Nervous System Opioid Tone / Human Contact

The time we all experience this the most is after work. At home, we eagerly hug our young children. We have been with people all day, but sitting on the lap, snuggling, feels great to parent and child, due to the increase in opioid tone.

By bedtime, most parents have entered the uncomfortable side of the inverse U. Contact hurts. Having the child transfer from the lap to their bed feels good. Reading a story that the parent knows precedes going to sleep feels good. Tiptoeing out of the bedroom without the child waking and demanding more attention feels like a triumph. High functioning!

Having a chronically low opioid tone is miserable. If one is conflicted about making contact because of a history of childhood abuse, wanting it but avoiding people out of FEAR opioid tone is low. PANIC is turned on. If one has been raped, sexual contact does not feel safe because FEAR is triggered. Snuggling is unpleasant.

High-functioning people do not seek opioids because taking a pill makes their optimal tone feel uncomfortably excessive, like a child who won't go to bed. One of my colleagues told me, "I took one oxycodone, and I was miserable. I felt like committing suicide."

Traumatized people who are in constant pain from low opioid tone find opioids a joy. "This is finally how I always knew I should feel!"

"I took an oxycodone, and I could clean my house!"

Note that they never say, "I took an oxycodone and snuggled." The pill gives the feeling of a snuggle. We saw this with Guillermo. He didn't use heroin to be close. He used it to tolerate his lonely existence.

We call opioid medications "a person in a pill." Opioids reduce FEAR. One patient told me, "I could rob a crack house on heroin." Patients who have been raped routinely use opioids to make having sex possible. In fact, some patients report that they have never had sex without using drugs. Opioids reduce PANIC, allowing a feeling of serenity in place of chronic anxiety. Opioids turn off RAGE. One patient told me that he had had it with his girlfriend. He had decided that he was going to go home after work and murder her. "But I stopped on the way, bought a bag of dope [heroin], and we had a nice evening together." Opioids make people with terrible emotional problems high functioning.

Notice the application to stigma. Saying that people want to get high from drugs sounds awful. The reality that the goal of using drugs is to be high functioning despite terrible emotional problems shows that drug use is a desperate attempt to address distress. We saw in chapter 5 that the goal of using upper drugs—nicotine, cocaine, and methamphetamine—was to enhance engagement with the world by turning on SEEKING. The goal of using opioids addictively is to turn off FEAR, PANIC, and RAGE to allow a façade of functioning normally in relationships in general and in sexual relationships for victims of sexual abuse.

Blaming people for having terrible emotional problems is a disease in itself. It is the narcissism of codependence. The defense involved is identification with the aggressor. Codependence, bullying addicted persons in a way that joins drug sellers by using identification with the aggressor, reduces anxiety at the expense of obscuring reality. Abusive people often do not notice consciously what they are doing. The victims feel the hostile stigmatization, but the perpetrators just feel calm and justified. Saying that people use drugs to get high is not accurate; it is codependent.

Patients on methadone or buprenorphine maintenance for opioid use disorder are already in the uncomfortably too high zone. They behave like autistic patients: gaze avoidance, disengaging behaviors, discomfort making emotional contact with words, not wanting to be touched.

On maintenance, one can make their children's lunches for school, but snuggling is not appealing. One patient on our buprenorphine maintenance service said, "I can hear my wife and daughter playing in the next room. I know I should go in there and be with them. But I don't feel like it. I sit on the couch and watch television."

We did buprenorphine maintenance groups for a while. Everyone on our service hated them. Feeling exasperated one day, nurse practitioner Tom Ringwood said in group, "All we talk about here is motorcycles, snowmobiles, and lawnmowers. Would someone talk about emotions or relationships?"

Tom reported two minutes of silence. Then one of the group members spoke up. "Hey. Have you guys heard about the Mars rover?"

An animated group discussion followed.

If this is true about opioid drugs ruining the opioid receptor system and making people unrelated, it seems to me that someone ought to find a way to measure that damage and find a way to fix it. One would think that if opioid drugs make people autistic/unrelated, there would be constant experiences in empathic treatments that the unrelatedness disappears with detox and correction of the receptor system.

One would never see this if one's only answer to opioid use disorder was opioid maintenance with buprenorphine or methadone or blocking the opioid system with naltrexone. Who provides treatment without prescribing these medications for opioid use disorder (MOUD)?

We do. We constantly detox patients from opioid medications and watch the autistic behaviors evaporate. Patients walk in on maintenance opioids for addiction, or opioids taken four times a day for chronic pain, acting flat, cold, unrelated. After detox, they are emotionally engaged and fun.

Jaylen arrived with his chief complaint being that he wanted our help to detox from buprenorphine. We get these patients because their buprenorphine providers refuse on the grounds that conventional guidelines recommend that no one is to be taken off, and because the providers have no idea how to do it. Patients report that getting off buprenorphine is far harder than detoxing from heroin. Standard practice is to use a taper from 16 mg to 14 mg to 12 mg and so on. I call this the "second-grade arithmetic approach." It requires mastery of subtraction.

Jaak Panksepp told me the human brain makes the equivalent of 0.5 mg/day buprenorphine as endogenous morphine, and Jaak published a review of the use of low-dose naltrexone (LDN) to stimulate endogenous morphine in 2009, just as I was starting Upstate Addiction Medicine.[26] If you do taper buprenorphine, the hardest reduction is 1 mg/day to zero, as if the receptors at 1 mg/day are still forced to activate less because so much more exogenous hormone had been provided above what the native state is like. Restoring homeostasis is painful.

This is what I found before 2009. Few patients can tolerate going from 1 mg/day to zero, and if they do, they have protracted withdrawal: misery, cold, anxiety, nausea, and inability to sleep for weeks or possibly months. Mostly, patients relapse and report that they need buprenorphine maintenance forever.

We have found that no taper is needed. One can go directly from 32 mg/day to zero, as long as you give LDN to stimulate the opioid receptors to grow back. Withdrawal usually ends in a few days.

When we first met Jaylen, he told us he had tapered down to 4 mg/day and "Buprenorphine saved my life. I go to work every day, and I am going to my kids' soccer games."

After his LDN treatment and some psychotherapy, Jaylen said, "Oh, my god! I used to stand alone and watch the games. Now I realize the sidelines are filled with parents. We talk constantly during the games, and I have become friends with some of them."

This is an example of switching from autistic behavior on maintenance to becoming socially related after detox. Practitioners who have never seen this change might advocate maintenance because "I go to work every day, and I am going to my kids' soccer games."

The goldilocks model of maintaining optimal opioid tone allows us to describe various phenomena, including pathological ones. First, we now understand why well-related people take one opioid pill and say, "Never again." They are dizzy, nauseous, out of it, miserable. Physicians, who tend to be high functioning, well-related people, wonder why opioid pills would be addicting in the first place. When they themselves tried opioid pills, they had a negative reaction.

Naïve physicians say, "Opioids are great pain relievers. I gave it to a patient in pain. They felt relief. What could the problem be?"

This is one origin of the tendency to stigmatize patients who get addicted to painkillers. "I am not interested in opioids myself, but I know opioid medications help pain. What is *wrong* with these people?

One minute, they are taking my oxycodone the way I have instructed them to. The next thing I know, they are injecting heroin. They want their reward system activated all the time, and with no effort!"

These physicians don't understand the goldilocks nature of opioids and that their brain is not functioning like the brains of their traumatized patients.

CHAPTER 8

Autism and Fibromyalgia as Disorders of the Endogenous Opioid Hormonal System

Why are these common diseases in this book? It is because autism, fibromyalgia, and opioid use disorder are due to changes in the opioid hormonal system. These are discoveries from Upstate Addiction Medicine that are not widely accepted. The reasons will be explained later. The reader may want to cautiously evaluate my evidence and see what they think. The consensus on autism and fibromyalgia is that the cause is unknown.

Autism

If the thyroid gland is making too much thyroid hormone, one has hyperthyroidism. This disease can be treated by administering medications that reduce the production of thyroid hormone, blocking it down into the normal range. Physicians follow thyroid hormone levels.

What about persons with too high endogenous morphine? These people are uncomfortable. They occupy the area past the right side of the bar on page 89. They would do anything possible to avoid human contact because it hurts.

The human disease like this is autism. Autistic people don't want to look at others, learn language, or be touched, the ways we contact others. Once again, we rely on Dr. Panksepp to give us empirical evidence about how the endogenous opioid system underlies the disease:

FIGURE 1. Plasma N- and C-Terminally Directed β-Endorphin Protein Immunoreactivity Obtained in 67 Children With Infantile Autism, 22 Girls With Rett's Syndrome, and 67 Normal Comparison Subjects[a]

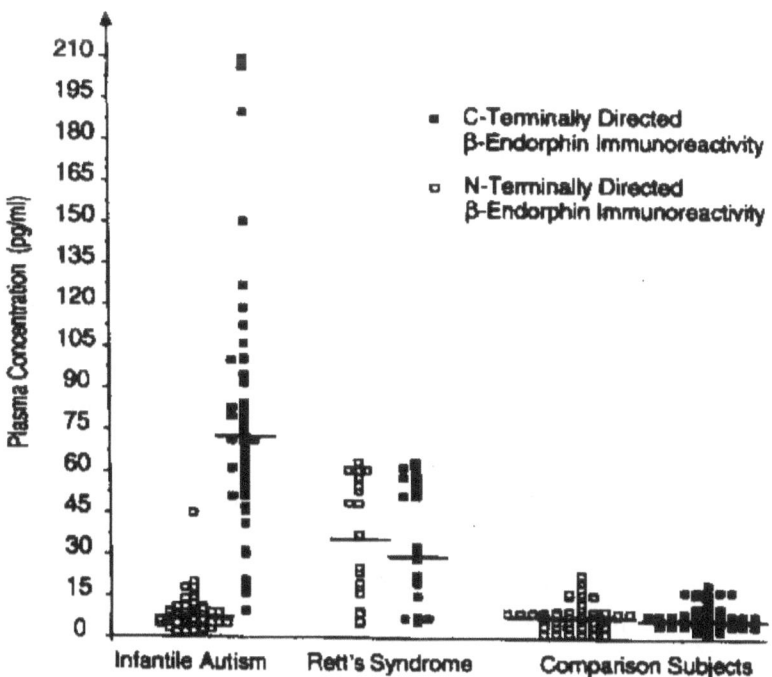

You can see that the level of C-terminally directed beta endorphin in autism is about ten times normal. One would want to measure C-terminally directed beta endorphin in autistic persons—and block it down to the normal range with the pure opioid blocker naltrexone, while observing the behavioral results such as lessening the gaze avoidance.

Notice the underlying concept that people with different brain systems behave differently. We feel good when we look in someone's eyes as we talk to them because it builds our opioid tone up to the top of pleasure. Autistic persons have way too much endogenous morphine. They live in constant emotional pain. When an autistic person's experience that human contact via looking in another person's eyes, it hurts, and they look away. Autistic persons don't act normal because their brains don't function normally.

Dr. Panksepp tried naltrexone with French child psychiatrist collaborators that he needed to work with because all his work was with animals. Naltrexone worked sometimes. A few other clinicians published small clinical trials in the 1990s that were somewhat successful. The field lost interest.

As a neuropsychoanalytic service that makes systematic observations combined with using neuroscience, we were in a perfect position to try out Jaak's approach and watch what happened. When I put "naltrexone AND autism" into PubMed on February 23, 2023, two of the top ten papers that came up were from our service. Only three of the papers had to do with treatment of autism.

The reason that we saw autistic patients on Addiction Medicine initially was because they arrived for treatment of alcohol, tobacco, and marijuana addiction—but never opioid addiction. Our goldilocks model of pain caused by too high opioid tone explains why. Opioid pills would cause pain! Now autistic patients also arrive because in the Upstate psychiatrist community, many have seen what naltrexone does.

Since C—terminally directed beta endorphin—is a test available only at a few research laboratories around the United States, we use the cold pressor test (CPT) as a proxy of endogenous opioid tone. The CPT is simply a beer cooler full of ice water, stirred by an aquarium pump so a sheath of warm water doesn't build up around the normal forearm of the patient we are testing.

Having one's forearm in the tank really hurts. We give the instruction, "Make sure your forearm is completely submerged and your fingers are apart. Keep it in as long as you can and take it out when you must." We time how long the patient can tolerate the pain of having their arm submerged. The longest we allow is three minutes.

Many autistic patients start at three minutes because of their high opioid tone. As we block them down with high-dose naltrexone to about one minute, they feel better and relate better. However, we are, for the first time in their life, creating the experience of emotional engagement for an autistic person who has not had the pleasure and pain of relationships since birth. What we found was that the naltrexone blockade had to be combined with psychotherapy to help patients tolerate feelings that they had never experienced before. Adding psychotherapy to the naltrexone treatment takes us an important step past where Dr. Panksepp was. But psychotherapy is a huge and complicated endeavor.

For example, in 2021, we published a case report typical of our approach.[27]

"The clinical diagnosis of autism in a 25-year-old man was confirmed by a Social Responsiveness Scale (SRS) self-rating of 79, severe, and a Social Communications Questionnaire (SCQ-2) by the patient's father scoring 27. CPT was 190 seconds—unusually long, consonant with the high pain tolerance of autism. At naltrexone 50 mg/day SRS fell to 54 and SCQ—2 to 9: both non-significant. CPT fell to 28, repeat 39 seconds."

Initially, Melvin had the odd thinking typical of autism. He thought more clearly and expressed himself nicely when his CPT came down. When Melvin started to experience feelings, he experienced interpersonal distress that resulted in stopping naltrexone and quitting treatment, only to come back when he bizarrely cut open his palm, requiring nine stitches.

No borderline patients cut their palms. It hurts too much. I think Melvin was trying to create pain to balance the misery of high opioid tone. Young autistic patients often bang their heads, I think, for the same reason.

Melvin eventually spent three years in twice-a-week therapy. His function improved immensely. Initially unemployable, he had a steady, full-time, well-paying job. Initially friendless and isolated, he spent time with friends and family. Initially addicted to tobacco, alcohol, and marijuana, he became sober and went to some AA meetings. But without psychotherapy, none of these gains would have persisted. Experiencing feelings he had never had before was super distressing.

We published an updated description of the goldilocks model of opioid tone:

PAIN / PLEASURE AS A FUNCTION OF OPIOID TONE

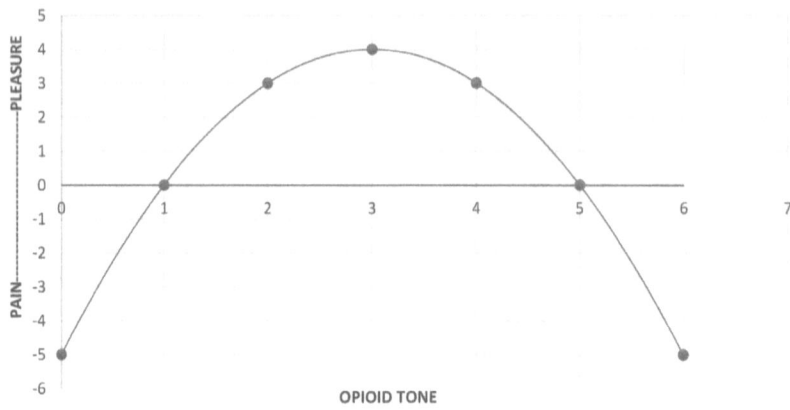

This model employs a quadratic equation to schematically show our understanding of pleasure-pain and human closeness regulating endogenous opioid tone. An underlying principle is that calculus seems to describe the natural world.[28]

Pleasure $(x) = 4 - (x-3)^2$

x = opioid tone, limit $x = 0 < x < 6$

This equation represents our clinical observations as follows:

When healthy persons feel the distress of loneliness, they seek comfort through the proximity of others to increase opioid tone. It feels good.

Prolonged intense contact causes discomfort. Healthy humans seek solitude to reduce high opioid tone to a pleasant level.

Human contact is used to modulate opioid tone between 2 and 4. Healthy persons can engage and disengage flexibly.

Autism's high endogenous tone, between 5 and 6, causes ordinary human contact to be uncomfortable.

A question that everyone asks is "Why is the prevalence of autism going up so sharply, from being a rare disease when first identified by Leo Kanner in the 1940s to one in forty-four births in 2021?"

A "three hit" model of autism posits:

A genetic neurodevelopmental vulnerability. Common and rare genetic variants contribute to autism spectrum disorder etiology. There are differences in polygenic architecture across clinical subtypes. Genome-wide association studies show five loci on chromosomes 1, 3, 5, and 7.

An environmental stressor that interacts with genetic vulnerability. With these in place, development is adversely affected.

We would want to look for the second "hit."

In our 2014 review of obstetric literature, moving from the "natural childbirth" ideal of the 1970s to the American College of Obstetrics and Gynecology encouraging opioid administration during childbirth in the 2000s, we suggested opioids given during childbirth were responsible for missetting endogenous opioid tone that is normally set by the pain of being born. Opioid pain treatment during childbirth was causing autism in genetically vulnerable newborns.[29] We offered this as a possible cause while appreciating that correlation does not require causation.

Here is the correlation from our 2021 paper, updated from the 2014 paper:

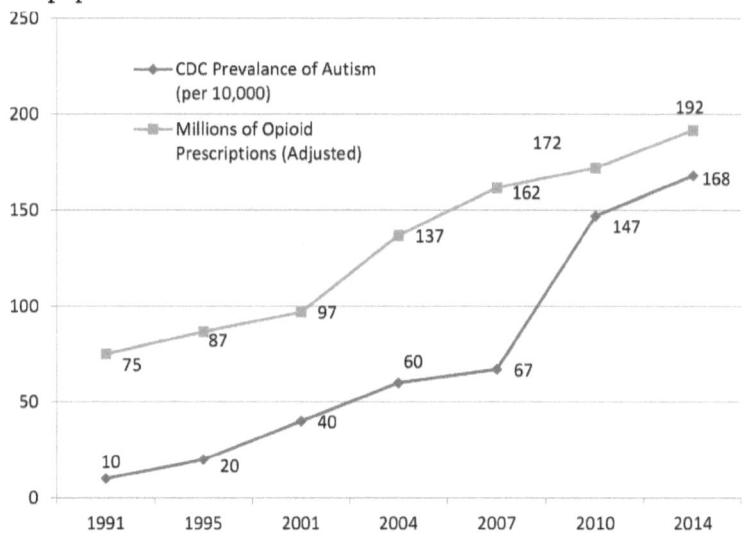

Autism rate and opioid prescription correlation. Correlation $p < 0.001$

High opioid tone provides an explanation for the diversity of findings in autism.

Development is influenced by aberrantly high pain that human interactions provoke. Looking, touching, and speaking augment tone, which worsens pain, forming the basis of social withdrawal, lack of speech mastery, and gaze avoidance.

Parents are in an impossible position. They seek empathic connections ignorant of the reality that empathy relies on everyone having similar brains. Conventional acts of parental love create pain in the child. Any parent would react with confusion when their child recoils from their loving ministrations. Different brains create different responses to human contact.

Intestinal problems could be a direct effect of opioids on the gut, analogous with opioid-induced constipation. There is an additional effect of opioids on immune functions located in the gut to prevent bacterial infection that toll-like receptors and opioids modulate. High opioid tone may turn on inflammatory cytokines that disrupt gut function.

Glial cells in the brain also have toll-like receptors. Endogenous opioids and inflammatory cytokines co-regulate at the toll-like receptors, type 4 (TLR4). High opioid tone may evoke inflammatory cytokines, accounting for brain inflammation in autism.

Endogenous opioids inhibit norepinephrine function in the locus coeruleus that fuel stimulation of corticostriatal pathways. Inhibited norepinephrine secretion may result in the high prevalence of ADHD in autism.

Disordered sleep is ubiquitous in opioid-maintained persons. High opioid tone would account for a similar symptom in autism.

Anxiety is a signal that one is distant from loving persons. Relationship avoidance to prevent pain creates distance, fitting the high prevalence of anxiety in autism. Autistic persons avoid the pain of closeness at the price of anxiety generated by separation.

The application of our experiences with autism to treating opioid-addicted patients is that exogenous opioids, whether obtained from doctors or drug dealers, makes our patients autistic when we first meet them. Detoxification results in a wonderful restoration of relatedness, as discussed about Jaylen earlier. But the same need to tolerate feelings that had been ablated by opioids results in the concept that psychotherapy is needed so that patients can tolerate newly restored feelings. Without psychotherapy, none of their gains persist. Experiencing feelings that opioids had eliminated is super distressing.

Fibromyalgia

Just as hyperthyroidism is a disease caused by too much thyroid hormone, and hypothyroidism from too little, seeing opioids as a hormone, we would anticipate a hormonal disease that is the opposite of autism, a disease where there is not enough opioid tone in the body. That disease is fibromyalgia.

The website of the American College of Rheumatology says, "*Fibromyalgia is not from an autoimmune, inflammation, joint, or muscle disorder.* There is most often some triggering factor that sets off fibromyalgia. It may be spine problems, arthritis, injury, or other types of physical stress. Emotional stress also may trigger this illness."

I will show what we know. I will make the case that fibromyalgia *is* an autoimmune disorder. But first, a simple concept about hormonal diseases with thyroid hormone as an example.

The thyroid gland in our neck makes thyroid hormone. It circulates through the blood and adjusts metabolism in our cells. We hope our thyroid hormone stays in the healthy range. If it is too high or too low, physicians have the technology to diagnose this hormonal disorder and to do something to correct the problem. The autoimmune disease that attacks thyroid tissue is called Hashimoto's thyroiditis. Autoimmune diseases run together. Sixty-two percent of persons with Hashimoto's thyroiditis have fibromyalgia.

Notice that no one labels too high or too low thyroid hormone as caused by a "triggering factor" such as spine problems, arthritis, injury, or other type of physical or emotional stress. In fact, all medical practitioners know that too high or too low thyroid hormone has to be corrected before psychiatric disorders will respond to treatment. For example, a standard workup for refractory depression is to evaluate thyroid function.

Blaming "triggering factors" is like saying, "My car had only 300,000 miles on it. When I got off at the Teale Avenue exit, my muffler dropped off. The Teale Avenue exit was the trigger." The sun also rose that day. But neither the Teale Avenue exit nor the sunrise had anything to do with the muffler falling off, and spine problems, arthritis, injury, or emotional problems have nothing to do with triggering fibromyalgia.

Fibromyalgia is three times as common in women as in men. It runs in families. It comes on in adulthood, sometimes triggered by the hormonal changes of the onset of menses or pregnancy. These are all aspects of an autoimmune disease.

In our hormonal model, an autoimmune process strikes the μ-opioid receptors. Since the gut is responsible for peristalsis, and the braking system is impaired because of autoimmune-injured opioid receptors, the gut would be hyperactive in the same way as in opioid withdrawal. Fibromyalgia patients are diagnosed with "irritable bowel syndrome," as if it was a separate disorder.

Endogenous opioids are responsible for an experience of being warm. Patients report that injecting heroin causes a sensation of warmth that spreads up from the lower back. They give energy. "One oxycodone, and I can clean my whole house!" If the system was low functioning, one would expect cold intolerance and chronic fatigue. In fact, fibromyalgia's symptoms are identical to opioid withdrawal, as we showed in this table from the 2014 paper:[29]

CONGRUITY OF OPIOID WITHDRAWAL AND FIBROMYALGIA SYMPTOMS

SYMPTOM	OPIOID WITHDRAWAL	FIBROMYALGIA
Feels cold	Common	Common
Diarrhea	Common	Common, often labeled irritable bowel syndrome in fibromyalgia
Restless Legs	Common	Common
Depression	Common	Common
Intolerable anxiety	Common	Common
Insomnia	Common	Common
Fatigue	Common	Common, often labeled chronic fatigue syndrome
Generalized pain	Common	Common
Can't work	Common	Common
Sweating	Common	Common
Trouble thinking	Common	Common, often labeled fibro fog

Since we were already treating protracted opioid withdrawal and opioid-induced hyperalgesia (OIH) with LDN, we decided to try it for fibromyalgia. Here is the first patient's six-month course:[30]

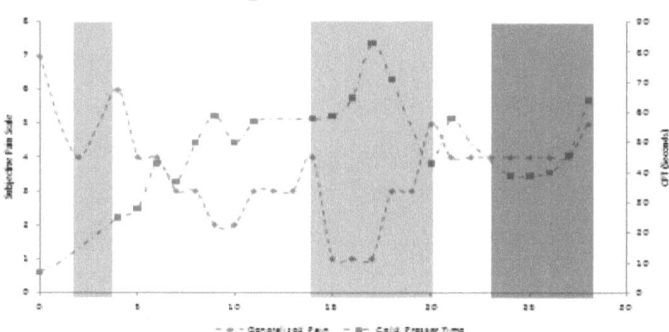

CPT in seconds.
Subjective pain scores on a scale of 0-10 (0: best & 10: worst).

The gray bars are times the patient was off LDN. The first time, it was because of a misunderstanding. The red line is the CPT. The blue line is the faces pain scale. You can see them varying inversely; CPT goes up as the faces pain scale goes down.

This was a tough, max-effort man. When he had to take his arm out of the ice bath after seven seconds, it was because he experienced immense pain. His fibromyalgia had been so bad that not only did he have most of the eighteen tender points typical of fibromyalgia, but he also had pain all over his body, including the soles of his feet. He would have to pull his car to the side of the highway to rest his eyes because his extraocular muscles hurt from keeping his eyes on the road while driving. His mother and brother had fibromyalgia.

LDN helped. At fourteen weeks, I thought I had cured fibromyalgia. I stopped the LDN. Initially, pain tolerance improved, and pain sank to almost nothing. Two weeks later, the fibromyalgia came back. The purple bar indicates that we eventually started to flex the dose of naltrexone to specifically match the patient's response. Currently, our patients say that twice-a-day dosing is best. Some of them notice pain and fatigue coming back in the afternoon. The second dose of naltrexone again improves their symptoms.

LDN works by turning on opioid growth factor, opposing the autoimmune receptor destruction. Whether LDN will be a long-term help, or the autoimmune process will continue to destroy the receptor system until there is nothing for LDN to bring back, is unknown. The response rate in a case series[28] was 80 percent. I suspect that the unresponsive 20 percent had such severe destruction of their opioid receptor system that the LDN had little to bring back.

I expect that a specific monoclonal antibody will be discovered to oppose the destruction of the μ-opioid receptor by an autoimmune antibody for fibromyalgia treatment. The monoclonal antibody would be used to stop receptor destruction. It would need to be used with LDN to coax back the receptors. Because 3 percent of Americans have fibromyalgia, the monoclonal antibody should be a blockbuster medication for some pharmaceutical company.

LDN seems to have a single, reversible side effect: pedal edema. This side effect occurred in two patients out of hundreds treated.

Overall, the "effect size" of LDN for fibromyalgia in one of our case series was 0.63,[31] moderate and higher than FDA-approved medications for fibromyalgia, milnacipran, a serotonin-augmenting antidepressant, duloxetine, a serotonin and norepinephrine augmenting antidepressant, and pregabalin, an anticonvulsant that suppresses the signal of pain. Our treatment specifically addresses the disease process, while the other agents have a small effect based on reducing the ability of the brain to feel signals from the body.

I have shown that our hormonal concept of the cause of autism and fibromyalgia yields treatments that work. Just as we receive referrals for high-dose naltrexone for autism treatment from our Upstate child psychiatry colleagues, we have received hundreds of referrals for evaluation and treatment of fibromyalgia patients from our Upstate rheumatology colleagues.

What has been missing is dissemination of these ideas outside of Syracuse, although treatment of fibromyalgia with LDN has caught on worldwide and I have been asked to review several papers by rheumatology journals and a LDN research proposal from Spanish colleagues sent by *BMJ Open*. A 2023 systematic review of papers worldwide found nine well-done studies, including four from our service.[32]

CHAPTER 9

Ignoring the Function of Opioids to Regulate Closeness

Pharmaceutical Dealers

The Right to Pain Treatment Movement

What some physicians don't know but is apparent on our neuropsychoanalytic service is that emotional pain and physical pain are sometimes so close in subjective experience that few can tell the difference. Patients in emotional pain want opioids. Why would they have emotional pain? Because they can't perform the interpersonal optimization of emotional closeness described above. We hate to categorize our patients since each one is so unique in their experience. However, we use standard rating scales to generate nomothetic information so that we can bundle individual patients into more general categories. Half of the opioid-addicted patients we take into treatment have borderline personality disorder.

Opioid Addiction and Borderline Personality Disorder

Borderline personality disorder might be described as, "The person is terrified of being close to others and keeps trying, but they use dysfunctional defenses." An example of a dysfunctional defense is splitting. At one point, we looked up my patient evaluations on the internet. Forty-eight percent said that I was outstanding; forty-eight percent said that I was awful. I don't think that the ratings had to do with me. I think our patients had to see me as either all good or all bad, splitting as a defense to reduce the anxiety of an intense emotional encounter.

Opioid Use Disorder: Drug-Free Treatment or Opioid Maintenance?

Opioids are the solution for many people. Let's return to Marta and Maria, who we met in chapter 1. Both had been raised in Mafia families.

I put Marta's first memory, going into the garage and finding the man chained by his arms, legs, and neck, into her discharge summary. Marta was on our harm reduction ward at Bournewood Hospital, the other ward being for patients in drug-free recovery. Marta left on buprenorphine maintenance. After discharge, she called me and asked me to take that story out of her discharge summary because her father had read it. I said no, we can't change records.

After I hung up, I worried that her father would come by the hospital to murder me. He didn't want to be identified as a Mafia member. Marta was using opioids so she could tolerate being close to her father, a man she knew murdered people. It is likely that she was using splitting so she could love her father.

Maria left her family. She lived briefly with a Black man. When she realized that her family planned to murder him because interracial relationships were prohibited in Mafia culture, she told him she was going out to buy some milk and took a plane to Los Angeles. It was an act of love. Maria valued his life over their relationship. She still loved him when I treated her.

When Maria moved back to Boston twenty-five years later, she was invited to parties that took place when relatives got out of prison and were welcomed back to continue to commit crimes. Prison time was regarded as part of the overhead cost of doing business. Maria was careful never to speak to her relatives again.

Maria was able to stay sober from heroin except for one brief period. I was seeing her for depression. Her daughter was struggling with addiction. When the daughter wouldn't answer the phone, Maria went to her daughter's apartment. She could hear the baby crying, but there was no answer. Maria had the landlord open the door. She found her daughter with her mother-in-law. The mother-in-law had split a month's prescription of oxycodone and clonazepam with Maria's daughter. The mother-in-law was stuporous, and Maria's daughter was dead.

I called the internist who had prescribed oxycodone and clonazepam so he wouldn't do it again. When he heard what had happened with his prescription, he hung up on me.

Heroin replaced the daughter Maria felt she could not live without. Maria's AA supporters and I helped her through a few weeks of use that recapitulated Maria's teenage addiction when she was all alone. But her recovery had surrounded her with loving people. She got sober again and finished treatment with me. She came back yearly to check in and get another year's prescription for bupropion. She resumed her leadership in the recovery community.

Like Guillermo, Maria had the capacity to allow herself to make a leap of faith that, despite her experience with her parents, some people would be dependable. Marta could not let go of someone abusive. She needed opioids, the "person in a pill" that allowed contact with her abuser. No judgment. Some patients who are addicted to opioids can make a drug-free recovery. Others need maintenance treatment with opioids.

Opioid Addiction and ADHD

Jaak Panksepp discovered rat laughter. He loved his animals. He played with them all the time. He realized that they must be laughing at a vocalization frequency too high for human ears to perceive. He put a transducer in the cage and showed that they laughed when he chased them around the cage with his hand and tickled them.

I am sure there is a genetic component to ADHD. Some children are hyperactive from the day they are born. Vigorous interactions with parents prevent or reduce ADHD.

When my grandchildren were preschoolers, and I would take care of them while their parents were away, all three of them would gang up on me. I weighed more than all three put together. But they would cooperate to see if they could knock me down and subdue me. We all had fun. PLAY is a lusty, exciting, pleasant instinctual system shared by all mammals.

Rats wrestle. Jaak showed that if a small rat is not allowed to pin the larger rat at least 30 percent of the time, the small rat walks away. No fair! Dr. Panksepp showed what happened when his rats were not allowed to play—social rats who wrestle all the time compared to rats who are raised in solitary confinement. When they are put in with other rats, they are hyperactive!

What about humans? So many of our patients describe bleak childhoods where they were left on their own. We find a high prevalence of attention-deficit hyperactivity disorder (ADHD) on our service, close to 50 percent of our admissions for opioid addiction. Patients with ADHD don't take information in from other people. One of the diagnostic criteria is "Doesn't listen when spoken to directly." The lack of interpersonal contact makes them a setup for addiction.

Below is a graph of comorbid disorders we found among patients in a case series who were labeled "addiction" (light bars) patients or "pain" (dark bars) patients based on whether they only met the criteria for opioid use disorder based on tolerance, withdrawal, and inability to stop their opioid medications on their own—pain patients—or had other symptoms of addiction such as spending large amounts of time obtaining, using, and recovering from the effects of opioids—addicted patients.[33]

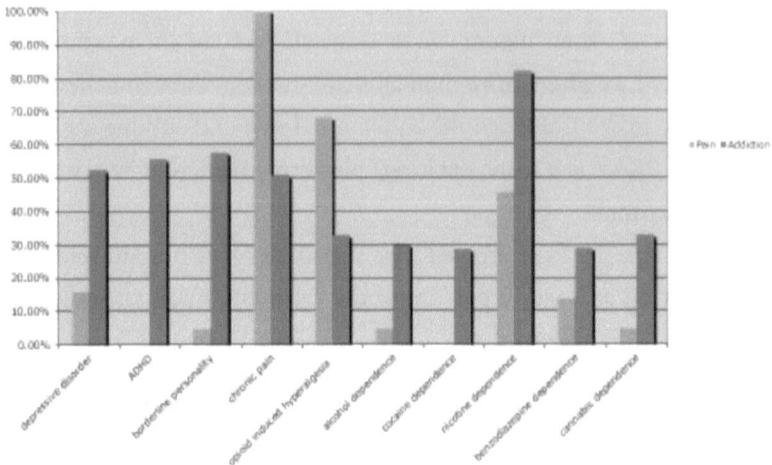

You can see that among opioid-addicted patients, we found 55 percent ADHD, and among the pain patients, we did not find one. This may reflect that ADHD afflicted persons, who can't take in much from relationships with others, are prone to take opioids, relish the "person in a pill" feeling, and keep taking them to reverse the misery of a hypofunctioning opioid hormonal system.

Might ADHD be reversed by intense play? As part of my publication on drug dreams in the *Journal of the American Psychoanalytic Association*,[9] I described the psychoanalytic treatment of Jane, who was addicted to many drugs, including alcohol and opioids, and who had severe ADHD. The diagnosis was independently made by another Harvard psychiatrist. As part of Jane's initial evaluation, checking that extensive cocaine exposure had not caused vascular damage that might be a contraindication to psychoanalysis, I had done a SPECT blood flow scan that showed the typical frontal hypoperfusion of ADHD.

Jane was a whirling dervish on the couch. I found Jane to be so inattentive that she was untreatable unless she took medication that helped the ADHD. If Jane did not, she reliably told me on the ninth day after she stopped her medication that she was quitting psychoanalysis.

I think this is because I could not contact Jane emotionally when she was not taking medication because she was so inattentive, and the treatment did not give her the good feeling promoted by our intense emotional engagement in psychoanalysis. I would reply that the treatment would not work unless she took her medication for ADHD. Jane would insist that the side effects were intolerable. I would pick another agent. Here is a table of our trials.

TABLE—MEDICATIONS PRESCRIBED TO JANE FOR ADHD

<u>Months Sober Medication Response</u>
1 imipramine intolerant of side effects
2 desipramine intolerant of side effects
4 methylphenidate markedly helpful at a dose of 60 mg/day; eventually refused because it caused insomnia
12 pemoline ineffective at dose to 90 mg
15 bupropion helped, but Jane was intolerant of headache, insomnia
24 Dexedrine definitely helpful, but Jane refused to take more than 15 mg/day because of insomnia, muscle pain.
42 Adderall, more helpful than Dexedrine at 30 mg/day
48 medications stopped

Each time I chose a different agent, it worked better than the previous one. By four years into the analysis, I finally got a clue that her ADHD was being improved by the psychoanalysis—probably because psychoanalysis is done in the PLAY mode. We had been playing together four hours per week for four years. The next time she insisted she could not tolerate the medication, I did not respond that she would be untreatable without medication.

The psychoanalysis proceeded nicely until we hit the next snag: when she had to take interferon and ribavirin for hepatitis C. I had consulted for a liver biopsy at the start of her analysis. When it was repeated four years later, there had been severe progression of the disease. The hepatitis C treatment again impaired her cognitive function.

Opioid Addiction and Depression

We find a high prevalence of depression on our service. We regard depression as another disorder provoked by inability to contact others emotionally. My Israeli friend Yoram Yovell and I have debated his practice, developed in collaboration with Jaak Panksepp, of giving a tiny dose of buprenorphine to suicidally depressed patients, most of whom have borderline personality disorder, at the Neuropsychoanalysis Congress.[34] We agree that this is providing "a person in a pill" to treat depression complicated by the urge to kill oneself.

The question we can't agree on is this: "Doesn't this just provide a solution that many borderline patients already adopt as a second problem that complicates their personality disorder, opioid addiction?" Yoram thinks this is an acceptable risk, and I do not. On Addiction Medicine, we find that just detoxing patients from opioids and correcting the opioid receptor system with LDN either makes depression better or puts it into remission.

Opioid Use Disorder and Drug Dreams

We used a database of 1,663 patients with substantial exposure to opioids, divided between 1,398 with opioid use disorder ("addicted") and 265 "pain-only" patients. 472 addicted patients reported opioid dreams (34 percent), significantly higher than the pain-only patients, among whom only 2 (<1 percent) reported opioid dreams ($\chi^2_{(1)}$ = 119.1, p<0.001). Having opioid dreams was associated with a more than threefold increase in the likelihood of experiencing dreams of other, non-opioid drugs. Nicotine use and a transition from sourcing from doctors to risky alternative opioid providers were the two strongest contributors to becoming addicted. This suggests that risk-taking behaviors involving drugs mediate the phenomenon of "addiction to painkillers." Dopaminergic changes underlie both addiction to opioids and production of opioid dreams. Opioid dreams are a marker of irreversible addiction. It may be helpful to include their presence as a criterion in future diagnostic manuals.

Opioids for Chronic Pain

Opioids are commonly prescribed for pain. They are frequently referred to as "pain meds" by many in the medical community. Unfortunately, calling opioids "pain meds" suggests that they are better for pain than medications like the NSAID/aspirin class of medications or acetaminophen (Tylenol). There is no evidence-based research that supports opioid use for chronic pain.

Opioids bring American manufacturers about $19 billion/year. The fine to Purdue Pharma, its president, top lawyer, and former chief medical officer, was $634.5 million for claiming OxyContin was less addictive and less subject to misuse than other opioids. Purdue Pharma was a key player in the opioid crisis.

How Do These Practices Get Started?

I was at the American Academy of Addiction Psychiatry (AAAP) conference in 2001 and 2002. The commonplace treatment for chronic pain in those years was to prescribe massive doses of opioids. This recommendation was being given at symposia sponsored by Purdue Pharma.

I stood up in front of all my colleagues.

"This is disgusting. The American Academy of Addiction Psychiatry should never have a symposium sponsored by Purdue Pharma. They are killing people."

I knew what I was risking. I am the most fired doctor I know of, not because I am obnoxious or low functioning but because I stand up for what I believe in.

As a result of two five-minute responses to the presentations in 2001 and 2002 that included emphasizing that "subjects" in the high-dose opioid trials had died, I was shunned. Some of my colleagues agreed with me, but no one else spoke up because it was going to have consequences for the individual doctor.

In 2018, after I had been on the "Controversial Issues Committee" of AAAP for years, my colleague Eric, the *only* colleague who spoke about my opposing Purdue Pharma, told me I had been right.

He went on to taunt, "But you are too controversial to be head of the Controversial Issues Committee." This was after Eric was named committee chair. He was affirming directly what had been made clear by behavior, that speaking up against Purdue Pharma was wrong because I had exposed the leaders' taking money from/being complicit with drug dealers.

It is amazing to me that no one at AAAP has ever discussed this openly. I know I am being shunned, Eric does, others who were witness to my public stance in 2001 and 2002 are, but none of the younger colleagues know. I am sure we can all feel that the way to success at AAAP is to go along and get along, not to take positions in opposition to the leadership. This problem in medical organizations will be developed with more experiences that I will discuss later.

Purdue Pharma's sponsoring the AAAP symposium was part of the "right to pain treatment" social movement in the 1980s, 1990s, and 2000s that advocated more widespread use of this addictive drug without any scientific evidence because it "helped" people with chronic pain. Purdue Pharma had clinical researchers present outcome data from trials of escalating doses of OxyContin. Accidental overdoses were blamed on trial participants. If oversight institutional review boards considered study participant death as a potential drug side effect risk for entering a clinical trial of chronic pain treatment with high-dose opioid medications, they never would have approved the trial. Purdue was taking advantage of this odd cultural convention that is part of mass denial about opioid medications; misuse is not a medication side effect but rather a sign of moral failing. Eighty percent of heroin users started their opioid use with painkillers. Is the problem with opioid overdose deaths the responsibility of drug dealers or customers?

Why the Doctors Prescribe Opioid Medications

Opioid manufacturers look for "thought leaders" in the medical community to give paid presentations endorsing their products. A 2009 position statement from the American Pain Society and American Academy of Pain Medicine stated, "Although evidence is limited, the expert panel concluded that chronic opioid therapy can be an effective therapy for carefully selected and monitored patients with chronic noncancer pain."[35] One had to read past page 100 to find out who was taking drug company money. Of the twenty-one authors, fourteen thought leaders were receiving payments from manufacturers of opioids, including Purdue Pharma.

Some doctors may have received kickbacks or incentives in the form of gifts, free lunches, high-end dinners, vacations, or money to promote opioid drugs. But the main driver of the quadrupling of opioid prescribing between 1990 and 2010 was the right to pain treatment movement. The health-care system ramped up the use of opioids and tended to avoid examining or acknowledging the risk of misuse. The American Pain Society invented "pain as the fifth vital sign" after height, weight, pulse, and blood pressure. Physicians who did not prescribe opioids freely were penalized financially and disciplined, and hospitals risked poor scores for care, based on addicted patients who complained about not being prescribed opioid medications.

There were a lot of frequent attenders of hospitals and emergency rooms who arrived specifically for opioids, often because they had run through a month's prescription in a brief time. As is the case with all addictions, people addicted to opioids spend a lot of energy and time working to procure their drug. They don't mind sitting in an emergency room for hours if they anticipate leaving with an opioid prescription.

The manipulative complaint of pain when the real issue was addiction would make providers angry, but the question was unfortunately physician self-care versus good patient care. Opioid pills might allow the patient to stave off withdrawal during the day, resulting in another "emergency" the next evening. Not issuing an opioid prescription at 3 a.m., sending that patient home with an aftercare summary saying, "Call your prescriber at 9 a.m.," risked a condemning score for patient satisfaction. This could cost the hospital millions of dollars for ratings issued by organizations such as the Joint Commission on the Accreditation of Hospitals.

Medicare.gov says, "A 1-star rating doesn't mean that you'll get poor care from a hospital. It means that hospitals that got 2 or more stars performed better on this particular measure of patient experience of care." As stated by a representative of the American Academy of Family Practice in 1999, "If we physicians don't get on board and try to make the data as good as possible and get our scores as high as possible, we're going to be hurt in the marketplace. We'll be noncompetitive."[36]

Imagine refusing a 3 a.m. prescription for OxyContin because you believed that the patient who was complaining of intolerable pain was manipulatively and hostilely spending hours to obtain the drug that they were addicted to, costing Medicaid $1,000 for the visit, clogging up your emergency department when terribly ill patients were arriving by ambulance, and then having your department chair call you in at 9 a.m., saying, "There is a patient complaint that last night you refused OxyContin because you don't listen, you don't care, and you know nothing about chronic pain. You are going to cost this hospital millions of dollars if you don't shape up. And you will not get any bonus money for good care scores." What would you do?

Physicians approach their patients with a sense of duty. This can be a dysfunctional countertransference. The patient asks, "Doctor, what will you do for my pain?" Instead of recognizing that this question involves a projection of responsibility from the patient, who needs to engage with active treatments like strengthening exercise/physical therapy, the physician accepts the projection and gives pills that create a vicious cycle of increased pain and increased opioid prescribing, sometimes killing the patient.

The result of the right to pain treatment movement, and guidelines such as those cited above from the American Pain Society, was quadrupling the prescriptions of opioids, accompanied by an acceleration of unintentional overdose deaths. Pain is the only condition in medicine where the symptom is never fatal, but the treatment is fatal for 3 percent of patients who take more than 200 mg morphine equivalents/day.[37] A million Americans have died since 1999 from a drug overdose. In 2022, 108,000 drug overdose deaths occurred in the United States. In 2022, opioids were involved in 81,806 deaths.

Problems related to OxyContin ("hillbilly heroin") use worsened when it gained popularity as a street drug, a cheaper drug than heroin if your insurance pays. Patients would grind up and sniff the pills. Sniffing and injecting opioids seems to produce cravings more reliably. This may be related to a second phenomenon, how quickly neurons are changed by the drug. Sniffing, inhaling, or injecting a drug brings brain changes faster than eating the drug.

Opioids given over time reduce the receptor system, resulting in OIH. Once dependent, patients who try to stop the opioids experience excruciating tapers because they are hyperalgesic, and therefore the brain-mediated pain they experience worsens during a taper. Both patient and physician attribute the pain to mysterious aspects of a back or knee rather than realizing that the pain is centrally (brain) mediated.

Opioids are the only class of "pain medications" that make pain worse. Technically, this is called "opioid-induced hyperalgesia" (OIH). Tolerance means that over time, there may be a need for a bit more opioid to help with pain. OIH is completely different.

In response to opioid medications, baseline pain increases, and the locations of pain spread. If one gives an opioid that reduces the drivers of misery—pain, anxiety, and depression—the body compensates and overshoots, as if pain is necessary for survival and shutting off pain signals makes the drivers upregulate to get back a lifesaving signal.

Pain protects the body. But the patient is more miserable.

This is described by the term "opponent process." The "a" is what the opioid does. The "b" is the body's response to try to restore homeostasis. The patient experiences that every dose of oxycodone helps, the "a" response. "Allostatic" means that homeostasis is no longer possible, that the "b" process has taken over and produced a state that is never seen in nature, the pain equivalent of a fever of 120 degrees. Pain has become super intense. The patient does not recognize the "b" process of pain, anxiety, and depression intensification.[38]

We published a 2018 paper, "The cold pressor test (CPT) as a routine clinical test on pain services," to alert practitioners to how easy it is to diagnose OIH.[38] But no one else uses it. Sometimes the patient demands opioids, saying, "Doctor, my pain is ten out of ten." The physician examines the back or knee and replies, "I don't find anything wrong." The patient complains that the physician can't know what the pain feels like and that they need their doctor's "help." Having no objective CPT to diagnose brain-mediated pain, there is little alternative to giving the patient what they are asking for. While the patient may obtain their prescription, the exchange makes the patient "feel like a drug addict."

Shaming is an aspect of opioid treatment of chronic pain that all patients encounter. While it may not be conscious, physicians blaming patients for getting addicted carries no liability for the physician. Blaming pharmaceutical manufacturers and professional organizations is not done, possibly because other physicians know what I know: there are consequences for taking a public stand against the system. The suggestion here is that physicians are mostly not conscious of the reason they blame the patient rather than the system. "System" here refers to all these powerful forces, pharmaceutical manufacturers, government regulators, professional organizations, and media who condemn not prescribing opioids as cruel or ignorant behavior by physicians, etc.

One common way to ally with drug manufacturers is to advertise their brand as you teach medical students. You don't say, "Morphine, diacetylmorphine, and buprenorphine are related drugs." You say, "Suboxone is the treatment for heroin addiction."

Amazing as it may seem, when I ask hospital physicians who treat heroin addiction what the generic name of heroin is, few know. I used the audience response system at an internal medicine grand rounds presentation. I gave five choices for the generic name of heroin, and 18 percent of the audience got it right: diacetylmorphine.

The application of this concept to mass psychology is that, if physicians were to say to their patients, "We would like to put you on hormone replacement therapy, oxycodone," many patients would recognize potential iatrogenic harm. If the physician does not even understand what they are doing and simply says, "Oxycodone is our best medication for your arthritis," the patient is lulled into submission to a toxic remedy.

Both physician and patient have no idea that because of coregulation of inflammatory and opioid functions in the brain glial cells, opioids are pain drivers, say, of chronic arthritic inflammation. The patient goes back to the physician, requesting more opioids. The physician responds "empathically," recognizing that the opioid is "helping." The physician prescribes a medication to help with the constipation produced by the opioid. The partner of the patient, loving the patient, puts up with the autistic loss of relatedness, the slide over to the right of the inverse U where human contact is uncomfortable. The partner gives unconditional love. In some cases, the patient eventually is killed, via unintentional overdose, by their physician.

How Common Is OIH?

A 2020 survey of anesthesiologists found that they estimated OIH to occur in 0.01 percent of chronic pain patients.[40] Since it is rare, nobody worries about it. Using the CPT, we have found that it is a universal response to long-term prescription opioid medications. If the anesthesiologists are right, with judicious use, the American Pain

Society guidelines are reasonable.

If I am right, physicians continually harm patients with chronic opioid therapy (COT), but they don't know that they are doing it. They have created a plague of chronic pain with opioid medications. Is OIH reversible if opioid medications are discontinued? Can an allostatic adaptation reverse back to homeostasis? No one knows.

Medical Treatment of Opioid Addiction

There is consensus that MOUD, opioid maintenance with buprenorphine or methadone, or injected naltrexone, are the only acceptable treatments. MOUD reduces harms, including overdose, incarceration, transmission of hepatitis C and HIV, and bacterial infections from intravenous drug use. But the most significant advantage is decreased mortality. All official addiction treatment organizations say this.

"We know detoxification from opioids increases the risk of overdose and death. . . . [We] need to move away from the philosophy that a 'drug-free' treatment is best . . . held not only by leadership and staff of in-patient or residential programs, but also other key stakeholders including clinicians at out-patient treatment programs, family members, people in recovery from addiction, policymakers, and patients themselves. Detoxification should be replaced by initiation of maintenance medication—methadone, buprenorphine or extended-release naltrexone." [41]

"Detoxification alone is not a treatment for OUD and increases an individual's risk for relapse, overdose and death when not followed with MOUD." [42]

Or more simply, "Future randomized controlled trials that withhold medication-assisted treatment are no longer ethical."[43] The all-cause mortality in the meta-analysis of 749,634 subjects that accompanied this last quote was 2.4 percent per year without treatment and 1.1 percent per year with opioid maintenance.

While the recommendation for medication-assisted treatment is "long-term," no guidelines advise any point of cessation.[44]

"Long-term, sometimes lifetime, continuation of opioid assisted treatment for the treatment of OUD results in optimal outcomes when measuring morbidity and mortality."[45]

The reality is that 95 percent of patients discontinue buprenorphine maintenance over the first ten years of treatment. Discontinuation incurs a six-fold increase in mortality. Most patients cycle on and off buprenorphine maintenance, incurring the risk of death repeatedly.[46] Saying that buprenorphine lowers mortality while on maintenance ignores the mortality that results from stopping buprenorphine.

The literature on treatment of physical dependence on opioids prescribed for chronic pain is mixed but favors maintenance.

"Based on 2014 estimates, as many as 4.3 million US individuals were current ('past month') non-medical users of prescription pain relievers. Of these, 1.9 million individuals meet diagnostic criteria for OUD." The consensus is "Maintenance therapy with either methadone or buprenorphine has been associated with improved patient outcomes compared to complete detoxification."[47]

In a study of 113,618 patients, average age of fifty-eight, about 1/3 of whom had their opioid medications tapered, per 100 person years, tapering was associated with 9.3 overdose events and 7.6 mental health crises compared with 5.5 and 3.3 during non-taper periods. Risk of overdose rose from 6.6 to 16.2, per 100 person years, as dose of opioid medication rose from 50-89 morphine milligram equivalents to 300 or more morphine milligram equivalents, suggesting that the most danger is invoked by tapering patients with high baseline prescribing.[48]

These dangers would make tapering of opioid medications an ill-advised treatment. Suppose you were a physician who knew that 3 percent of patients receiving 200 morphine mg equivalents per day die of an accidental overdose that is blamed on the patient, but if you reduce the dose from 300 to 100 morphine mg equivalents, the patient sues you for malpractice because you are not compliant with the conventional wisdom embodied in the statements above, the community standard of care. Suppose the patient became depressed, an expectable withdrawal symptom. Do you do what is safest for your patient or practice defensive medicine? If the patient dies from an accidental overdose, the cultural convention is that they are to blame. If the patient is hospitalized for depression when you taper them down to a safe dose, it is your fault. Which option do you choose?

The cost of providing lifelong treatment is substantial, estimated at $10,000 per year (all amounts adjusted in 2022) for methadone maintenance.[49] One injection per month of long-acting naltrexone costs $14,000 per year. Buprenorphine maintenance also costs about $14,000 per year.[50] Veteran's Administration treatment is less expensive.[51]

What exactly is the treatment? One of my colleagues wrote to me, "I see all my buprenorphine patients using Zoom or whatever they make me use. Now it has become VHV—virtual home visit."

Note the "whatever they make me use." My colleague, a well-published full professor, is an employee, required to carry out administrator-generated treatment, and he knows it.

On conventional addiction services, administrators hire practitioners who do as they are told. Appearing to be treated by experts, the reality is a disengaged encounter. I can't imagine what is talked about during VHVs, maybe motorcycles or the Mars rover.

On Addiction Medicine, we tried virtual treatment during the pandemic. We found that not being in the same room as the patient multiplied the lack of emotional contact. We currently do virtual treatment only if the patient is sick, to minimize the chance of our staff being infected.

Sunny Aslam, MD, from our service complained that it was torture, because of emotional disengagement, to see his buprenorphine maintenance patients for twenty minutes once a month, at a buprenorphine maintenance workshop at the American Society of Addiction Medicine. Sunny reported that the workshop feedback was "See them for less time. You will enjoy it more."

Treatment of comorbid disorders is difficult. While 80 percent of patients on methadone maintenance treatment have one or more psychiatric disorders,[52] noncompliance with psychiatric care is the most common outcome.[53] Comorbid psychiatric disorders tend to persist.

Treatment recommendations are to tolerate other drug use and not to make it a ground for dismissal from treatment.[54] This approach leaves providers of opioid maintenance treatments in a position of providing one type of opioid while patients use other opioids, including IV heroin/fentanyl and also cocaine, cigarettes, alcohol, etc. Outcome measures for opioid maintenance do not account for the long-term effects of these other lethal drugs, especially tobacco, because although tobacco is lethal, the deaths come after the period of measured mortality because most cohort studies recruit relatively young patients, clustering around age thirty-five in the study of mortality for 749,634 cited above.[43]

Neuropsychoanalyst Claudio Colace reported another important finding. When he interviewed patients on methadone maintenance who had been using diacetylmorphine (heroin), they still reported using diacetylmorphine in their dreams.[55] This finding represents something important about methadone maintenance. The conceptual model used for methadone maintenance is that the high doses of methadone administered will substitute for the diacetylmorphine or other opioid drugs that are so urgently wanted. Methadone doctors look for a "blocking dose." Dr. Colace documented in this work on drug dreams that losing the appetite for heroin does not happen. There is no such thing as a dose of methadone that shuts craving off.

Dr. Colace's finding is completely consistent with the Hser papers[56, 57] documenting that after an average of 4.5 years on opioid maintenance, 32 percent of urine drug screens are still positive for use of other opioids, and within the last month, 66 percent of 795 subjects maintained on opioids, whether methadone or buprenorphine, still report injecting drugs in the last month, after years on maintenance. Apparently, opioid maintenance by doctors doesn't end the craving for opioids that is satisfied by dealers.

Earlier, we discussed Jane and the PLAY system that underlies at least part of ADHD. I reported the five-year course of drug dreams for her.[9] She began four-days-per-week psychoanalysis after six months of psychotherapy that had been initiated when she left an inpatient detoxification treatment for heroin addiction. Taking advantage of the fact that I took nearly verbatim notes of what she and I had said over that interval, I tabulated all the dreams she reported.

Of 240 dreams Jane reported, 58 had manifest content involving the seeking or using of drugs. There was never a change in the frequency of drug dreams, although other dream researchers have reported a lessening of frequency with abstinence. Many patients also report less frequent drug dreams over the months following drug use cessation. But this is what I found with close observation, about one drug dream a month for five years.

One of my friends told me she had stopped drinking alcoholically when she was a law student. Thirty-two years later, when she was a judge, she was still having drinking dreams. Mortimer Ostow, one of the original neuropsychoanalysts, now deceased, told me he was still having cigarette dreams fifty years after he stopped.

What sense does this make? The SEEKING/dreaming pathway is built into animals so that we don't forget items linked to survival. If it was 10,000 years ago and your band of humans stumbled on red fruits on the ground, you would eat all the strawberries you could find. Unfortunately, strawberry season only lasts two weeks in June. Soon, you would be starving again. You might return to the area all summer and fall, looking to see if there were more strawberries.

The next June, there would be more. To conserve energy, you would start to assemble "cues" that the strawberries might be there. The smell of the air in June. The vivid green of the leaves that have just come out. The color of the sky. Only when you noticed these cues would you expend the time and energy to go look for strawberries.

In June, you might start dreaming about strawberries—an experience that would promote survival. But if the strawberries did not come out one year, or for ten years, you would still want to give it a try—when the air smelled right, when the leaves were vivid green, when that color in the sky gave you the thought, "Strawberries. Maybe there are strawberries."

This system is taken over by drugs. When the bar is dark, the wood paneling is beautiful, the smell of stale beer is in the air, and you might think, "Maybe I can drink in safety. Maybe I am over my alcoholism."

The drug cues have turned on craving. The SEEKING pathway is tuned to alcohol. It has been wanting alcohol since you stopped drinking ten years ago. Drug dreams are continuing, warning you that you still urgently want to drink.

What is one to do? There are two choices. One is to try to battle the urge to drink alone. Use "willpower." The cruel joke here is that the very nature of having SEEKING taken over by alcohol means that your will belongs to people who make alcohol and who run the bar.

You might say, "I'll just have one." But if you have insight, you will remember that last time you said this to yourself, the first one tasted great, the second was okay, and the rest of the night's drinking disappeared into a blackout.

You could call your AA sponsor. This is called "turning it over" in AA. You turn your will and life over to god (group of drunks) as you know him. Your sponsor recognizes intuitively by her or his experience that you are in danger.

Lovingly, the sponsor tells you, "Leave immediately and meet me/go to an AA meeting/go home and take a bath," whatever fits the situation. If it is midnight, the sponsor is in bed, AA meetings are closed for the night, the bath immobilizes you, and allows the craving to die down.

Drug dreams, craving, drug cues—all these things are discussed at AA. Uncle Harry who tells you to "just have one" does not understand. People in AA do. Craving is forever, as seen by the persistence of drug dreams. Treatment must fit reality, not the fantasy that a drug-induced change in the craving/dreaming system can be reversed. The AA slogan, "We drink because we are alcoholics," is a reality that matches the neuroscience-based SEEKING model described here. So does the slogan, "You can't change a pickle back into a cucumber."

Notice the similarity of persons with autism and their parents, who have different-functioning brains. It doesn't occur to Uncle Harry that your brain is changed forever due to alcoholism. Uncle Harry doesn't know that different brains respond differently to the same drug.

Drug dreams are like a form of brain imaging. Like imaging, they signal a brain lesion. Drug dreams alert the clinician, who can alert the patient with a neuroscience-based clarification that the urge for, say, opioids, will always be there. The relapse model for opioids—PANIC, FEAR, and RAGE—drive relapse, comorbid ADHD and depression drive relapse, lack of a recovery community drives relapse, use of other addictive drugs drive relapse, and damaged opioid receptors drive relapse; they can be strengthened by interpreting drug dreams as a chance to discuss permanent brain changes caused by opioids. The psychotherapist performs a function similar to what I just explained about the AA sponsor. "You have a craving that you have not been aware of. It showed up in your drug dream. What might you do about this evidence that you are in danger?"

Psychotherapy while on opioid maintenance is generally not tolerated, and in addition, it is ineffective for anything except retention in treatment.[58] Medications can be prescribed but are generally of low effectiveness. For example, the effect size of antidepressants on depression ranges from 0.26 to 0.31 for unaddicted people.[59] It may be lower for patients on opioid maintenance. I am not aware that anyone has ever studied this.

In contrast, the effect size of psychoanalytic therapies is 0.78 to 1.46 and increases after termination of treatment.[59] By detoxing patients from opioids, we make them available for our main treatment: twice-a-week transference-focused psychotherapy. Is our mortality higher? No. We have examined our mortality for drug-free treatment compared to buprenorphine treatment over a ten-year period and found no difference.[60]

Patients are sometimes told that substitution opioids are not addictive. When I submitted the paper on abolishing neonatal abstinence syndrome by getting pregnant buprenorphine-maintained women off all other addictive drugs to AAAP's American Journal on Addiction, it was vituperatively rejected with a comment: "Buprenorphine is prescribed by doctors and is NOT an addictive drug."

Older chronic pain patients put on buprenorphine arrive at our service astonished that they will have to go through opioid withdrawal when they stop buprenorphine. They were not warned by the physicians who initiated the drug.

The field of addiction medicine has gone from "Opioids are the treatment for chronic pain" to "Opioids are the treatment for addiction to painkillers." Either this is true, or there is some physician dynamic of wanting to give out addictive drugs that is not conscious. Somehow, the entire field of addiction medicine believes that opioids prescribed by addiction specialists are not to be counted as the identical class of drug sold by dealers.

You can see that labeling drugs with the names Suboxone and heroin, and not knowing that the generic name of heroin is diacetylmorphine, may contribute to prescribing Suboxone in a way that using the generic names morphine, diacetylmorphine, and buprenorphine would not. I notice that when I ask patients what diseases are caused by cigarettes, often they "don't know," as if they don't want to know. I wonder if 18 percent of academic internists being able to pick diacetylmorphine off a list of possible generic names is caused by the same motivated ignorance. They don't want to know that buprenorphine is being substituted for diacetylmorphine or that when they give morphine for pain in diacetylmorphine-addicted patients, they are fueling future diacetylmorphine use.

Seeing articles that report that opioid maintenance therapy reduces the use of illicit opioids is like reporting that providing vodka reduces the use of bathtub gin. I have never seen a paper where replacing drug dealer opioids with an equivalent dose of physician prescribed opioids is discussed. Say, if the average use of heroin had been 5 bags per day, 3,000 morphine equivalents per day, and when put on 100 mg per day of methadone, 2,000 morphine mg equivalents per day, and heroin use had declined to 2 bags per day average, 1,200 morphine mg equivalents, that the effective daily opioid dose would remain the same. I assume the objection would be "Methadone is prescribed by doctors and is NOT an addictive drug."

Psychological trauma cannot be addressed when opioids render the person unrelated. A therapeutic alliance is not possible when the patient has an incentive to be dishonest so as to procure the drug that they urgently, for both psychological reasons and because of SEEKING drug craving, want to add to other drugs they are using. Opioid maintenance services set up a cops-and-robbers relationship where patients bring in drug-free urine to submit for the urine drug screens (UDS) or find other ways to avoid the treatment service, knowing that they are using other drugs.

One of our patients was proud of using a "whizzinator," a device that has a fluid reservoir connected through a hole that he cut in his pants pocket to a tube that he ran under his penis, combined with synthetic urine that he bought at a head shop, to pass hundreds of UDS administered by a methadone maintenance service, while he was injecting heroin. He was finally caught when his wife was so angry about his heroin use that she replaced the synthetic urine with water.

We do UDS when we use buprenorphine maintenance. One woman went into the bathroom with someone else's urine in a Red Bull can that she had inserted into her vagina.

Recently, requirements to stop using other drugs have been relaxed in the name of "harm reduction." Functionally, this means one can inhale forty cigarettes a day, smoke marijuana, take buprenorphine or methadone from a prescriber, and in many cases be told that you are "sober" because you are not taking drug-dealer opioids. If you are, you are likely to continue to be prescribed buprenorphine or methadone anyway.

A true informed consent for opioid treatment should acknowledge the cost of loss of relatedness. The patient should be informed that their partners and children are likely to experience them as less available emotionally. To my knowledge, the effect of opioid maintenance treatments on the children of these patients has never been evaluated. Do they get depressed? Do they develop more ADHD? And patients should be warned that they are likely to develop OIH/brain-mediated pain—before they start a maintenance drug.

CHAPTER 10

Benzos and SSRIs

Psychiatric diagnoses have continuously changed from the initial DSM-1 in 1952 until DSM-5, adopted in 2013. In 1960, Dr. Hamilton published his Rating Scale for Depression (HRSD). Twenty-one symptoms of depression are rated according to severity, yielding an overall score. There are many anxiety symptoms in the HRSD. The DSM-5 committee decided that there are anxiety disorders such as generalized anxiety disorder and panic disorder that are independent of depressive disorders.

Dr. Panksepp suggested that anxiety is built into humans as a survival strategy. Lone humans millennia ago were picked off by saber tooth tigers or, more commonly, by rival bands of humans. There needs to be an internal signal that warns us that we are in danger because there are no other people present to help protect us against attacks. Therefore, as distance from humans increases, anxiety increases, the PANIC system.

In his fable of how life might have been, Dr. Panksepp suggested that the "separation distress vocalizations" observed in many animals would increase with time but require a shutdown mechanism, depression, to preserve energy and shut off vocalizations that could be a beacon for predators. The depressed human would lie quietly waiting to be found by their people. This means that anxiety and depression are all one response to interpersonal distance. Depressive symptoms are added to anxiety symptoms as the distance gets greater and the time of illness gets longer. This idea fits with how the HRSD is constructed.

We all notice anxiety feelings. They are prompted by a lack of clarity about one's human environment. When you are with close friends or family, engaged in a shared activity, there is likely to be no anxiety. If you are just starting a new school or job, anxiety is likely to be high. As you get to know people, as you make friends, your anxiety goes down again.

If you were in a new environment and didn't make friends, eventually you would become depressed. This would be typical of someone who is ostracized for gender or racial reasons, because they have a disability and are excluded, or because they have a feature that is picked out by people in their human environment and used by hostile individuals to mark them as undesirable.

Benzos

Benzodiazepines, sometimes called "benzos," calm or sedate a person by raising the level of the inhibitory neurotransmitter GABA in the brain. Common benzodiazepines include diazepam (Valium), alprazolam (Xanax), lorazepam (Ativan), and clonazepam (Klonopin). Although most of these drugs were meant to be administered on a "per needed" (PRN) or temporary basis, physicians often prescribe them for years. Notice how the generic names group them while the brand names give no indication that Xanax and Valium are nearly identical.

In the drug culture, everyone wants Xanax brand alprazolam. Drug dealers sell Xanax. College students use "Xaniebars." The use of brand names is part of the idealization of the drug. Should physicians talk to their patients about alprazolam or Xanax? Gee. Prescribing alprazolam sounds so pedestrian.

Benzos mimic the action of alcohol. Alcohol also raises the level of GABA in the brain. On our service, we call benzos "dehydrated alcohol."

Alcohol is metabolized at about one drink an hour. If you have three drinks in the evening, alcohol is gone in three hours. The problem with benzos is their long half-lives. If you have three drinks in the evening, you are mildly intoxicated for a brief time. If you take a benzo, you are mildly intoxicated all the time. Who would want their patients half intoxicated all day?

My mother-in-law, then about eighty, took benzo temazepam to help her sleep. My warnings to her that it was dangerous were ignored. Feeling cold at a hotel, she got on a chair to get a blanket out of the closet. She fell off and fractured her hip. The ambulance ride back to Boston was 150 miles. She said, "I only had one glass of wine at dinner, but I felt drunk."

Why patients are prescribed benzos is a mystery to me. They temporarily cancel out the distress/anxiety caused by being too alone. Since patients complain about their feelings, our approach is to ask what comes to mind about feeling anxious. Practitioners who pride themselves on helping patients to get rid of feelings prescribe benzos. This results in addiction, with harms such as cognitive impairment, dangerous driving, falls, fractures, and enhanced risk of suicide. For sober alcoholics, providing dehydrated alcohol turns on craving for liquid alcohol.

The Ashton Manual, the bible of benzodiazepine addiction, recommends a slow taper. Patients have come to me months into the discomfort of this approach: insomnia, anxiety, odd sensory distortions, hearing too loud, smells and tastes odd, feeling unstable because they can't tell exactly where their limbs are and where they are in space, distorted proprioception.

My colleague from Honolulu, Jon Strelter MD, taught me that almost anyone can be easily detoxed by switching to chlordiazepoxide. Chlordiazepoxide has four active metabolites, including diazepam (Valium) and oxazepam (Serax). We give ten 25 mg pills. Addicted patients feel that they have *scored* since this is so many mg. We don't tell them that chlordiazepoxide is fifty times weaker than alprazolam. Twenty-five mg of chlordiazepoxide is equivalent to 0.5 mg of alprazolam.

We tell patients to take a chlordiazepoxide pill any time they are anxious. We tell them that after a while, since their blood level keeps rising with each dose because of the long half-life, they will stop wanting to take any more pills. From there, the drug tapers itself over almost a month (five five-day half-lives). This usually works fine. On average, patients take eight of the pills. If someone were to take the entire ten pill prescription, it would not be dangerous. It would be the equivalent of 5 mg of alprazolam, but slowly absorbed and slowly metabolized. No one has taken all the pills at once on our service.

Even if the patient dreads withdrawal, since we meet with them twice a week, they can discuss their concerns and experiences. Because of our sober support person system, older patients on benzos commonly come back with a middle-aged child who coaches them through the withdrawal.

Benzos are not as effective as antidepressants for anxiety/depression. We use the HRSD to document target symptoms. The antidepressant prescribed on admission will take over symptom reduction, along with psychotherapy, exploring the meaning of symptoms. The HRSD can be repeated after a month to measure progress.

Becoming more isolated as one loses work colleagues through retirement, friends through death, and mobility due to the older patient's physical decline, anxiety increase with aging is common. We help patients become aware that losing relationships needs to be reversed through conscious efforts such as calling old friends one has lost touch with, moving to assisted living, or attending senior centers. Helping troubled children can crowd out social activities without the patient having been mindful of the fact that their own welfare needs priority over helping others.

SSRIs and SNRIs

Selective serotonin reuptake inhibitors (SSRIs) include medications such as sertraline (Zoloft), fluoxetine (Prozac), citalopram (Celexa), and escitalopram (Lexapro). Serotonin/norepinephrine reuptake inhibitors (SNRIs) include venlafaxine (Effexor) and duloxetine

(Cymbalta). These medications work on serotonin, an important neurotransmitter that plays a role in feelings of well-being and happiness, as well as thinking, memory, sleep, and digestion.

There are several problems with this class of medications. First, although prescribers know that serotonin is important, they seem not to be aware of *how* it is important. Drive activities such as sleep, sex, and eating feature low levels of serotonin during the activity. The activity is terminated by a surge of serotonin.[8]

It seems likely that it is the fluctuation in serotonin level that we find pleasing. Serotonin is low during sleep. One wakes up with a surge in serotonin, accompanied by the feeling, "Oh, what a glorious day!" Orgasm terminates a sexual experience with a flood of serotonin that makes you feel close to your partner.

Constant high serotonin levels induced by SSRIs and SNRIs work against this variation. Patients describe feeling flat on SSRIs "As if I am observing life through a pane of glass." Busy primary-care doctors are unlikely to hear this. We hear it all the time.

An enterprising research group asked patients prescribed the antidepressants fluoxetine, sertraline, and paroxetine (Paxil) what the duration, intensity, and latency of orgasm was like compared with other patients who had been treated with bupropion.[61] SSRIs degraded sex relative to their baseline experience prior to taking the antidepressants. Bupropion moved things in the other direction, causing more interest, more intense and longer orgasms and, unlike the SSRIs, did not make it harder to have an orgasm.

In a more rigorously conducted study with 3,114 subjects, where interviewers carefully asked about sexual interest, lubrication/erection, and orgasm, 96 percent of women and 98 percent of men experienced disruption of function.[62]

Since sex is a wonderful way of connecting, prescribing SSRIs works against the goal of fixing the driver of the symptom, shutting down because of distant relationships. On our service, bupropion and trazodone are our first line medications.

One woman came back to me after I prescribed bupropion and said, "Honey, my sex drive is through the roof. My boyfriend can't keep up with me." She was pleased with this side effect.

Trazodone is so sex positive that it is necessary to warn young men about a rare side effect that trazodone can produce a long-lasting erection. One of our female patients had to discontinue trazodone because spontaneous orgasms disrupted her trips to the supermarket.

Patients worry not only that antidepressants will ruin sex but also about the common side effect of weight gain. The average person loses five pounds on bupropion.

The shibboleth that "SSRIs are the first line drug for anxiety and depression" was taught to every student; it is not evidence-based. It is based on the widespread hiring of thought leaders in the 1990s to advertise for pharmaceutical manufacturers as the SSRI group came out as proprietary drugs.[63]

One of my nurse practitioner colleagues bragged to me that in the year 2000, she had made $200,000 by giving "drug talks." Calling SSRIs the first line medication for feelings of anxiety and depression "evidence-based" medicine is false advertising.

The language is confusing. Anxiety and depression are universally experienced feelings. Anxiety and depressive disorders cause significant trouble functioning. But which antidepressant to choose is a matter of side effects since all antidepressants are equally efficacious.

Long-term use of SSRI/SNRI drugs can be noxious, and detoxification from them is not simple or straightforward. First, no one in the medical community is going to call getting off SSRI/SNRI medications detox, even though it fits our definition of the term, referring to reversal of alterations in neurotransmitter systems caused by the drug. Calling "discontinuation syndrome" detox would attack the system of expert panel guidance requiring compliance by practitioners. Second, when patients have flu-like symptoms and bizarre experiences, most commonly referred to as "brain zaps," they uniformly tell us that they were not warned about this before being prescribed the drug, despite the incidence of discontinuation symptoms being 50 percent.[63] Bupropion and trazodone don't have a discontinuation syndrome.

One worry is that antidepressants cause depression. Imagine how we would test for this. Let's propose to the institutional review board (IRB) that we would like to have 10,000 participants screened for depression. Of all those not depressed, we will put half on placebo and half on an SSRI. We will taper them off after a year and observe them for another year. We would like to see if any of the previously healthy patients develop depressive disorders from the antidepressant exposure due to rebound from alterations in neurotransmitter systems caused by the drug—for example, chronically low serotonin function after the abnormally high serotonin levels induced by the antidepressant. We expect a few normal participants to commit suicide—the reason there is a black box warning on antidepressant prescribing information regarding young patients dying as a side effect.

Although no IRB would approve this study, it is carried out daily in primary-care practice. Patients who have reactive depressions, depressive feelings caused by recent job loss or loss of relationships through death or divorce, are often given antidepressants by overtaxed practitioners.

"Feel depressed? Here, take paroxetine." Patients then encounter unexpected side effects and discontinuation syndrome.

In summary, patients complain about symptoms that are a natural signal that something is wrong because the signal makes them uncomfortable. The choice for practitioners is to help the patient ignore the symptom with a medication, "The fire alarm is bothering me. Can you help me shut it off?" or try to make an alliance with the patient, like "I know that the alarm is bothering you. Let's see if we can find the fire, put it out, and then the alarm will shut off."

Benzos immediately reduce distress. Benzos can change the SEEKING pathway. Drug dreams involving SEEKING of benzos are common. Benzos are addictive drugs.

SSRI/SNRI medications are prescribed in response to distress.

SSRI/SNRI medications can act like addictive drugs by getting rid of feelings. SSRI/SNRI medications can, like addictive drugs, add a brain-alteration component to emotional distress, an alteration that requires detox. But SSRI/SNRI drugs do not alter the SEEKING pathway. They require detox but are not addictive.

Antidepressants are used for all DSM-5 anxiety and depressive disorders, as if these were all one disorder. If the treatment for anxiety disorders and depressive disorders is identical, chances are that the disorders have been mistakenly broken into pieces when they are one illness.

PART 3

TREATMENT

CHAPTER 11

Tricks and Tips for Counselors

Sensitive Treatment May Get You in Trouble

Counselors have a nearly impossible job. The two main sources of distress are countertransference, the difficulty of listening to material that elicits strong disagreeable feelings, and lack of support from treatment facility administrators who don't value their work, either emotionally or financially. In facilities that provide buprenorphine, methadone, and injected naltrexone, there is no acknowledgment about how overactivating or blocking the engine of relatedness, the opioid receptor system, makes talking with patients frustrating. We treat counselors on our service, so observe and interpret the healthy need to try one employer after another to find the most support and the best fit. Working for someone who reenacts your own trauma by ignoring your feelings is miserable.

Counselors do their best. If they go to AA, they usually make the backbone of their work "twelve-step facilitation," helping their patients understand that attending and following the programs of AA and/or NA leads to the best outcomes.

Counselors who have more book learning have been taught a version of the cognitive-behavioral school of psychology, which incorporates the concept that the psychotherapist is the expert teacher and the patient needs to learn recovery skills. This is the opposite approach from psychoanalysis. We are the humble students of patients who we ask to teach us how and why they make choices that lead to suffering.

One way to negotiate this difficulty is to espouse motivational interviewing (MI). MI is a technique where the questions, not the answers, are the key. The counselor has no interest in the patient's responses, as long as they represent careful thinking. The counselor attends to the process of thinking and helps the patient sort through their own values to decide what is right for them. The counselor doesn't want to stir up trouble, to contradict, or to offer their own opinions. This stance creates a warm bond with the person being treated, unless they are on opioid maintenance, in which case, no approach creates a warm bond.

The two basic responses in MI are called "reflexive listening," where one repeats back what the patient just said in one's own words: "You decided to drink because your sponsor said she/he was out of town? Tell me about that." And "double-sided reflection," where one notes a contradiction in the patient's thinking: "You didn't call because your sponsor was out of town, but your sponsor has asked you to call every day, and you know cell phones work everywhere. What do you think?"

These two interventions are identical to what psychoanalysts call "clarification and confrontation." You can advocate MI without getting into the trouble you would incur if you said, "You don't need to go to a psychoanalytic institute to use its methods. I am going with the psychoanalytic approach."

You can also incorporate these interpretations into twelve-step facilitation, starting with reflexive listening/a clarification. "I hear you are not going to AA. Tell me about that."

This can be followed with a double-sided reflection/confrontation, like "Most people with good recovery get to know people in AA, join a group, and get a sponsor. You are not even going. Tell me about that."

When the patients say, "I don't want to go to meetings to hear about other people's problems," you can respond with another double-sided reflection/confrontation: "I understand your reluctance to go to a meeting to listen to other people's problems, but you have never been to one AA meeting. How do you know that that happens at AA?" This is the most common interpretation of the defense of avoidance that is used on our service.

The nice thing about the MI/psychoanalytic stance is that you have less work than the patient. If they don't talk, you start with a clarification: "I notice you are not talking in your psychotherapy hour."

If they respond in the most common way, "I don't know what to say," you can respond with a confrontation: "You made a giant effort to get here to talk with me. I would think you have something on your mind. But you are not talking. Tell me about that."

Or you can establish the frame of the relationship: "I am trying to understand you as your partner. I am in no position to know what you are dealing with unless you tell me what you are dealing with. That is why I am leaving the topic up to you."

You make it clear that you work for the patients. They are in charge. In one aspect, you are taking step 1 of Al-Anon, the twelve-step group for those who love alcoholics: "We admitted we were powerless over alcohol—that our lives had become unmanageable."

You are helpless, but you know that if the patient will make that leap of faith that the two of you are more powerful than either one of you alone, something good will happen. It was exactly by having this insight that Bill Wilson started AA by getting together with Doctor Bob. That working together with at least one other person is required for recovery has been discovered independently by Bill Wilson, Sigmund Freud, and, I am sure, many others. One of the creators of the twelve steps of Alcoholics Anonymous was R, who had had a psychoanalysis with Carl Jung.[93] It was Carl Jung's idea that alcoholism requires a spiritual solution. What about leading groups? Counselors often look up ideas on the internet for what to have groups about. Being an "expert," they educate the patients. The leader introduces material by giving a lecture and then invites comments from the group. This approach can lead to emotionally flat encounters.

When I have done group work, I have used psychoanalyst Wilfred

Bion's approach.[57] One starts with identifying the work of the group, say, talking about opioid addiction. As long as there is a working group, the leader says nothing. This leaves the most time for group members to think out loud and respond to each other. It models that the patients are the experts but need to be more conscious of their own good thinking.

There are three resistances that Bion called "basic assumptions": the dependency group, the ideal couple, and fight/flight. Dependency means the whole group depends on the leader to carry the content. Drained of responsibility, the members disengage. The ideal couple is two group members that the group depends on to carry the content. The rest of the group members disengage. Fight/flight means the group takes a paranoid stance and projects all their trouble into the leader, then attacks the trouble there.

One can see why giving a talk on a topic in a rehab group could be dismal. The leader initiates a dependency basic assumption. If not aware of this, the counselor could be frustrated that after the facts are presented, no one wants to say anything—resistance. By giving a lecture, the counselor has drained the group of responsibility to do the work of the group.

One group my Harvard resident Cody led at the Dimock Health Center, with me sitting next to him, devolved into an escalating set of attacks on Cody for doctors prescribing opioid pills to patients.

"You are responsible for our addiction!" one patient after another said in their own way.

I let Cody squirm for a few minutes, then interpreted a fight/flight group with some version of "It is such a relief to have all the responsibility for changing behavior in Cody!"

The whole group laughed, Cody relaxed, and we went back to discussing what everyone could do about their addictions after they left the Dimock inpatient rehab. I debriefed with Cody afterward.

Trauma Work

If you find a job where you can work on the reasons people use drugs, you will have to understand why victims of childhood sexual abuse have dysfunctional adult behaviors. The first problem we face is, what about the word victim? Isn't the victim stance a bad one?

The answer is "It depends on the situation." Children are victims. They are smaller, lack the ability to think like an adult, and most decisively, can't tolerate emotionally being in an unsafe environment. Being alone with hostile adults sets off annihilation anxiety. They are helpless.

Claiming to be victims is the way predators justify attacks. This is the origin of the idea that claiming to be a victim rings false.

Guilt is the experience that you have violated your values. If you think you should always be honest, and you lie, you should feel guilty about it. But children haven't done anything wrong when adults have sex with them. For children, helplessness is immediately replaced by guilt and shame about "what I have done."

Neurotic guilt is feeling guilt about violating someone else's value system. If your patient feels guilty about explaining childhood sexual abuse when the perpetrator has told them not to talk about it, or people in their family have told them not to talk about it, the guilt is a problem to be addressed by the treatment.

For example, incestuous families keep secret what they are doing to their children. Victims of incest know that if they discuss what happened, they will be attacked again with nonsensical statements such as, "That happened years ago. Get over it!" or "Think of what this will do to your poor uncle!" (Who raped you as a child). In AA, they say, "You are as sick as your secrets."

Shame is the experience of being told that you are viewed unfavorably. "You got all As except for one B. Why didn't you get all As?" is shaming.

Or you can be out for a team, the stands are full of parents, and yours never come. Instead of being angry at your parents, because it is psychologically impossible to acknowledge as a child that they don't love you, you feel ashamed of your family and fear being judged by your teammates. Helplessness is defended against with shame.

Let's consider Sarah, who was forced to perform fellatio on a babysitter when she was eight. She did not tell her parents. She was not able to say at eight, "You left me with him. I trusted you to keep me safe. I am angry at you."

Therefore, she must think, as a defense against annihilation anxiety, "It is my fault." The defense reduces anxiety at the expense of obscuring reality. In many cases, I have heard reported, the parents knew the teenage boy wasn't a safe babysitter.

The babysitter came back several times over the next year. Every time, he demanded that Sarah perform fellatio again. When she was ten, her parents decided that she didn't need a babysitter anymore.

When Sarah was twelve, she started smoking weed. This was followed by pill parties, where kids brought all the pills they could find in their parents' medicine cabinets. Sarah was found passed out and brought to the emergency room.

"Après-Coup" again, French for "after the blow." In this case, as sexual feelings come up in Sarah at puberty, the result of estradiol lodging in her hypothalamus and tuning SEEKING to LUST the wish to have sexual encounters with boys, Sarah's guilt and shame over the trauma at eight were intensified by her sexual wishes.

We are all helpless about wanting sex. We just want it, just as we want to sleep or eat. Without drugs, children enter adolescent sexual development carefully, often with protective parents who don't discuss sexual feelings directly but who say things like, "Here are some condoms in case you find yourself in a certain situation." Drugs get rid of FEAR, so Sarah, when intoxicated, is more likely to engage in sex because she can't use the natural feedback of FEAR that protects us all.

Sarah started using cocaine and alcohol and going into drunken rages. She got pregnant at sixteen. Her much older boyfriend went to prison. Sarah went to rehab and relapsed to drinking the day she got out. Her parents don't want any contact, saying to Sarah, "You are nothing but a whore and a drug addict."

Sarah started having seizures. On EEG, there was no seizure activity. She has been told by the neurologist both, "You don't have seizures," and "You have psychogenic, non-epileptic seizures (PNES)." She is ashamed of having seizures since the neurologist said, "These are *not* seizures. Go see a psychiatrist!" Sarah's defense, using shame to counter helplessness, has now been exacerbated by a shaming neurologist. She has no control over the seizures.

Sarah got sober at your facility. As you take her history during the first visit, when you ask, "Have you ever been forced to have sexual contact when you did not want it?" Sarah falls on the floor and starts seizing. You call the ambulance to take her to the emergency room.

Sarah comes back for the next visit and tells you that the emergency room visit was unproductive. She said she had had a seizure. She was put on levetiracetam (Keppra) and now feels worse, dizzy and tired. What do you think? What do you do?

This is the complexity that addiction is built on. Every patient who comes for treatment is like a 1,000-piece jigsaw puzzle. You are never more confused than at the very beginning. It takes a while before you can see where some of the pieces fit. The more you see, the more confident you get about being able to put the puzzle together.

You don't know what has been driving the illness. This is why you have to turn the agenda over to Sarah. She knows how this all fits together, but not consciously. You are a team; her role is to say what comes to mind, and your job is to make the interpretations that help her gradually become conscious about what she has been explaining.

Let's let Jaak Panksepp help us. When faced with a predator, animals have three choices: fight, flee, or freeze.

Fight engages the RAGE system. The cornered rat strikes out at the cat. But the rat knows she will never win. If she fights, she will lose and be killed.

Flee engages the FEAR system. The rat can run. But if the cat is too close, the cat will catch the rat and enjoy playing with it until the kill.

Freeze is playing dead. The rat lies motionless, hoping the cat will lose interest and walk away. This is the safest of the options.

PNES is the human equivalent of the rat freezing. Explaining this to Sarah is the first thing to do; then politely call the neurologist's office to request the levetiracetam be discontinued.

You may think to yourself that none of us tolerate helplessness well, that doctors can prescribe pills, and whatever the neurologist's conscious thought was, although prescribing a medicine for PNES comes across as bad practice, perhaps he was motivated by wanting to do *something* when confronted with a patient in distress. His neurologist skills couldn't alleviate the distress. Prescribing levetiracetam was an unconscious, dysfunctional, countertransference action to get rid of his helpless feeling.

What about Sarah's guilt and shame, intensified by her parents' shaming her and the neurologist shaming her?

Shame is the experience of being condemned as inferior because of some personal attribute. You gain Sarah's trust by asking her directly if she experiences you shaming her and responding effectively to her answer. Acknowledging that, of course, she feels ashamed to talk about all these awful things, you go over the fact that she, like every child, was unable to tolerate that her parents would not back her up. Shame was put into her emotional experience to camouflage the even more awful experience of helplessness.

People stay the same unless they have asked for help. Sarah is likely to change with your guidance. But her fantasy that her parents will switch from condemning to loving is a continuing defense against the reality that, until she constructs a recovery environment, she is truly alone. Seeing you is step 1 in being loved.

Is it okay to tell Sarah that you love her? Of course. Love is being there when a person needs you. It has nothing to do with sex.

Humans use fantasy to escape reality. A common fantasy to escape having been a helpless victim is for Sarah to imagine that she did something to provoke the attack. Did she look at the babysitter in a seductive way? Did she wear something that turned the boy on sexually?

One way to show guilt as a defense against the reality of helplessness is to ask, "Is it the rat's fault that the cat wants to eat her? Did she look at the cat? Did she groom her fur in a way that made the cat hungry?" Dr. Panksepp said that the cat's wish to eat the rat is "cold aggression," SEEKING tuned by ghrelin. The cat was just hungry and scanning the environment for food.

Child sexual abuse is not sexual. The goals for predators are to behave in a way that makes them feel powerful by demonstrating that the child is helpless and to ruin sex for the entire life of the child.

These goals are not conscious, but they are confirmed by treating recovering predators. For example, one man in treatment for cocaine/alcohol addiction was terrified of women because of almost being killed repeatedly by intoxicated, violent people with guns, who his mother would take him to for childcare.

He had a hard time maintaining an erection while with lovers, who, by association, recreated his fear of his mother. He reported that as soon as a woman cried out in fear, he would get an erection. The defense was identification with the aggressor. Because he wanted to get better, he recognized this meant something, knew that he did not want to make any more victims, and discussed his experience in therapy.

Treating victims of childhood sexual abuse requires helping them to think through what they will do the next time they are attacked.

"Fight, flee, freeze, what will you do next time?"

You want to be sure they understand identification with the aggressor because begging for mercy will communicate "I am prey." The man will intensify the attack. The only response that keeps us all safe is being aggressive.

One aggressive approach was taken by a woman who knew she could not win a physical fight against a man who had taken her by surprise, and she could tell, he intended to rape her.

Instead of resigning herself to rape, she said, "Honey, let's make this fun. Let's go to the bar, have a few drinks, then go back to my place."

This maneuver gave her time to plan her next move. At the bar, she excused herself to go to the bathroom. There, she found a window large enough for her to climb through and escape.

Patients tend to be afraid of aggression, confusing it with the abuse they were exposed to. It is true that the predator was aggressive. But the predator's motive was harm. We all need to be constantly aggressive to obtain our goals. Trying not to be aggressive by using avoidance and passivity has just compounded Sarah's distress and impedes her recovery.

PTSD means that the victim can't keep the past in the past. FEAR keeps being triggered in the present. Drugs will get rid of the signal temporarily. But it is a dangerous, dysfunctional response that cancels out a signal one needs to pay attention to in a present filled with more predators.

Dreams that recapitulate the trauma are a creative way to bring up memories in ways that allow modification of thinking about what happened. They are often also a way to retrieve memories about what really happened, memories that need to be shared with you as part of recovering. Fighting off practitioners who want to "help" by prescribing drugs such as prazosin that suppress dreaming may be part of advocating for your patient's well-being.

Addictive drugs also suppress dreaming, a fact that you may want to alert your patients to. Marijuana suppresses dreaming. When marijuana is stopped, patients report constant dreaming from REM sleep rebound.

I will try to help counselors and other practitioners by showing them what we do.

CHAPTER 12

Neuropsychoanalytic Treatment of Addiction

Preliminary: What Is Neuropsychoanalysis?

Neuropsychoanalysis is no more than psychoanalysis that uses neuroscience as its basic science,[67] the same way that medicine in general uses biology as its basic science. Neuropsychoanalysts constantly go back and forth from psychological mechanisms to neural mechanisms.

We consider our approach completely scientific. Sometimes light is best conceptualized as a wave, other times as a particle. We know that the observer changes the nature of the phenomenon, not only by simple observation but also by the intersubjective influence of each actor on the other.

How do we employ the explosion of neuroscience information about addiction? Thomas Insel, then director of the National Institute of Mental Health, said in 2013, "Patients with mental illness deserve better" than descriptive psychiatry. He created the research domain criteria (RDoc), saying, "Mental disorders are biological disorders involving brain circuits that implicate specific domains of cognition, emotion, or behavior."

Dr. Insel started with categories and then tried to put mental illness research into those categories. We do not use RDoc because it is not well founded.

The concepts used in neuropsychoanalysis were created principally by psychoanalyst/neuropsychologist Mark Solms and Jaak Panksepp. Astrophysicists have to use tools to look out at the cosmos and build their scientific models on measurements combined with good thinking. Neuropsychoanalysts studying human subjectivity have the benefit of two independent sources of information: subjective reports of patients filtered through the analysts' own subjectivity and measurements from scientific instruments. If we are doing good science, the two sources of information should line up. This approach was labeled dual aspect monism, two kinds of observation about human subjectivity.[68]

Mark Solms has a brilliant lecture[69] on YouTube where he draws a distinction between the clinic-anatomic approach and the statistical approach to treating disease, idiographic and nomothetic. When a patient walks into the emergency department with crushing chest pain radiating down her left arm, the physician does not think statistically. She or he thinks anatomically and mechanistically. The physician immediately envisions one or more coronary arteries so narrowed that the heart muscle can't get the oxygen it needs to survive. The pain is generated by hypoxic heart muscle. The physician immediately takes action to confirm their hypothesis. If confirmed, the action taken revolves around remediating the hypothesized anatomic problem of the coronary stenosis and imperiled heart muscle.

We do the same with neuroscience. When a patient walks into Upstate Addiction Medicine with a complaint of addiction, we immediately think about one or more predisposing conditions. Are there other addictions? Do they use drugs to get rid of feelings? Have they been traumatized? Are they depressed? Do they have ADHD? Is their opioid receptor system damaged? Has their SEEKING system been taken over by drugs so that even while asleep, they pursue drugs in their dreams? We count things: HRSD, 3MS, faces pain scale, CPT, etc. This is a third aspect of neuropsychoanalysis.

If confirmed, the action taken revolves around our understanding of intersecting and synergistic problems mostly rooted in changed neural function, in the context that a central brain function is to maintain life by embedding us all in a protective web of human relationships. We refine our understanding as we do an extended evaluation by having the patient free-associate. We remediate what we can.

In summary, neuropsychoanalysis discovers things by combining the systematic observations of psychoanalysis, neuroscience, and counting things. It incorporates the psychoanalytic premise that every treatment is research, that in a good treatment, the analyst is constantly surprised by what occurs. Is this any more than old time psychoanalysis? Yes. Discoveries fill this book.

Why Is the First Neuropsychoanalytic Addiction Service at Upstate Medical University?

I was at Cambridge Hospital for my first eleven years in Boston. When I was recruited to teach residents at Beth Israel Hospital, the avuncular chair, Freddie Frankel, MD, kidded me that "This is a Jewish hospital, and we don't have addictions." He asked me to take the residents on addiction rotation to the Dimock Community Health Center in the poor and nearly 100 percent Black neighborhood of Roxbury.

Freddie retired, and a new chair came in who I did not have an alliance with. I had been training as many as twelve residents a year at Dimock and at Bournewood Hospital in Brookline, where I was medical director for addiction.

I was a clinical assistant professor at Harvard Medical School when I proposed starting a neuropsychoanalytic addiction service to teach residents. My department chair did not respond to my request for a year off to pursue this.

I rented an office and applied to the Department of Public Health in Massachusetts for a license to operate a detox. Part of licensing paperwork involved obtaining a letter agreeing that I could send a patient to Beth Israel Deaconess Hospital for emergency treatment. My chair didn't respond to this request either, saying she was too busy.

I went to community relations for the letter. The person I spoke to said they needed to ask my department chair.

My chair called me at 7 p.m. one evening, clearly furious that I had gone around her for the letter. She said, "There is an unwritten rule at

Beth Israel Deaconess Hospital (BIDMC) that we do everything we can to be sure that addicted patients *never* come to the hospital, and you will *never* get that letter."

Freddie hadn't been kidding. There really was an unwritten policy. Three days later, I received a snail-mail notification that my services were no longer needed at Harvard Medical School.

I was being recruited to Upstate. I realized I needed institutional backing to have a neuropsychoanalytic service. I let Mantosh Dewan, MD, then the department chair in psychiatry at Upstate, know that I had been fired. He still wanted me.

My practice before I left Boston had been to see four analytic patients starting at 6:30 and then drive over to wherever my Harvard residents were seeing inpatients. After four or five hours, I would drive back home and see two or three more psychoanalytic private patients at my home office.

By 2008, I had done about 15,000 inpatient detoxifications with residents or in other settings, such as the "level 3" staffed intermediate care CASPAR detox that trained Harvard medical students, psychiatry, and internal medicine residents. Between my training at Cambridge Hospital and constant iterations of improvements in how we did detoxification, especially in partnership with Lance Longo, MD, when we were both training Harvard residents at a beautifully organized private psychiatric hospital, Bournewood, in Brookline, I could bring any kind of withdrawal into remission in a few hours.

Mantosh offered to give me a clinical position anywhere he could within the Upstate teaching services. I chose Crouse Hospital because it had the largest addiction service and was the site that the Upstate psychiatry residents worked at to fulfill their training requirement for at least a month on an addiction service. I came back a second time to consult with all principals at Crouse Hospital, including the chief medical officer and chief executive officer of Crouse, cautioning that my approach was not conventional but rather innovative. We agreed that outpatient detox would be part of the change I would bring.

I started at Crouse. The first thing I did was take down about 100 drug advertisements that were taped all over the walls of my office by the previous addiction psychiatrist. I refused to see drug detail representatives, who had brought the staff donuts and coffee on many occasions.

At that time, the methadone maintenance doctor saw about one of her 600 patients per month, usually to document the encounter as part of an administrative discharge. The rest of her time was spent conferring with staff and signing orders about methadone doses. She was carrying out the administration's policies. She was frequently absent, and I covered her duties for methadone maintenance. I noticed that half the men on the maintenance service were on transdermal testosterone because methadone suppresses sexual function based on the opposition of opioids to a precursor neuropeptide necessary for testosterone production. None of these men had been warned about this methadone side effect before starting the drug.

I refused to prescribe benzos to methadone maintenance patients. This was against Crouse policy. Two maintenance patients died from methadone/benzo accidental overdoses during my tenure at Crouse. But refusing to prescribe benzos was a demonstration that I exercised my own medical judgment rather than being a company man.

Crouse had the common organization that an administrator hires physicians to approach the patients according to the administrator's policies. You may think of going to your primary-care doctor and getting expert input. You are. But in addiction treatment, the physician is commonly a beard.

Mantosh's backing was essential because I was fired after fifteen months, apparently because I had been advocating for all outpatient detox. Crouse made a significant income from inpatient alcohol detox. Insurance companies wouldn't pay for inpatient opioid detox, but since Crouse operated a large methadone maintenance service, the need for opioid detox had not been responded to. Physicians had asked me to detox chronic pain patients, and I had been unable to help.

I then started an outpatient addiction service as a clinical service of Upstate Hospital and was again fired, apparently because Mantosh's leadership conflicted with the hospital and university administration. He was fired as chair soon after I was fired. The Upstate president had used removing me as a way to undercut Mantosh's power. The transgressions in both my case and Mantosh's had to do with principled leadership.

One of my colleagues who runs a department at Harvard told me that at leadership meetings, "I keep my head down and my mouth shut." This is one way to pursue an administrative career.

The president of Upstate Medical University who had fired Mantosh was fired for corruption. Mantosh became University president in 2019.

Mantosh and I started Upstate Medical University Addiction Medicine in my private practice staffed by medical students and psychiatry residents. There was no way I could be fired from my own practice. It has expanded since then to incorporate, at the time I had to retire in 2022 because of illness, physician assistant and psychiatric nurse practitioner students, medical students and internal medicine, family practice, and neurology residents, and pain and addiction psychiatry fellows and psychiatry residents. It continues in modified form as nurse practitioner Tom Ringwood's neuropsychoanalytic Addiction Medicine Service.

Starting a Neuropsychoanalytic Addiction Medicine Service
When I came to Syracuse in 2008, the question was how to put the neuropsychoanalytic approach into practice. I published a paper soon after arriving called "What makes a treatment 'neuropsychoanalytic'?"[70] It was a study based on reviewing verbatim notes taken from behind the couch over the first sixty hours of five-days-per-week treatment of Beatrice, who had been injecting cocaine, including during part of her analysis.

I had four categories of intervention from my side: psychoanalytic interpretations, neuroscience interpretations, medication interventions, and twelve-step clarifications. One example would be an interpretation made in hour sixty, where Beatrice had a dream that her husband injected her with cocaine. This was interpreted psychoanalytically as both a communication to me and to her conscious self that her wish and fear was about her husband codependently facilitating her addiction. As a neuroscience interpretation, the dream revealed that her ventral tegmental dopaminergic SEEKING pathway was permanently altered so that Beatrice would always intensely desire cocaine, whether she used it or not.

An example of a medication intervention would be a suggestion originating from my side that Beatrice take dopaminergic and noradrenergic bupropion to counteract the neurotransmitter downregulation that made her life boring without cocaine. This was combined with disulfiram (Antabuse) that simultaneously made it impossible to drink and inhibited dopamine decarboxylase, the enzyme that degrades dopamine.

I had made it clear that my one-hour-per-day treatment would never be sufficient to tip Beatrice into sobriety without more human intervention. Twelve-step clarifications would have to do with asking, at the point of relapse to injecting cocaine, whether she had been talking with her sponsor in Alcoholics Anonymous.

During the psychoanalytic treatment, Beatrice was going to at least one AA meeting per day. She had a sponsor who sounded connected and deeply caring. Beatrice reported that her sponsor would make herself completely available and make comments about relapse such as, "Honey, I don't want you to die."

This paper became, for a while, a part of the eight-seminar series that our psychiatry residents and fourth-year medical students on elective at Addiction Medicine would read and report on to the other students to understand neuropsychoanalysis in general and its application to treating addiction. We constantly vary the seminar as new papers come out and to keep the senior staff from growing bored.

Conventional addiction services are set up with relatively unskilled counselors at the base. They are cheap. The most common degree is "certified alcohol and substance abuse counselor" (CASAC). There are fewer social workers, even fewer PhD psychologists and nurse practitioners (NPs), with the fewest staff members being physicians. When I worked at Crouse Chemical Dependency, counselors did all the intakes and presented them at a meeting presided over by the one psychiatrist for the entire service, responsible for 1,000 patients: 600 methadone maintenance and 400 other outpatients.

An innovation at Upstate Addiction Medicine is to turn conventional treatment on its head by having the staff be all skilled medical practitioners. New patients are presented by trainees to the NP/MD staff. Trainees carry out transference-focused psychotherapy. By 2016, I saw 2,650 outpatient patient visits and 334 UH consults. I went from room to room to watch trainees work and billed only for my time with the patients. We see mostly poor people with Medicaid and Medicare insurance, but based on volume, they make the Psychiatry Department money.

Dr. Dewan and Tom Schwartz, MD, the Psychiatry Department chair who followed Dr. Dewan and Dr. Gregory, helped me to get funding from UH to expand the service. In 2017, we had the financial resources to add more senior staff. The apex of staffing was in the beginning of 2021, when we had three psychiatrists, a nurse practitioner, and a physician's assistant—and zero counselors.

Transference-Focused Psychotherapy Combined with Neuroscience Interpretations, Medication Interventions, and Twelve-Step Facilitation

Every student and psychiatry resident receives a one-hour seminar at the first day orientation on how to make psychoanalytic interpretations. We use Dr. Otto Kernberg's four basic interpretations: clarification, confrontation, defense, and transference interpretation.[71] Clarification involves picking out emotionally salient associations and repeating them with a "marked response."

"The weather has been rainy. . . . Syracuse University's basketball team did great last night. . . . I was raped three times last year."

The clarification is, "OMG, you were raped? Three times?" The earlier associations are disregarded. Clarification begins when the material "drops" to the level of emotional salience.

Confrontation involves repeating back associations that seem to conflict with each other.

"You are saying you have a boring life, and you also say you were raped three times. Tell me about that."

These two types of interpretations, clarification and confrontation, were relabeled by William Miller, PhD, inventor of "MI," as "reflexive listening" and "double-sided reflection." [72] When I explain this, we are on solid ground. The trainees have often heard about, or even practiced, MI.

If the patient were to say, "Rape, it isn't such a big deal, and I should be over it by now," a defense interpretation is in order. Defenses reduce anxiety at the expense of obscuring reality. An interpretation of minimization would be something like, "Might it be that you are so upset about this that you try not to think about it by labeling it as 'not a big deal'?"

If the patient were to then angrily respond, "You don't really want to hear about it, do you?", the transference interpretation might be something like, "You have been telling me that no matter how badly you are hurt, your [mother, father, family, etc.] keep telling you to suck it up and stop using drugs. Making me just like them might also help you avoid the anxiety of discussing the family web of abuse and neglect, but we have agreed that you seem to be using drugs because you are so upset. Making me just like them would make me equally unavailable to help you."

When I don't have a fresh dream from the day of the introductory seminar to fall back on, I use one I published because it is so simple.[73] This is a dream from Jane's psychoanalysis.

"You know the feeling you get when you hold a baby? They smell so good, you could eat them up. The mother handed me the baby; it smelled so good that I bit off the toe. Then I thought, *OMG, what am I going to say to the mother?*"

I ask what the trainees think the dream is about. When I get the usual silence, I commend them on not opining without the patient's associations. I explain that dream interpretation starts with asking the patient to make associations to each element of the dream.

Biting off the toe?

"This morning, I woke up with bloody footprints leading to my bed. I followed them and realized; you know that Ambien (zolpidem, a benzodiazepine receptor agonist sleep aid) that you have been telling me not to get from my internist? I must have taken Ambien, gone into a blackout, gotten the munchies, tried to put a glass dish in the microwave, dropped it, stepped all over the glass, and gone to bed."

"The mother/baby?"

"When I was twelve, I told my mother I was going out to play after school.

"She said, 'No you are not.'

"I said, 'Yes I am,' and left.

"She said, 'You'll be sorry.'

"When I came back, my mother didn't seem to be home. Then I saw a trail of blood in the living room. I followed it. My mother was lying behind the couch in a pool of blood. She had drunk a quart of vodka, cut her arms, and passed out."

I explain Freud's concept of day residue and childhood antecedents of dreams. I explain the function of the dream to bring up items for the therapist that are emotionally difficult and at least partly unconscious. Jane had wanted to tell me both about taking zolpidem, with consequences, and childhood abandonment.

Now the students are set to see patients.

Pain service was Wednesday afternoons. Tom Ringwood has had to stop this service because only I had the broad range of medical knowledge needed to lead this treatment/teaching conference.

We took referrals from all over a huge catchment area. For Pain Service, we added a neurology resident, an internal medicine resident, and a pain fellow to our core trainees: medical, psychiatric nurse practitioner and physician assistant students, psychiatry and family practice residents, and our addiction psychiatry fellow. Holistic evaluations and presentations to a large group of trainees resulted in careful diagnosis and treatment plans. Pain patients then entered the general treatment service. Often, but not always, pain patients had been maintained on opioid medications for chronic pain, and we started with detoxification and daily psychotherapy. We took in 200–300 new pain patients per year.

The service ran and now runs on this model. All patients come in for treatment of at least one addiction. Every new patient must arrive with a nonaddicted support person, most commonly a relative. The support person is involved with all parts of the evaluation. Every patient gets a ninety-minute evaluation with a trainee, who then comes in with the patient and support person to present their findings to the senior staff.

Evaluations come up with an average of five diagnoses. The most common psychiatric disorders are depressive disorders (major depressive disorder, persistent depressive disorder), ADHD, borderline personality disorder, persistent somatic symptom disorder with pain predominant, and PTSD. PTSD is usually not diagnosed the first day. It requires some therapeutic alliance before the patient describes what they have been through. In addition, most patients have multiple addictive disorders.

Some patients need an alcohol, benzodiazepine, or opioid detox. Some come in other states of addiction, such as early recovery. If they need detox, they are seen every day for the first week, excluding weekends unless the patient really needs to be seen, in which case a senior provider may come in and see them. Otherwise, they come twice a week for an "extended evaluation."

Treatment episodes for our pain patients average thirteen visits. The average includes the patient left prematurely, the patient completed treatment and was not interested in anything additional, the patient has a comorbid psychiatric disorder that responded to brief treatment, is in twelve-step recovery, and seems to be in a lifelong process of recovery, the patient elected longer term treatment on our service despite the need to see trainees who change every four to eight weeks, or the patient is stable enough to go to Dr. Rich O'Neils systems centered therapy (SCT) group.

SCT has a psychoanalytic core. The focus is on how members of the group relate to each other. For some patients, we recognize the need for long-term individual psychotherapy, and a trainee is found who is likely to do them good over time such as an addiction psychiatry fellow, a Syracuse University PhD candidate training on the service, or a fourth-year resident who provides leadership on the service for a year.

Senior staff move from room to room, observing the neuropsychoanalytic therapy. Earlier in a trainee's experience, senior staff are likely to show them how to make interpretations that they missed. If the trainee is good, by the end of their training period, the patient is glued into a therapeutic alliance, the patient disregards senior staff entry into the room, we say nothing, and treatment issues are discussed during the group supervisions that occur at least three hours per week.

The financial result of being able to see so many patients in a day is that by 2021, my last full year on the service, my private practice income had been $550,000 despite most patients being on Medicaid or Medicare insurance. Other senior staff exceed their expenses so that we can contribute 30 percent to the Upstate Psychiatry Department and pay our front office staff. Is it really feasible to provide psychoanalytic therapy to a wide range of addicted patients? Our model shows that with good leadership, yes, patients can get exquisite care.

Probably the most common reason for relapse is that the patient tries to continue to inhale cigarettes and stay off alcohol or opioids. Another common pattern is that the patient is off opioids and nicotine for a while, then uses denial to say to themselves and then us, "I wanted heroin, but I just had a cigarette instead." The nicotine invariably precedes relapse to heroin use.

Getting patients off nicotine is easy. Initially, we tell them to stop, which doesn't have a high success rate. Sometimes, the support person is also addicted to cigarettes. We tell them, "You want X to stop heroin? The most loving thing you can do is stop cigarettes along with them."

Since about half our patients have ADHD, our most common antidepressant is bupropion, a "dirty" (psychiatrist slang for multifunction) drug that also treats depression and lowers interest in cigarettes. Senior staff tell these patients during the initial evaluation, "My bupropion is going to lower your use of cigarettes from twenty to three. I am going to take total credit for this. I am the prescriber. But when you go from three to zero, we are going to give you huge credit because nicotine is the most addictive drug in the world, and you will have achieved something difficult."

The best medication for nicotine addiction is the nicotinic agonist varenicline, marketed as Chantix brand. It gives the experience of just having had a cigarette without the drug influencing the SEEKING pathway. If the support person is also addicted, or if our patient lives with cigarette inhaling persons, we invite everyone to stop at the same time. Cigarette addiction is treated like a sexually transmitted disease; you don't treat a patient without treating their partner, roommate, parent, etc.

Sometimes patients are asked to stop cigarettes at midnight and come in in the morning holding their box of varenicline. Some can't even stop for a few hours. We ask these patients to just stop long enough to be craving a cigarette when they walk in the door. The patient, and sometimes their support person, take varenicline in front of the trainee at the start of their psychotherapy hour. Twenty minutes later, they are asked if they want a cigarette. Usually, the answer is no. If the patient still wants a cigarette, they take another 0.5 mg of varenicline. The exercise demonstrates the power of varenicline.

That is it. They are off cigarettes. If they inhale one more, the topic of the psychotherapy hour would be, "You have a replacement for cigarettes, yet you are still inhaling them. What is your thinking?"

The answers are unique. This is the nature of good psychoanalytic therapy. The therapist is surprised by the answer.

Joe became so angry at his drug dealers that he participated in a sting with the local police to get the biggest dealer in his town arrested. But he continued to inhale cigarettes. As we thought about it together, there were two impediments that he came up with. The first was that he needed a big dose of varenicline, 4 mg/day.

When Joe arrived, he had been inhaling forty cigarettes per day. The packaging for the drug indicates that two milligrams is the maximal dose. Why two? Who cares? Varenicline is mimicking the nicotinic action of inhaling cigarettes. If one follows one's inner reactions, it doesn't matter how much one takes. As you now know, nicotine is an insecticide made by the tobacco plant to kill insect predators. Poison makes one nauseous as a defense of the body against dying. If one starts to feel nauseous from nicotinic varenicline, one doesn't want to take more. At that point, a nicotinic cigarette would cause nausea too.

A second problem for Joe was that he wanted a cigarette after dinner. Dinner had become a drug cue. Yet the dinner would slow the absorption of the varenicline so much that he couldn't hold out.

Joe read on the internet that varenicline works faster when used sublingually. He didn't need to use his dinner-filled gut to get the drug to his brain. With this final amendment to administration, he stopped his cigarettes. Joe taught us. Learning from our patients is so much more fun than following the directions on the varenicline box.

Relationship of Neuropsychoanalytic Therapy and Twelve-Step Recovery

One of my psychoanalytic colleagues disagrees with my suggestion that neuropsychoanalytic therapy and twelve-step recovery are complimentary.[74] He often cites a study that found that Alcoholics Anonymous helps only 5 percent of people suffering from alcoholism. I don't know if this is true.

On the continuum of active and passive treatments, passive treatments are most susceptible to "percent of benefit" studies. You can give half of a population placebo pills, half the active drug, and measure targeted outcomes. One can do urine screens to find out if the subjects are taking the active treatment.

I don't see how such a study could be done with AA. One thing that psychoanalytic therapy and Alcoholics Anonymous have in common is that participation is voluntary, and only those who feel benefited continue to attend. This makes "What percentage of people does it help?" a difficult question to answer.

One of the aphorisms of our service is "We can't help people who need help, only people who want help." Alcoholics Anonymous is for the segment of the population who are able to walk into a meeting terrified that they will die from addiction, appalled at the losses they have incurred because they are being controlled by drug dealers, and willing to take a chance that depending on people, not drugs, might save their lives.

We make it a treatment goal to help our patients be well enough to use Alcoholics Anonymous. If we do an outpatient detox, fix comorbid ADHD and depression, work on issues of relatedness with a transference-based psychoanalytic model, ameliorate persistent opioid withdrawal with LDN, or have a support person administering disulfiram for alcohol use disorder while the patient has a chance to get their brain and relationships in a more stable state, we hope that we would get a higher rate of engagement in Alcoholics Anonymous or Narcotics Anonymous.

We watch our ADHD patients, over the month it requires for the drug to have a full effect, have wonderful responses to bupropion and psychotherapy done in the PLAY mode. We get reports of emotional engagement, school achievement, job success, and warm and emotional engagement from patients. A constant clarification I made was "OMG, you talk as if your IQ has jumped twenty points since you started. It is not that you are more intelligent. It is that you are finally able to take information in and use it to go back and forth with us!"

Jerome was so ill with alcoholism at age sixty that he was hospitalized with cellulitis, a bacterial infection in his leg that was probably contributed to by immunosuppression caused by alcohol. The hospital referred him.

Jerome had never had a sober period. The only comorbid disorder we found was ADHD. He was started on bupropion and disulfiram the first day, the disulfiram administered by his brother, who had accompanied Jerome as his sober support person.

We discussed AA. Jerome said that he would never go to a meeting. I understood this to mean that Jerome's ADHD was so bad that he couldn't take in what other people were saying. This made the anxiety about trying AA intolerable. The anxiety was generated by feeling alone.

Jerome's brother came back for some of the psychotherapy hours. If he had not come, Jerome may have been so anxious that, like Jane, he would have quit treatment because the ADHD made it impossible for him to feel us.

The bupropion helped Jerome take in our discussions. Jerome agreed to try one AA meeting. Jerome reported that he found an old friend at the meeting who immediately agreed to be his sponsor. Jerome went to that AA meeting every morning from then on. After a few more visits, Jerome was seen for monthly check-ins.

Jerome was discharged after a year sober. He had gone to his AA meeting every day for the previous year. His primary-care doctor took over prescribing bupropion. Disulfiram was stopped.

Another aspect of our psychoanalytic brand of twelve-step facilitation is that patients don't do well sometimes because of social isolation. Janet reported that her husband was abusive and did that thing that controlling men do: insist that she dedicate every minute of her life to serving him and their children. An initial improvement in depression, an initial engagement with AA, was followed by an intensification of her husband's demand that she spend every minute at home. He probably knew that his control was based on her alcoholic drinking, and he needed to undermine her being influenced by caring people. Janet came to a psychotherapy hour desperate to drink because she felt so helpless about her rage at her husband.

The confrontation was "You can drink to feel better, or you could call AA Central Service and ask for a woman to take you to an all-women's meeting."

Janet decided to call, went to the first of an ongoing series of women's AA meetings, and de-emphasized what to do about her husband, along the lines of "Don't make any major decisions during your first year sober."

Given such stark choices, why might Janet choose staying with her controlling husband? Not every woman wants to be free and self-determining. They might like being free and autonomous and at the same time not want it, the liking/wanting conflict.

Why might anyone have this wish? Growing up with a controlling, abusive parent. It wouldn't have to be the father. It could equally well be the mother. Resolving the question prematurely could result in submissive alcoholic drinking to counter annihilation anxiety. "Don't make any major life decisions for your first year sober" allows time for character change with improved function so that drinking, the previous go-to when faced with unpleasant feelings, is not chosen.

This way of thinking then makes the question "What percentage of people with addiction are helped by Alcoholics Anonymous?" an odd question.

Questions worth investigating for research-funded treatment providers might include

- Of all the patients on whom you do intakes, what percentage of those patients would be a match for AA?

- How would you know?
- What are the characteristics of those patients, and how do they change over time?
- What other kinds of patients are taken in?
- Is there a better treatment for those patients?
- How do those patients do?

Countertransference

The most difficult problem on our service is how awful reality is. We have to carefully prepare our trainees emotionally to withstand the trauma of witnessing what addicted patients' lives are like. We have lost a few trainees, who asked to be transferred to other services for their psychiatry experience.

Kat, one of our physicians' assistant students, missed the 8 a.m. orientation for new students because she was having training on the electronic record. Orientation is a discussion about countertransference starting with the senior staff, then progressing to newly arrived trainees, to discuss personal stories about addiction. I have explained one version or another about growing up with addicted parents and siblings. Almost everyone has had family members or friends ill or dead from addiction. Orientation ends with assurance that we will help trainees with their countertransference feelings. But Kat missed orientation.

When Kat arrived in the afternoon, I said a brief, "Great to meet you," and asked her to see one patient with me, Darla. I spent part of the hour reviewing with Darla and Kat how we had taken Darla in a few weeks earlier, helped her stop drinking alcoholically and using cocaine and tobacco, and started talking with Darla about the difficulties that had provoked a severe depression, as well as starting her on trazodone and bupropion. I left, instructing Kat to just listen for another thirty minutes.

Kat almost didn't come back the next day. She listened to Darla explain that when she went to her grandmother at age eleven about being molested by older cousins, her grandmother only said, "Honey, that is the way men are."

Darla told Kat that when she joined the Marines to escape her abusive family, her drill sergeant listened empathically to her emotional difficulties—grooming—and when he felt she was vulnerable, he raped her. He told Darla that if she tried to expose him, she would be the one to leave the service. Darla complained and was dismissed from the Marines.

We have group supervision or a neuropsychoanalytic seminar six times per week to give students a chance to share the unusual and often horrific stories they hear. Of course, the senior staff are mindful that some of our students have been sexually abused, raped, or are addicted to drugs. We strive to make ourselves available to hear from these trainees individually. Kat was able to recover her emotional balance with a combination of talking with me individually and talking during countertransference group.

Another example is that our senior resident in addiction, Sutanaya Pal, MD, was treating a woman who had come in for marijuana addiction. As the therapeutic alliance strengthened, the patient, Stephanie, was able to explain that the boyfriend, who was assaulting her, demanded that Stephanie get a tattoo with his name clearly visible to all.

Sutanaya urgently wanted to tell Stephanie, "No! Please don't do that. He is demanding you be branded, as if you are an animal." But analytic neutrality required that Dr. Pal explore Stephanie's wish to submit to abuse, along with Stephanie's growing awareness that she was already making choices that made her life a horror.

The Senior Staff

We strive to be diverse, in recovery from addiction and not, physician assistants, NP, and physicians. Our addiction psychiatry fellowship is the only one I have ever heard of with 100 percent of the full-time faculty of at least partly African descent. Senior staff go into psychoanalysis as part of the hiring agreement.

Goals of Treatment

The first encounter is a holistic data collection. Trainees start with chief complaints, history of present illness, and psychiatric, medical, family, and social histories. We carefully ask the drug history, including onset and frequency of use, periods of abstinence, treatments, last use, and drug dreams—present or absent—for ten kinds of drugs. We ask about twelve-step recovery, abuse as a child or adult—and what kind—and whether gambling is a problem. We conduct a basic physical examination. Then the HRSD and 3MS are conducted—the latter to look for subtle cognitive impairment that is a common consequence of drug use. We have new patients self-rate for borderline personality disorder, Fagerstrom nicotine dependence, faces pain scale, adverse childhood experiences, and the ADHD Self Report Scale. If the latter is positive, the trainee conducts a structured confirming interview, called the DIVA. If the patient is addicted to tobacco, expired carbon monoxide is measured. If set up that day, a CPT is measured for patients who use opioids or marijuana. We have found that, like opioids, marijuana, when used daily for chronic pain, causes hyperalgesia.[75]

The assessment is then presented to trainees and senior staff who are available with the patient and their support person sitting at the head of the conference table. A senior clinician asks the patient and support person whether the presentation is complete. They are invited to speak first. Often, further physical examination is done. Then a list of problems and potential treatments is discussed.

For example, "You came in for back pain. You have been on oxycodone for eight years, every day, except for a month when you endured horrible withdrawal symptoms and had extreme pain that drove you back to oxycodone.

"We can see what the pain drivers are now. There is inflammatory pain in your lumbar facet joints, with paraspinal spasm to try to keep the joints from moving. You have neuropathic pain from the sciatic nerve trapped as the nerve roots come through the spine. Your CPT of twenty seconds means that all the time on oxycodone has gradually ruined the pain-damping system in your brain, centrally mediated pain. Each kind of pain—inflammatory, neuropathic, and brain-mediated—makes the other pain drivers more intense.

"The other condition that makes this worse is that you are inhaling tobacco and cannabis. Each drug may help a little each time you use it, but they are probably making your pain worse overall. Tobacco is a lethal drug, and you are committing suicide with it.

"You have severe depression and ADHD, the inattentive type.

"You have come to the right place!

"We recommend you come for an extended evaluation twice a week so we can go back and forth with you to develop your treatment plan along with you. Tentatively, nortriptyline is an antidepressant that is also good for neuropathic pain. It takes a month to work. We will prescribe gabapentin at bedtime and suggest ibuprofen, 600 mg, four times a day in the short term.

"You need to be the captain of your recovery. Core strengthening is the most important way to address the lumbar pain and sciatica. We may send you to a physical therapist to advise you about the most effective ways to strengthen the core muscles that hold your lumbar facet joints in place.

"We will help you with inhaling drugs. The antidepressant bupropion will reduce your interest in tobacco. It will help your ADHD and depression.

"We will help you off oxycodone by having you stop it by midnight Thursday, come in on a Friday to take a single dose of the long-acting opioid buprenorphine, and then come in every day the next week to talk with us and have us work with you on the minor withdrawal symptoms we expect, possibly gut cramps, anxiety, insomnia, and restless legs. There are medications for each. You will see my cell phone number at the top of your handout. Call, day or night, if there is a problem. You will start LDN as soon as you take your buprenorphine. It will restore your pain-damping. We will follow your response with the CPT. We hope you will go from twenty seconds to three minutes over about three months."

This is the start of making a treatment plan. Any treatment requires that the goals be specified at the outset. We have lots of handouts. The treatment plan is refined over time.

This initial plan yields evidence about whether oxycodone is being taken out of ignorance as a treatment for chronic pain or if it is being used to treat emotional issues. In the first instance, the patient agrees to take our help immediately.

If addiction is present, some patients will storm out, saying, "You don't listen, you don't care, and you don't understand anything about treating pain! I came here for help, and you don't want to give me the only thing that helps—oxycodone."

They are objecting that we are getting between them and an addictive drug they intend to continue. That makes all addicted people angry. A true statement would be "You understand that I urgently want a drug that is hurting me, and you disagree with continued use, rationalized by pain."

It is rare that patients arrive on either the Pain or Addiction Medicine Service with a single problem. Multiple psychiatric conditions and multiple drug addictions are the rule. In this example, a leading diagnosis is, "persistent somatic symptom disorder with pain predominant." This means that the patient uses passive treatments such as oxycodone, tobacco, and cannabis, sits on the couch all day worrying about their back pain, and waits for a brilliant doctor who realizes that escalating the oxycodone dose is the best treatment.

Neuroscience Interpretations

Trainees need to learn when to use clarification versus using a neuroscience interpretation. For example, if the patient were to say, "I need to keep smoking cigarettes because I need something to do with my hands," a psychoanalytic clarification would be "What comes to mind about doing something with your hands?"

A neuroscience interpretation says, "Doing something with your hands makes no sense outside of your brain. The tobacco companies control you. They have you using their drug to commit suicide, and the explanation about your hands is nothing but a restatement of 'I urgently want the drug.'"

A common comment is "I came here to get off heroin/fentanyl, not to stop smoking cigarettes."

The neuroscience reply is "You know that when you are injecting opioids, you urgently want cigarettes. On heroin, you chain-smoke. You are less aware that when inhaling cigarettes, you urgently want opioids because you were already addicted to tobacco when you got addicted to painkillers. When our patients try to stop one drug but continue others, we can't help them. When patients stop all drugs, we win with you against all the drug dealers, legal as well as criminal."

Notice the lack of stigma involved. The way we are detoxifying stigma, in part, is by blaming drug dealers. This is not done in conventional treatment.

Social Setting of Treatment

Trainees are taught that language embodies cultural denial. I don't understand why trainees are taught to use the "one drop of blood" racist characterization of patients. No one on Addiction Medicine presents a case starting with "This is a thirty-four-year-old African American male." Looking at someone and placing them into the racial caste system is not done.[76]

We don't treat females and males on our service. This is regarded as dehumanizing language used to make the treaters superior to the patients. Dogs, cats, and turtles are labeled female or male. We only treat women and men.

The senior staff don't advertise their favorite brands of medications to trainees. We don't prescribe "Wellbutrin"; we prescribe bupropion. Sometimes I ask physicians who use brand names how much they are being paid to advertise proprietary drugs to patients.

We don't use terms that minimize drug use such as "packs of cigarettes." Trainees learn that "smoking one-half pack of cigarettes" sounds safer than inhaling ten cigarettes per day. Inhaling ten cigarettes per day sounds terrifying, matching reality. We can't do psychotherapy that considers the harms of inhaling tobacco unless the patient knows those harms. Early on in our extended evaluation, we make sure patients who inhale tobacco know how it kills. Often, surprisingly, they say they don't know or give a completely inadequate answer. I think this is motivated ignorance to deny the danger. We discuss the patients' experience of starting to inhale tobacco as a child, and having their opinion about tobacco changed from frightening—"Mommy, Daddy, please don't smoke"—to "Cigarettes are cool."

We don't take away patients' "pain medications." Sadly, most physicians join their patients' denial system by calling opioids "pain medications" when opioids increase chronic pain. I have often clarified, "We strongly believe that patients should be given pain medications such as the aspirin family of anti-inflammatories, the anti-inflammatory food turmeric, tricyclic medications such as nortriptyline, or anticonvulsant medications such as gabapentin. We are against opioids for chronic pain because they destroy the brain's pain-damping system, resulting in increased pain."

We don't care about frequency of use of alcohol or amount. We care about consequences of use. After a presentation of a patient who came with a chief complaint regarding drinking, if consequences are unclear, I would ask the patient and support person to convince me that this is alcoholism. We fit the patient into a spectrum of drinking: light—often defined by me as less than your doctor drinks; heavy—more than your doctor (I hope it is clear that these are jokes told to convey a tone of nonjudgment); symptomatic—a brief period brought on by stress such as loss of a loved one or a job, with consequences; alcohol abuse—your drinking is getting in the way of your life and work; and physical addiction—your life and work are getting in the way of your drinking (more jokes that also convey reality). This way of describing drinking is backed up by psychoanalytic research.[77, 78]

As is typical of our treatment, the power and responsibility are with the patient. We don't tell them what to do. For example, some depressed and guilty patients present to our service with a complaint of alcoholic drinking. The support person opines that there is no alcoholism. We perform an extended evaluation. The depression goes into remission, as do the guilty statements about having alcoholism. The patient decides to keep drinking.

Some patients with heavy drinking have success with the "Sinclair Method." They take 50 mg of naltrexone before starting to drink and report a drop from nine drinks to two drinks. They are happy to drink less.

The onset of drinking dreams is regarded as evidence that alcohol has captured the craving center and attempts to drink in safety are futile. The support person, if cohabiting or nearby, is asked to administer disulfiram daily for the first year sober. Or patient compliance with disulfiram can be witnessed by the support person by FaceTime.

Racism

If these ferocious attacks on humans are part of our culture, then they are part of every patient's experience. By making it clear that we are interested, using clarification, we facilitate patients describing awful experiences of being hurt on the basis of who they are. This propitiates recovery from the damage.

Isabel Wilkerson's *Warmth of Other Suns*—about the great migration of African Americans from the southern United States to escape the constant risk of death and her *Caste*, educating us that the United States has the most effective system of racism in the world—is part of "cultural competence." Cultural competence is knowing that one can't know others' experiences without education and openness. Wilkerson's work is recommended on our service.

Sexism

Myrna, sober from the alcoholism that had brought her in, better from depression and ADHD, and off cigarettes, had a dream about a boss who had harassed her and successfully fired her when she refused to have sex with him. What was he doing in her dream? Dreams are from the SEEKING pathway. Why might she SEEK him?

The answer, based on her associations, was that she was looking for a job and wanted to be conscious that it might happen again—she might be attacked in a sexist way by the next boss.

SEEKING is not only tuned to pleasure. It can be activated by danger. Myrna wanted a job, and she wanted to stay conscious that abusive men are everywhere. She needed to land in a safer place.

Racism and Sexism

Teenage drug use is a marker of distress. Sixteen-year-old Isabella came in as a daily marijuana user, often vaping multiple times a day. Isabella was referred from our child psychiatry service because she wouldn't stop using drugs despite psychotherapy and psychopharmacology.

A social worker had been providing weekly psychotherapy while a nurse practitioner prescribed sertraline and aripiprazole, an antipsychotic drug used for anxiety and depression. Isabella's description of psychotropic prescription visits was that her father would meet with the nurse practitioner for forty-five minutes to talk about her problems. Then they would call her in to tell her what she would be taking.

The previous treatment seemed to honor her father's wish for the patient to carry responsibility for difficulties in the family. A constant on child services is "The problem is her, not us." Often, projective identification is used; the parents behave in a way to induce their children to act out their issues—in this case, a sense of inferiority. The expression of the parents' issue is then condemned in the child.

Initially, Isabella had rages that resulted in breaking things and assaulting family members. The behavior was "about something." The first thing I did in her treatment was remove all medications.

Isabella had a substantial psychotherapy on our service that included a consideration that her European American family had adopted her from Guatemala because they could not conceive. Isabella looked like she had Mayan ancestors. She was regarded by her family as belonging to another race. "Race" is used as a social construct, used only by us to understand attacks against singled-out persons. Immediately after her adoption, her parents got pregnant.

Isabella would say, "I wish I had a body like my sister." Why? Because there was racism in her family directed at her. The defense of idealization protected her from experiencing her family's hostility. A European American body would have protected her from the attacks. Realizing this consciously helped.

Boys would demand sex, and Isabella would comply. Why? Because in her teenage drug culture, girls had one function: sex. Boys asked her for naked pictures. The boys circulated the pictures to many other students. Having been devalued by her family, Isabella's SEEKING was tuned to abuse, tuned to want boys who treated her as inferior.

Interpretations were about "boundaries," recognizing that the family was racist, was attacking her, and that she was using drugs because it hurt so much. As the trouble from racist attacks was understood as an outside force—not something that needed drugs to escape the pain of having been adopted from a part of the world where she might have been loved and into a family that found having a "mentally ill drug addict" fit its expectations—rages and drug use ceased.

The last medical student to work with Isabella looked like her cousin. This medical student had grown up in the same part of Guatemala that Isabella had been adopted from and had come to the US as a teenager. Isabella had the capacity to use identification. She talked in an animated way with the student while I was in the room. Isabella used our help.

Marijuana was behind poor school performance since the cannabinoid system is inhibitory and responsible for functional forgetting. On marijuana, one forgets what one learned in school. Drug use had been transient enough that after a year with us, Isabella was able to go on to normal development, including college.

Using Awareness about Social Factors in Treatment

Treaters need to convey their awareness of how patients are hurt to be helpful. This includes

Not thoughtlessly using labels that carry racist or dehumanizing values.

Not creating a power differential where we tell patients what their path to recovery is. We make it clear that we work for the patients. They are in charge.

We start from our first encounter to convey that addiction means repeated harm from use. Inhaling tobacco is terrifying. We make sure that patients are consciously aware of self-harm.

We make explicit that selling pharmaceuticals is a business that we are not engaged in. We use generic names of medications.

Whether patients need to stop drinking is a question we are happy to think through along with them. If they can drink safely, we can go on to other issues. If they learn consciously why the drinking is destructive, it stops.

The sellers of drugs are always included in our discussion. "Do you want to altruistically give up your life to help a stockholder get that third vacation home?"

"Do you want to protect a drug dealer who kills for a living and who might kill you?" The way to counter stigma is to blame the right people for addictive illness.

Use of Psychotropics

Relatedness is the goal of medication. We are social animals. We want our patients to be happy by functioning well, being loved, and loving others. This is in the context of neutrality. We help our patients do their own good thinking rather than imposing our goals on them.

Our first line antidepressants are bupropion and trazodone—because of their side effects. Our patients want their drive systems to work. They want to eat well but not gain weight. They want to have sex. They want to sleep at night. Patients are afraid that psychotropics will make them gain weight and ruin sexual functioning. The average person loses five pounds on bupropion. Both medications are sex positive. We almost always prescribe 450 mg of bupropion. For antidepressants, higher doses of medication generally give the highest response rate. The therapeutic range for trazodone is 200—600 mg/day. Our usual target is 300 mg.

Addictive drugs usually cause insomnia, so large doses of trazodone are appreciated. Gabapentin 600 or 1,200 mg only at night is a nice combination with trazodone. Gabapentin has an odd latency of onset of action, about three hours. Trazodone puts one to sleep, and gabapentin is both sedating and good for pain—it keeps you asleep. We do not give gabapentin around the clock because it is less effective that way. We are mindful that gabapentin has some overlap with benzodiazepine effects and can become compulsively used with adverse consequences.

Bupropion has an odd reputation for increasing anxiety. The reality is that it reduces anxiety as much as any other antidepressant.[80] My guess is that when the SSRI and the SNRI groups of drugs were being introduced by "thought leader" psychiatrists who were being paid to advertise the new, expensive medications, they worked to discredit the competition.

Bupropion is not used for ADHD on most addiction services despite the fact that its efficacy and tolerability are equal to stimulants.[81] This may again have to do with the cultural convention of blaming the patients who get addicted to medications, as if it is their fault that they have a side effect. In an anonymous study of college students, Garnier found that 35 percent of students said that they would misuse an opioid prescription: sell it, take it recreationally, take large amounts at once, or bring it to parties. Sixty-two percent said they would do this with a stimulant. Seventy-one percent said they would misuse mixed amphetamine salts (Adderall). Garnier actually asked about bupropion. Zero percent of the students would misuse it.[82] Why wouldn't every physician use bupropion, desipramine, or atomoxetine—all effective and not addictive—for ADHD? I don't know.

Trazodone was the most widely prescribed antidepressant in the United States before fluoxetine (Prozac) started the avalanche of "me too" medications in the SSRI class. The competition for market niche resulted in searching for FDA-approved indications when, in fact, antidepressants have equivalent therapeutic effects. With 50 percent of chronic pain patients having comorbid depression, duloxetine (Cymbalta) was marketed effectively for pain, despite the fact that it is inferior to tricyclics in terms of side effects.

On our service, we joke with our patients that we give SSRI and SNRI medications to three classes of patients: masochists who want to suffer with the common "discontinuation syndrome" of feeling like you have the flu, electric shocks in your brain, and odd sensory distortions that can go on for weeks, patients who are trying to be celibate, and sex offenders—the latter two groups wanting the sexual side effects ubiquitous to those classes of drugs.

If trazodone and bupropion do not work for depression, or if neuropathic pain is an issue, we most commonly prescribe tricyclic antidepressants. We pick up rapid metabolizers and noncompliant patients by getting blood levels. There is no other class of antidepressants that allows routine lab-drawn blood levels. Nortriptyline is great for neuropathic pain and has few side effects.

This covers all situations, except transient anxiety, that may trigger relapse. We use norepinephrine blocking propranolol or clonidine, occasional major tranquilizers such as olanzapine, perphenazine, aripiprazole, and risperidone, and anticonvulsant valproic acid, until the antidepressants have had their usual month to work—or not, requiring another medication trial.

Almost all these uses of medications are "off-label," which means that there is no FDA approval for, say, bupropion for ADHD, tricyclics for neuropathic pain, or taking variable doses of varenicline whenever our patients crave nicotine. Bupropion is a vastly safer medication for ADHD than Adderall, but Adderall has FDA approval. Shouldn't we be following FDA guidelines? This question requires an understanding of how FDA approval works.

Let's consider varenicline. The FDA requires that a phase 1 trial be done for safety. No one had much experience with the newly formulated drug at that point. Since the inventors thought it might work best if smokers were told to take varenicline at low doses while inhaling nicotine for the first week, the way they might fail after investing many millions of dollars was what we see when patients disregard our directions and follow the instructions on the box. Inhaling poison while taking a nicotinic agonist causes nausea and sometimes vomiting. Varenicline could have failed its phase 1 trial if nausea and vomiting were too common. Early on, there were worries about changes in mood, including depression and mania, psychosis, hallucinations, paranoia, delusions, homicidal ideation, aggression, hostility, agitation, anxiety, and panic, as well as suicidal ideation, suicide attempts, and completed suicide. It was in the drug company's interest to dose it low to pass phase 1. Phase 2 is a small and phase 3 a large, multisite efficacy trial. Sure that varenicline was effective, the phase 3 trial continued the low dosing.

There is no money to be made by modifying the dosing of an FDA-approved drug. Once approved, it is up to practitioners to learn off-label uses. The reward for the drug company by taking this approach was just under $1 billion per year until the patent ran out in 2020.

If we save lives by using varenicline the way it works best, we take a tiny risk of being sued. Is the trade-off worth it? If Adderall addicts 71 percent, but bupropion causes an occasional seizure, is it worth the risk to use it off-label? What about prescribing bupropion for depression when every textbook says SSRIs are the first line drug? How does one balance the lives of patients against the risk of suit?

Every physician has to decide for themselves.

Upstate Addiction Medicine has several patient deaths every year. Having graduated from medical school in 1976, I am approaching a half century without any indication that anyone has ever wanted to sue me for malpractice. I believe this is because my wish to help my patients is apparent.

Medical Culture

The culture we practice in is full of denial. Some of my colleagues might attack me for killing patients by offering opioid-free treatment. The term used in insisting on opioid maintenance in all cases is "client-centered treatment." We can be regarded as performing malpractice by violating the community standard of care by detoxing patients.

Our opinion is that insisting that anyone who arrives on opioids be maintained on opioids is the opposite of "client-centered treatment." It is imposing on patients a treater's opinion. We offer our patients a choice of opioid-free or buprenorphine maintenance care rather than the "client-centered" one-size-fits-all.

When patients return to their primary-care physicians with diagnoses such as persistent depressive disorder, somatic symptom disorder, opioid use disorder, tobacco use disorder, osteoarthritis, or opioid-induced hyperalgesia and says, "No one listened, no one cared, they have no idea how to treat pain, and they don't understand that I need my pain medicine," a common response is for the primary-care physician to feel bad that we did such a terrible consult and say to us, "What could I do? The patient insisted on oxycodone."

To the extent that it is possible, we try to help the primary-care doctor recognize that it is likely they feel the hostility in the devaluation of us and provide oxycodone to avoid the hostility being directed toward themselves. Some physicians use language that suggests the origin of opioid prescribing is the will of the patient rather than the medical judgment of the prescriber: "They insisted on oxycodone."

This same dynamic is present in prescribing benzodiazepines to patients.[83] Issuing a short-acting drug that is frequently addicting takes the place of provoking a direct expression of hostility toward the prescriber. The horrible side effects of long-term benzodiazepine use are constantly seen on our service, especially the cognitive effects.[84]

We have been supported by our hospital and university leadership to provide outpatient and inpatient consultation on addiction. We are met with ambivalence by some providers. For example, our consulting psychiatrist would be excluded by some outpatient primary-care providers because he offered to help with tobacco cessation. Their opinion was that their patients did not want to give up cigarettes. When allowed to see the patients, he experienced a variety of responses from "I like smoking cigarettes. I am just here to get help with my COPD" to "OMG, you have a pill that takes away the craving! I want to try it!"

Primary-care providers are often heavily invested in medical management of complications of addictive drug use, as if this relieves them of having to face the diversion of hostility from drug use to provider, whereas we see this as a wonderful progression of treatment.[85] In other words, patients who give up their addictive drugs often then complain that their doctors are awful.

This has nothing to do with the doctor. It is a transference. The patients were abused as children. Take away drugs, and they experience being abused by their doctors. Of course! That feeling had to go somewhere. If it goes to us, the drug does not hurt the patient. On our service, we treasure hostility. We can help our patients with it, help them locate the source of the feeling.

Internal medicine practitioners tend to take it personally, as if it has to do with them. This intolerance of countertransference is deadly; preferring to have the hostility manifest as drug use is more dangerous than hating your doctor.

Medical providers often don't recognize addiction until it has reached the skid row level of progression. When these patients are consulted on, there is often little we can do for them. They have given away their entire life to pursue drugs.

A common hospital admission is for abdominal pain where the cause cannot be found. When the physicians administer morphine, the pain disappears because the pain driver was gut cramps from heroin/fentanyl withdrawal.

Floyd, admitted with endocarditis, was tying everyone, including my consulting nurse practitioner, into knots when he demanded, "Benzodiazepines or I leave," while on buprenorphine 16 mg per day. Our nurse practitioner consultant had already advised that he be given the anticonvulsant gabapentin and the major tranquilizer olanzapine. Floyd said that these did nothing for his anxiety.

I went to see him. He was short of breath from a partially destroyed heart valve. Floyd's first comment was "I may have to leave because my anxiety is not being well managed here."

I replied, "Yes, you may have to leave. You are likely to die from addiction. The mortality is twenty-five percent in a year, mostly because patients leave without treatment." My tone made it clear that I was concerned for Floyd's life but not influenced by his threat to leave.

I asked Floyd what happened since I detoxed him from spike earlier that year, while he had been on methadone maintenance. He had come in with his father, saying that the methadone maintenance service simply told him to go inpatient. His experience was that the withdrawal symptoms were intolerable within a few hours. He knew that if he applied to be admitted, he would be in withdrawal long before medications were considered. We did an outpatient detox with valproate 2,000 mg and olanzapine loading while he and his father sat in our office until the withdrawal went into remission. We saw him a few times more and sent him back to methadone maintenance.

Floyd had been administratively discharged for constant methamphetamine and cocaine-positive urines, tried a second methadone maintenance program, then went back to injecting street opioids. He had not used any more spike. He had had a number of losses of close relationships, including with one of our patients who had been mysteriously killed.

I suggested first, given the amount of drug exposure his brain had endured, that medications were unlikely to help. Second, I interpreted that his anxiety was due to feeling alone. The solution for this was to go on a charm offensive with the nurses so they would not avoid him to escape his negativity. In other words, maximize human contact.

We parted friends. I gave him my business card and warmly invited him to come back to outpatient Addiction Medicine when he had finished his six-week course of intravenous antibiotics. He had "lost" the card given by our consulting nurse practitioner, which I regarded as an expression of feeling.

My thought was that my card would represent a transitional object, a thing that stood in for our relationship. Therefore, the card could have some antianxiety properties. Hostile behaviors are an expression of distress. If he felt accompanied by me/my card, he could possibly be less hostile with the hospital staff.

I wrote a careful note explaining this to the hospitalists who were managing his medications. Our service is constantly trying to teach the hospital staff to use their feelings as a guide to treatment. If one thinks about it, psychiatry is the only medical specialty that teaches tuning in to one's countertransference response to the patient as part of providing good patient care. We frequently hear from physician patients that expressing one's feelings about patient interactions is condemned on other medical services.

As a contrasting example, the usual response from hospital medical providers is to accede to the demands for benzodiazepines, saying they are saving the patients with antibiotics provided for life-threatening infections, while doing little harm by agreeing to the patients' terms. This approach violates the medical dictum that one is to address the primary illness along with secondary consequences. Diabetic ketoacidosis requires acute hospital treatment. No physician ignores the need for better long-term blood sugar control. Providing addicting drugs to patients admitted for medical complications of addiction fuels the illness. At an extreme, this is lethal.

For example, our consultant suggested that an endocarditis patient be given buprenorphine maintenance at UH and not be given 6 mg/day of alprazolam. He was found dead in his hospital bathroom after injecting drugs, successfully revived, and discharged with alprazolam. His mother found him dead from an accidental buprenorphine/alprazolam overdose the day after discharge.

There are only three classes of medications that have addictive potential: stimulants, benzodiazepines, and opioids. A part of our medical community has recognized that Addiction Medicine has the resources to evaluate demands for these classes of medications. A larger part of our medical community prescribes these medications with little thought, although our academic neurology, internal medicine, and family practice clinics now refuse benzodiazepines and opioids. And we have seen that there is no reason to give stimulants since bupropion, desipramine, and atomoxetine treat ADHD with no risk of addiction.

TRANSFERENCE-FOCUSED PSYCHOTHERAPY WITH NEUROSCIENCE AT THE CORE— CASE EXAMPLES

Opioid-Induced Hyperalgesia

One primary-care physician with a clever and spiritual orientation, Dave Page, MD, spent three years working on Toby to come to us for a consultation. Toby had taken oxycodone for arthritic back pain for many years. He arrived for a pain consult, saying that oxycodone was "the only thing" that helped his pain.

Toby was not addicted, so when we diagnosed OIH as a pain driver, he acceded to our advice to let us detoxify him and put him on LDN. After two months of discussing the persistent somatic symptom disorder Toby suffered from and helping him with active rather than passive treatment—core strengthening and weight loss—he returned to Dr. Page with no back pain. His pain had been brain-mediated and/or caused by a lack of self-care.

Fibromyalgia and Carbohydrate Addiction

Candace, sixty, presented to Pain Service. She had had forty years of back pain and was referred by her orthopedist to see if there was an alternative to back surgery. Fibromyalgia and osteoarthritic back pain had been "treated" with a combination of fentanyl and oxycodone, total morphine milligram equivalents 200, and medical marijuana.

Physical examination showed 15/18 fibromyalgia tender points. CPT was thirty-six seconds. There had been an onset of depression and fibro fog, which resulted in going on disability ten years earlier. Her Hamilton Rating Scale for Depression was twenty-one—severe. She had contracted type 2 diabetes: height 68 inches, weight 166 pounds. Metformin had been prescribed for her diabetes at 1,000 mg twice a day.

Candace was detoxified and suddenly a charming, interactive delight. Nortriptyline was used for neuropathic sciatic pain and depression. LDN mildly improved fibromyalgia symptoms, with an increase in CPT to three minutes a month later.

Eliminating carbohydrates from her diet resulted in a thirty-pound weight loss. Metformin was stopped. Blood sugars remained in the normal range. This means that her type 2 diabetes went away. Depression in remission and functioning well, Candace was discharged after a three-month treatment that required a total of nineteen visits.

Opioid, Cocaine, Alcohol, Tobacco, Gambling, Sex, Carbohydrate Addiction

Gil, at fifty, with a history of two inpatient rehabs and previous alcohol, cocaine, and cannabis addiction, presented initially for help stopping opioids. He was detoxified, took LDN, and left treatment. He came back a year later still off opioids, but he was worried that he would die prematurely from the combination of tobacco and weighing 300 pounds. He was seen along with my Addiction Psychiatry Fellow Ben Milczarsky, MD.

Gil's father had been a brutal bookie who ran a bar. Part of the initial engagement involved our suggestion that he come twice a week. He refused, insisting on once a week. His concrete defense was that he had a job that did not allow the flexibility to make the second hour. Our repeated transference interpretation was that he feared a fatherlike attack and was keeping his distance from us, as he did from all humans. Addictive behaviors enacted the fear and abuse from his father while making close relationships impossible. Gil's bastion against relatedness with us was refusing to come more. What follows reflects a year of weekly transference-focused psychotherapy.

We took up one addiction after another. Gil had lost $40,000 gambling, nearly a year's take-home pay. We had to wade through the usual idealization of his denial system: his romance with his bookie, "a great guy," details about internet sages of football betting, and the excitement of smoking cigarettes and betting on horse races. As we analyzed his denial system, gambling went into remission except for specific emotional relapses, as explained below.

We heard repeatedly about the excitement of taking a Saturday with a friend to go to private venues that allow smoking and drinking. He knew that at exactly three beers, he would start to inhale cigarettes, about twenty, after a period of abstinence. Gil went on and off cigarettes repeatedly. He said that the smoking/drinking companion was his only friend.

Gil's concern about smoking grew. Denial and idealization were interpreted repeatedly. By the end of the treatment, he had a stress test for his heart and computerized axial tomography of his lungs to look for cancer. As self-care improved, the hostility of the addictive behaviors entered the relationship with Ben and me. I would often come in, as Gil said that Ben's office furnishings were lacking, Ben's shaving wasn't adequate, and Ben's dress was not up to Gil's standards.

There was a peculiar criticism that we were withholding discipline. Gil idealized carbohydrates. He loved "kettle corn," which we learned was popcorn dusted with sugar. He described brownies that he bought at the farmers' market as if they were a work of art. After binging on one of these, he would come in and attack us for "withholding discipline. You have it right over there in the filing cabinet," or, "Where are you hiding the discipline this week?"

This was a paternal transference. Gil's father told teenage Gil he should join the Marines to get discipline and be a man. Gil's father was a violent drunk, lacked discipline, and constantly attacked young Gil for lacking it. This defense is projective identification, condemning another for what you can't tolerate in yourself, combined with behaving to get the behavior enacted by the person you wish to condemn. Gil's father didn't want Gil to have discipline. Not really.

One night, Gil's father drove home from a bar with a state trooper in pursuit. The father ran in the door, throwing his car keys at teenage Gil, who was having a sleepover with a friend in the living room—as if to say it had been Gil driving. There was then an intoxicated conflict with the trooper at the front door. The message in throwing the keys at Gil was, again, that Gil was responsible for his father's lack of discipline, for lacking the discipline to always drive sober.

Carbohydrate addiction started to go into remission. Gil lost forty pounds by the end of the treatment. As hostile comments toward us were noticed and associations asked about, Gil began to consider dating women. He averred that women were "crazy" or "difficult." He had not had a relationship with a woman in fifteen years. He had employed prostitutes for most of his sexual encounters, including when he had been married.

Gil went on a date with a woman he found appealing. The following day, Superbowl Sunday, he bet and lost. He went to the farmers' market and bought brownies and kettle corn. He considered quitting treatment. The interpretation was that he was in a panic about being close.

The last three months of treatment involved a resolution of our relationship so we could openly discuss the closeness and caring from both sides. He went on more dates and was able to contain his panic about the closeness, usually without the help of brownies and kettle corn.

Early in the treatment, a work colleague's father died. Gil said, "I hate wakes." He did not attend. Late in the treatment, a colleague's mother died. Gil brought over dinner. He said, "When I handed it to him, I could see that he knew I cared."

In summary, Gil did not know how to have relationships without expressing hostility toward the other. This repeated his experience with his father that closeness was frighteningly hostile. The addictive behaviors enacted hostility. There were no relationships that did not center on addictive behaviors. Gil was alone.

As Ben and I analyzed the denial and idealization of the addictive behaviors and they started to go into remission, the hostility was brought into our relationship, where it could be gradually shown to be unnecessary given the love between us. Having resolved this trouble in the therapeutic relationship, Gil became capable of having loving relationships with others. Self-care improved. The reason that the addictive behaviors existed was gone.

Opioid Use Disorder in Pregnant Women

As much as we would like to detoxify pregnant women who arrive addicted to opioids, we have no evidence base that we can do this successfully. Pregnancy is complicated. Women want to have healthy babies. Most pregnant women are super serious about stopping all drugs, especially tobacco, alcohol, and marijuana.

Pregnant opioid-addicted women seem to go the other way. They seem to feel their life is out of control and that pregnancy is another manifestation of being hopelessly addicted. Pregnancy accelerates drug use.

The most authoritative study of opioid-addicted pregnant women is called MOTHER. Its first author, Hendree Jones, is regarded as one of the foremost experts. She advocates a form of contingency management therapy. Women are paid for "drug-free" UDS. The reason for the quotations is that nicotine is not considered an addictive drug.

In MOTHER, 33 percent of women treated with buprenorphine

maintenance dropped out. Eighty-five percent of women used tobacco. The payments for "drug-free" urines averaged $1,167. Fifty-six percent of neonates had neonatal abstinence syndrome (NAS). NAS caused an average of ten days in the hospital.[86]

NAS, also called "neonatal opioid abstinence syndrome" by Dr. Jones,[87] is a horror. Families watch helplessly as newborns go through a withdrawal syndrome that features high-pitched crying, nasal congestion that makes breathing difficult, hyperreflexia, and gut cramps, with diarrhea leading to dehydration. In the MOTHER study, newborn detoxification included the use of opioids, such as methadone and morphine.

Where would we ever get $1,167 to pay our pregnant women to stop addictive drugs other than buprenorphine? Almost all our pregnant women have Medicaid insurance that pays small amounts for our treatment.

Two titans of addiction psychotherapy, Carroll and Weiss, reviewed the efficacy of psychotherapy during buprenorphine maintenance. Psychotherapies that require relatedness had no effect. Contingency management had a small effect.[88]

Using the idea that emotional contact hurts, we make a contract on the first visit, that our single treatment goal is the birth of a healthy baby. The support person is almost always either the father of the child or the mother of the patient. We have the couple take a quiz about how tobacco or vapes influence the fetus.

The quiz is written to also convey that our treatment is done in the play mode. "Which of the following is NOT a danger of using tobacco during pregnancy?" After listing sixteen horrible potential consequences, such as losing, on average, seven IQ points, a half-pound of birth weight, and increased risk of sudden infant death syndrome and ADHD, answer seventeen is "Alien abduction soon after birth." All our intake patients enjoy the quiz and are gratified that they got the right answer. We do not seek to judge, only to inform.

The "reward" for stopping drugs other than buprenorphine is

that the psychotherapy will stop, replaced by check-in visits. We meet once a week with UDS and expired carbon monoxide to verify what drugs the pregnant women are using. We tell them that as soon as the UDS turns negative, they will have the option to come once a month, have a UDS to be sure they are still abstinent, and leave with a buprenorphine prescription.

If things don't go well, if after four weeks, the UDS is still positive, we will meet twice a week to work on having a healthy baby. If the UDS is still positive after eight more twice-a-week visits, we will meet daily until the UDS turns negative.

Memorably, one of the mothers in our published case series[89] told me, on the first return visit, when her UDS was positive for cocaine and nicotine, "What do you expect? I'm a drug addict!"

The most common interpretation about continued drug use was identification with the aggressor, that the women respond to their own history of being abused, currently and as children, by attacking their fetus. This is the hostility of addiction.

Frequently, that hostility comes out of the relationship with the fetus and into the relationship with us. We become the monsters of the relationships they are engaged in. One mother started in our case series and continued on buprenorphine maintenance for years. Every visit after delivering a healthy son started with how much she hated former Psychiatry Resident Swati Shivale, MD, who had a lot to do with creating and piloting this approach. I loved it. Better that they have angry feelings toward us than unconsciously harm their fetuses with cigarettes or chewing tobacco.

Our retention in treatment is the highest I have seen reported: 84 percent. The dropouts were almost always because of external circumstances such as, "I found a closer provider, so I don't have to drive two hours each way." The women really wanted to take care of their fetuses. Our therapeutic alliance sustained the engagement.

Almost all pregnant women stopped other drugs. Tobacco was the last to go. One hundred percent stopped tobacco. Only one woman out of twenty-five in our case series had to be seen daily. She kept getting mad and grabbing chewing tobacco at the convenience store she worked at. One woman would not give up clonazepam, and her child had NAS.

Five of the nineteen women who were off all drugs except buprenorphine at delivery reported transient NAS, always less than a day in duration, none requiring opioid treatment. The longest stay required was six days for one child—for monitoring, not treatment of NAS. We effectively abolished NAS as a clinical concern.

Treatment of Comorbid Depression and Fibromyalgia

To my surprise, it may be impossible to treat depression successfully unless one concomitantly treats fibromyalgia. We discovered this when we took a sophisticated man, Hector, with refractory depression for over thirty years, so bad that he was disabled, into treatment for fibromyalgia on our pain service. His HRSD was 20, CPT 21 seconds, faces pain scale (FPS) 8/10. He had eighteen of the eighteen fibromyalgia tender points.

Hector came across as icy and narcissistic. He was taken off the SSRI vortioxetine, gabapentin was reduced from 2,400/day to 600 mg at bedtime, he was detoxed from clonazepam using the ten 25 mg pills of chlordiazepoxide, and trazodone was increased from 200 to 300 mg at bedtime.

Once his fibromyalgia was much better, his depression went completely into remission. After ten weeks, HRSD and FPS were zero. Hector became wonderfully engaging, jokey, and fun. The problem had been that he did not have the endogenous opioid function to be related! This case supports my contention that the driver of depression is unrelatedness. His long-term supportive psychotherapist said that he had never seen Hector related and not depressed over a decade of care.[90]

Alcohol Detoxification

If the patient needs an alcohol detox, we ask the patient to stop drinking at midnight and arrive at 8 a.m. the next morning. If alcohol withdrawal is diagnosed during the initial evaluation, we recommend continued drinking until midnight and arriving at 8 a.m. the next morning. "Enjoy your last day of drinking" sounds good to new patients.

The patient starts at Upstate Hospital to pick up medications and have blood drawn for blood alcohol level, electrolytes, complete blood count, liver, and pancreatic enzymes. They get to us at about 9 a.m. Since alcohol withdrawal starts about eight hours after the last drink, pulse and blood pressure are just starting to go up.

We use a breathalyzer to be sure the patient has a low blood alcohol level, as it takes about ninety minutes for blood results to come back. The patient is loaded on 2,000 mg of valproic acid and an amount of chlordiazepoxide determined by the severity of withdrawal. If vital signs are not elevated, only the valproate is given. If there is a significant elevation of vital signs—pulse over 100 and blood pressure over 140/90—chlordiazepoxide is started, usually 200 mg. Chlordiazepoxide has the virtue that it is metabolized to norchlordiazepoxide, metabolized to diazepam, metabolized to nordiazepam, and metabolized to oxazepam. All five are cross-tolerant with alcohol, meaning that the brain can't tell the difference between alcohol and benzodiazepines. The functional half-life is five days. While all the alcohol comes out of the patient in a day, chlordiazepoxide takes a month to disappear. The patient stays until the withdrawal goes into remission. Chlordiazepoxide is given hourly after vital signs are measured. Sometimes pulse and blood pressure go up for two hours, then trend downward. Sometimes the withdrawal is in remission by the first hour. No one has ever needed more than seven hours for a detox.

Before leaving, the patient takes 1,000 mg disulfiram and is cautioned that drinking at this point may be fatal. They leave mildly sedated. Dehydration is common, so patients and their support person are encouraged to be sure fluids are taken in abundance. The support person has pledged to attend the patient for twenty-four hours and drive them back the next morning.

The patient sleeps in their own bed, often for many hours after getting home. They take another 1,000 mg of valproic acid and 250 mg of disulfiram on waking and are brought in by their support person. The support person is there briefly. Valproic acid, 1,000 mg, is again taken at bedtime.

If there is no resolution of withdrawal by twenty-four hours after the detox starts, the only cause is continued drinking. A breathalyzer blood alcohol level is obtained, and more disulfiram is taken in front of treaters. Psychotherapy/extended evaluation begins via free association. Valproic acid seems to provoke no interest for any use except to ease the withdrawal. 1,500 mg is taken at bedtime on the third day, and it is usually rapidly tapered. Propranolol, 10 mg four times per day as needed for anxiety, is often helpful once the acute withdrawal is in remission. Trazodone and/or gabapentin are used for insomnia of post-acute withdrawal.

We have detoxified forty-two patients a total of sixty-nine times. If a patient relapses, they come in for another detoxification, and we investigate the reason for relapse. We completed 97 percent of our detoxes. One patient had a blood alcohol level (BAL) of 475 mg/dl (50 percent of people die at a BAL of 400). She looked fine when she walked in. This is called "behavioral tolerance," learning to function while intoxicated because of lots of practice. We had to call the ambulance and have her taken to UH for admission to be sure she kept breathing. Behavioral tolerance was so profound that I encountered her chatting with someone on her cell phone as she was wheeled out by the ambulance crew. One patient filled prescriptions for his third detox and was never heard from again.

Fifteen (22 percent) of detoxifications required more than 3.5 hours, either because the patient did not stop drinking at midnight as requested and medications had to be held until withdrawal symptoms allowed them to be administered safely or the withdrawal was so severe that more time was needed. We used our records to calculate the prediction of alcohol withdrawal severity score (PAWSS). A score of 4 or more predicts moderate or severe withdrawal. The PAWSS score was > 3 for 59 (86 percent), 3 for 9 patients, and 2 for 1 patient. Patients who scored 3 included one whose BP went from 158/90 to 130/70 two hours after loading on valproate and 200 mg of chlordiazepoxide and one whose BP went from 150/120 to 140/80 two hours after loading on valproate and 300 mg of chlordiazepoxide. One detoxified patient had ascites caused by alcoholism. Every patient returned for post-detox treatment.

Post-Detox Treatment of Alcoholism

We tell students that the right answer on their psychiatry rotation test to the question, "What is the best medication for alcohol use disorder?" is naltrexone. The clinical reality we find is that naltrexone does almost nothing for alcoholic drinking, although for the rare heavy drinker who wants a medication to cut down their intake, the "Sinclair Method," taking 50 mg of naltrexone an hour before starting to drink, does work.

Having the support person pledge to create a network of persons who will observe the patient taking disulfiram every day, sometimes via FaceTime, addresses codependence problems in families. For example, one mother, whose son had alcoholic myopathy so severe that he became wheelchair-bound, said that her son spent so much of his disability income on alcohol that she was "forced" to drive to the discount liquor outlet to conserve his money. In other words, with this rationalization, she ensured that he could drink more.

The patient got better, regained his ability to walk, dropped out of treatment, and came back months later with his mother. The alcoholic myopathy and need for a wheelchair had returned. This puts us in a position to investigate with the codependent why they might decide to stop the observed administration of disulfiram.

OUTPATIENT THERAPY WITHOUT SUBSTITUTION OPIOIDS

Opioid Detox

Intakes to outpatients who need opioid detox have a preliminary visit with a support person. They are instructed to arrive for detox in early opioid withdrawal—just the beginning of increased pain and anxiety, gut cramps, feeling cold and crawly. The patient takes buprenorphine 2 or 8 mg at a time, depending on the amount of opioid they had been taking, until the withdrawal goes into remission. Patients mix up LDN by putting a 50 mg pill into 50 ml of water and drawing up and swallowing the first 0.1 mg of naltrexone using an insulin syringe. The patient goes home with some minor symptomatic medications, such as hyoscyamine for gut cramps and clonidine for anxiety and insomnia. The most important item on the instruction sheet is the phone number of a senior clinician: "Call day or night if you need help." We are marking the relatedness issue. Often, we add, "Call your doctor before you call your dealer." Thousands of people in Syracuse have my phone number. I get a few calls.

We measure damage to the opioid receptor system with the CPT and use LDN to fix the receptor system, monitored by expecting and finding increasing CPT/pain tolerance. It takes an average of three months for CPT to normalize.

Post-Detox Treatment of Opioid Addiction

Psychotherapy starts immediately. We treat drug addiction, not opioid use disorder. Our approach, "We can't help people who need help, only people who want help," is, in fact, how medical care is delivered. Everyone goes to the doctor as infrequently as possible, for as short a time as possible, as long as they are well. We work like a conventional medical care practice. Patients stay as long as they want, often having relatively brief treatments.

On intake, we offer buprenorphine maintenance harm reduction treatment for those who prefer it to active treatment. Maintenance patients have monthly visits and work on comorbid addictions like tobacco and take prescription antidepressants like bupropion for ADHD. We note that tobacco addiction and comorbid psychiatric disorders go into remission less frequently with harm reduction. We carefully tell the patient and the required (for intake only) support person that they can start with maintenance and shift to drug-free treatment at any time or that they can start with drug-free treatment and shift to maintenance.

Since drugs get rid of feelings, if our patients can't talk through their trauma, they are going to go right back to using drugs to quash their feelings. Withdrawal is not one of the drivers of relapse. Detox has become a minor event. It is because of the single dose of buprenorphine and the LDN.

Feelings such as anxiety and depression indicate something is wrong that can be explored in psychotherapy, other comorbid addictions need to stop to prevent relapse to opioids, and impressively, no one in conventional addiction treatment practices seems to have noticed that measuring OIH with the CPT and fixing damage to opioid receptors with LDN is essential to treatment of opioid use disorder. Let's see what happened with three patients who have been discussed so far, whose treatment included CPT and LDN.

May arrived drinking alcoholically. A conventional addiction service had been injecting her with high-dose naltrexone. It blocks opioid receptors twenty-four seven. As usual, naltrexone had no effect on her drinking vast amounts of alcohol. But it prevented her opioid receptors from regenerating after opioid exposure.

She said on intake, "I had a right knee replacement in 2011. The surgery was technically proficient, but I was still left with continuing pain, which the surgeon could not explain. In total, I have had over twenty surgeries on my knees and feet and have muscle injuries, including a ruptured deltoid and a ruptured gluteus maximus. I have numbness and tingling in both knees and feet, as well as a buzzing that occurs between the two joints. I ache all the time, especially when walking. I have a sharp, stabbing pain while walking. I have done physical therapy continuously and been prescribed opiates in the past. They have not been effective in treating my pain.

"The pain has affected my life greatly. I have had to stop swimming. I used to be an avid rock climber but had to stop these activities in 2005 due to the pain."

Her initial CPT was forty-seven seconds. We stopped injecting naltrexone, started LDN, and asked her support person to give her disulfiram every day. Two months later, her CPT was our three-minute maximum. I started tricyclic antidepressant nortriptyline for chronic low-level depression and for neuropathic (nerve injuries from surgeries: "buzzing") pain and also bedtime pregabalin to block the signals from injured nerves.

With this treatment, May had so little pain that walking and swimming became her two main forms of exercise. Her depression went into remission. This initial improvement helped deepen the therapeutic alliance that allowed her to start talking about being raped and being afraid of being murdered.

Reuben arrived injecting heroin. His CPT was fifteen seconds. He had chronic abdominal pain from recurrent alcoholic pancreatitis. It took a while for our alliance to allow for taking LDN.

By seven months, his CPT was three minutes. As he relapsed repeatedly, his CPT would go down, with him describing the ice bath feeling "like razor blades," and then back up to three minutes. In his psychotherapy, we learned that noncompliance with LDN was a marker of intending to go back to injecting heroin/fentanyl. When he took his LDN, his abdominal pain was mostly absent. When he achieved abstinence from alcohol, the pancreatic pain disappeared.

Holistic Treatment of Chronic Pain

Having a pain service embedded in our Addiction Medicine Service has been essential for treating opioid addiction. As of 2016, 3–4 percent of

Americans were maintained on opioids for chronic pain.[91]

There are three kinds of pain: inflammatory, neuropathic, and brain-mediated. The first is the ordinary, meaningful kind of pain we all experience. You twist an ankle, it swells—the inflammatory response that generates pain. If it is a bad sprain, you take an anti-inflammatory pill immediately and apply ice to limit the swelling. If the pain is still intolerable, you could add acetaminophen. If it kept you up at night, you could add gabapentin, an anticonvulsant that hyperpolarizes the nerve that innervates the ankle.

The pain is generated by swelling-activating pain receptor nerves called "C fibers" that transmit a signal through a waystation in the subcortical brain called the thalamus. The thalamus has lots of receptors for endogenous morphine. Your amount of pain is a combination of the degree of swelling in the ankle, the signal transmitted from C fibers that innervate the ankle, and the ability of the thalamus and communicating brain structures to notify you about how much your ankle hurts. This is "functional pain." You "let pain be your guide" as you walk around gingerly until the ankle heals. As the swelling goes down, the pain goes away. You start to use the ankle the way you did before the injury.

Finally, we could take opioid hormones, such as morphine or oxycodone, that diminish the recognition that there is something wrong with the ankle.

One can see that the optimal management is ice the ankle, start with an anti-inflammatory, add acetaminophen if the anti-inflammatory alone does not make the pain bearable, add an anticonvulsant if the anti-inflammatory and acetaminophen together are not enough, and finally, take out the brain with an opioid.

Jon Streltzer, MD, described it this way: "I had hip replacements on both sides. I only took aspirin. But when they took out that meningioma, it hurt like hell. I took opioids for the first two days." This judicious use of opioid medications was good for Dr. Streltzer but would wreak havoc with opioid pill sales that rely on selling to patients with chronic pain who take the pills four times a day for years.

When I broke the ulna in my forearm and the acetabulum, a pelvic bone, in half in a bad bike accident for which I was hospitalized for three days, my first thought upon hopping up from the pavement and recognizing the ulna was broken was *Cool, I get to see what severe pain is like from the inside.* The surgeons screwed my ulna back together that evening at Beth Israel Deaconess, my hospital in Boston. I took acetaminophen for a day and a half and nothing thereafter. When I moved, my pelvis killed, but in a week, I was able to use my wheelchair without pain because the bones had knit back together. This used to be the most common approach in the United States until that odd "Right to pain treatment movement" campaigned for more opioid prescribing starting in the 1980s.

We treat neuropathic pain with nortriptyline and, less-effectively, with anticonvulsants. Brain-mediated pain is treated with LDN, following the CPT and function and subjective pain. We sometimes use patient handout #1 that has a menu of pain treatments divided into "Inflammatory, neuropathic, and brain-mediated pain." We perform back exams, shoulder exams, fibromyalgia exams—whatever we need to do to establish drivers of chronic pain.

Physical examination of pain patients often shows arthritic changes in the facet joints between vertebral bodies and in weight-bearing joints such as knees or the sacroiliac joint where the spine sits in the pelvis. One common comment is "Doctor, my joints are bone on bone. I need my oxycodone!"

Often, surgeons have looked for "herniated discs" that they can operate on, and the patient tells us that this is the pain driver. Joint fusions in the back force adjoining facet joints to flex more, intensifying arthritic pain, often prompting repeat fusions for more "herniated discs."

We respond, "Surgeons say 'herniated discs'; medical practitioners like us say, 'Arthritis features disks that herniate at times and go back into place at other times,'" but surgery makes arthritis worse. Surgery is never the treatment for chronic arthritis pain.

Screening for Opioid Addiction among Chronic Pain Patients
The classic question for pain service is "Are you here for help with your pain, or are you seeking a source of opioids?" Opioids make pain worse. Buprenorphine appears to be the least noxious, and methadone appears to be the most effective way to increase pain. By knowing this, and by having empirical evidence for this generated on our service,[31, 92] we can say that the 3 or 4 percent of Americans on opioid maintenance for chronic pain are masochists, and their physicians are sadists—or they are not reading our papers.

Why the CPT is not in general use on pain services is a mystery to me. I call it "the blood pressure of the pain system." One cannot know someone's blood pressure by interview, and one cannot know someone's pain tolerance by interview. So many patients assured me that they had huge pain tolerances only to show themselves pain-intolerant on CPT.

One man, at his initial evaluation, when we discussed his five-second CPT, said, "I could have kept my arm in there longer. I just didn't try."

I said, "Okay, go do it again."

The repeat time was four seconds.

Relying on the patients' self-report misses emotional reasons to request opioids and fails to notice where OIH has become the main pain driver. The CPT is an empirical measure of pain/pain drivers while the FPS that pain specialists use is an opinion. The underlying assumption of the pain specialist is that all brains are the same, which the CPT shows to be untrue. Remember the case earlier where Dr. Page's patient, Toby, complained that oxycodone was the only thing allowing him to function and that when he focused on active self-care and was detoxed and put on LDN, his back pain disappeared? Is this a unique case? No. We have published multiple case series showing that our holistic treatment improves pain.

Holistic treatment is most commonly built around persistent somatic symptom disorder with pain predominant (PSSDPP). These are patients that sit on the couch, smoke cigarettes, and wonder when their doctor will figure out how to fix their chronic pain—the external locus of control. I notice that my trainees routinely go to the gym and make sure they eat in a way that keeps their body weight low.

One of our trainees slipped on a wood floor at midnight going to the bathroom, fell down a flight of stairs, had his humerus screwed back together, and arrived for work a week later with an ice pack on his arm.

Our PSSDPP patients are the opposite. They report that their opioid maintenance started after they took time off work to rest the injury in bed. They report that using the injured area hurts, so they avoid functioning fully. They need psychotherapy work on avoidance, so that they start to be the captain of their recovery from chronic pain, aided most notably by physical therapists.

The most common two questions for physical therapists is "Why don't my patients keep coming?" and "Why don't my patients do the exercises I show them at home?" We work on our side of these questions by interpreting avoidance as a defense and helping patients get off addictive drugs such as opioids, alcohol, nicotine, and marijuana.

But wait, isn't marijuana a great drug for pain that helps patients get off opioids? No and no. Opponents process once again, "a" and "b." We find patients who use marijuana have short CPTs.

A well-done four-year prospective series shows that, relative to pain patients who did not use marijuana, there was more pain and anxiety over baseline four years later when using marijuana for chronic pain.[93] There is no evidence that using one addictive drug, marijuana, reduced the use of another addictive drug, opioids.[94] My opinion is that any news coverage suggesting that marijuana be used for pain is a covert advertisement for investors who want to cash in on the sale of yet another addictive drug.

Addiction with Chronic Pain

I met Coleen at UH when she was on a ventilator for respiratory failure, not able to breath on her own. She arrived for her outpatient evaluation on maintenance opioids and cigarettes—combined with an oxygen tank at 3 liters per minute. We detoxed her and fought a titanic battle against cigarettes. She left after six months of twice-a-week psychotherapy with vastly improved function. She was back at work and walked briskly, as opposed to barely being able to use a walker when she arrived. We were doing a case series of failed back surgery patients who rated their pain and function before and after treatment. Coleen rated her pain and function as far worse.

Coleen was off opioids and cigarettes. The hostility of the addiction had entered the relationship with me. She was furious at me. Coleen's way to express her anger seemed to be saying that I had made her worse. This dynamic is not accounted for in studies using numerical self-rating scores. It is not accounted for in physician ratings.

Addressing Weight Issues

Patients gain weight, intensifying arthritic pain in weight-bearing joints in the back, knees, and feet. Large amounts of abdominal fat jutting out above the pubic symphysis put constant pressure on lumbar paraspinal muscles. You see people with this kind of pain bent over their shopping carts at the grocery store, using the support of the cart to rest their lumbar paraspinal muscles. This is referred to by pain specialists as "myofascial pain." I often have joked to patients that physicians shift to Greek when they want to confuse their patients, often after the pain fellow has summarized the pain drivers during our multidisciplinary pain service evaluations using the term myofascial pain.

The overall solution is psychotherapy to help chronic pain patients stop externalizing responsibility for their health so they can embrace active treatments. The central need is often the need to get stronger and lose weight. But losing weight has been recommended to many chronic pain patients. Most people can't do it.

Literature searches on PubMed, Cochrane Library, and Web of Science found that the Atkins diet showed the most evidence in producing clinically meaningful short- and long-term weight loss.[95]

It starts with complete abstinence from carbohydrates but suggests gradually reintroducing them. What has been missing from the diet literature is the concept of addiction.

Our response has been patient handout #3, "Sober Diet." We explain to the patient that they are addicted to carbohydrates. Principle one is that one can never again eat for pleasure, only for health. Principle two is that addiction to carbohydrates means that one cannot "cheat" at all, any more than someone with alcoholism can have a "cheat day" for vodka.

Upstate Medical University Addiction Medicine

Brian Johnson, MD

Sober From Carbohydrates Diet

There is no exact definition of a sober diet. We all crave food just as we can crave sex or drugs. Craving food is built into your brain at the same level as the urge to breathe. You just want to breathe, and you just want to eat.

Keep in mind that everyone works on their eating for their entire life. There is no success or failure. There is only daily effort to eat better.

Two Main Principles of a Sober Diet:

Principle One—decide each morning what you should eat for the day. Your goal each day is to eat what is good for you. Eat only what is good for you.

Principle Two—eat as few carbohydrates as possible. Experiment with yourself. You will see that when you eat carbohydrates, it turns on your craving. Eating one potato chip, one bowl of ice cream, is like someone with alcoholism having one beer. It makes you urgently want more.

For many people, carbohydrates cause an endocrine disorder. Here is how it works:

1. Carbohydrates cause a surge in blood glucose.
2. Blood glucose causes a surge in insulin, the hormone that puts glucose into fat cells where glucose is turned into fat.

3. The surge of insulin causes a crash/low blood glucose that turns on hunger.
4. You eat more carbohydrates, gain more weight.

Here is how it turns into type 2 diabetes, a potentially fatal disease:

1. You reach your genetically determined maximal fat storage.
2. The pancreas puts out even more insulin, and you get even fatter.
3. All the insulin the pancreas can make is not enough to stuff more glucose into fat cells.
4. Blood glucose starts to go up. You have type 2 diabetes.
5. Sometimes, physicians prescribe insulin that is injected into you. This allows even more glucose to be forced into your fat cells, and you get even fatter. If you lose weight, you may no longer have diabetes.

The National Weight Control Registry has found that of people who have lost thirty pounds and kept it off for a year:
- 90 percent exercise, on average, about 1 hour/day.
- 78 percent eat breakfast every day.
- 75 percent weigh themselves at least once a week.
- 62 percent watch less than 10 hours of TV per week.

The underlying brain mechanism has to do with the action of insulin. Blood glucose is sensed by receptors in the lateral hypothalamus. If one has eggs, meat, and vegetables as one's food intake, insulin levels stay low. Eating candy, bread, fruit, pasta, etc., provokes an outpouring of insulin to drag glucose into fat cells. The fat cells grow fatter, and the blood glucose plummets in response to the crescendo of insulin, provoking more hunger mediated by the lateral hypothalamus and more carbohydrate ingestion.

Like any addiction, carbohydrate addiction is forever. The only way to stay slim for a patient who has accrued substantial abdominal fat, with resulting chronic pain, is to stay sober from carbohydrates. Lacking this concept results in the "yo-yo" experience of weight going down when sober and boomeranging back up when relapsing on carbs.

When type 2 diabetes has ensued, we use Robert Sapolsky's[96] explanation that everyone has a genetically mediated maximal capacity for glucose storage as fat. When the maximum storage is reached, the pancreas increases insulin production. This is the beginning of "insulin resistance." When the pancreas can no longer make enough insulin, and fat cells cannot take in any more glucose without more insulin, physicians begin prescribing medications to reduce insulin resistance, or they directly provide exogenous insulin to further abet the process of gaining subcutaneous and visceral fat.

The sober diet puts the patient in an active role. It is up to them whether they decrease the pain of their joints bearing more weight than their frame was built for. It is common that back pain goes away with core strengthening and weight loss.

Inflammatory pain is a helpful signal to take action to protect the part of the body that hurts. Disregarding this helpful signal is a bad idea. Going for "help" to get rid of important feedback from your brain, which is interpreting information it receives from the body, brings up an important question in medicine: "Is our job to help our patients interpret their experience that something is wrong to guide treatment, or is our job to help them disregard the signal that something is wrong?"

Summary of Innovations of Neuropsychoanalytic Service
By using students to provide most of the care, and by having senior clinicians circulate to deliver both service and in-the-room teaching, we can bill enough to provide sophisticated care.

Outpatient detox from alcohol, benzodiazepines, and opioids is easy, safe, and cheap and can be used to engage patients in ongoing treatment with an alliance built on delivering them from a frightening situation where they are intimidated by the ferocity of the withdrawal syndrome.

Recognizing social determinants of addiction is a key to good treatment. Using the racist "one drop of blood," the dehumanizing use of "female" and "male," and advertising practitioners' favorite brands of medications to students and patients is not done. Analyzing the impact of racism, sexism, homophobia, etc., is essential for helping.

We constantly apologize to our trainees about having to hear about reality. Countertransference is brutal, listening is anguishing, yet learning transference-focused psychotherapy is possible for naïve trainees who spend four to eight weeks on the service. The key is the senior staff's participation—showing how to make interpretations and observing the trainees' work—teaching in the room.

Having neuroscience models helps us understand our patients. If they are depressed, we notice the disengagement from us during psychotherapy. We use words as a clarification to describe the disengagement we see in our interaction. If they would like to return to the recreational use of drugs, we explain that drug dreams are a biological marker of irreversible brain change. We explain that weird statements, such as "I have been told to do one thing at a time, and besides, I did not come here to get off cigarettes," are simply a reflection of brain changes caused by the drug and have nothing to do with reality.

We don't stress about the unrelatedness of buprenorphine-maintained patients. We appreciate that they can't feel their emotions. Many benefit from being able to march through life with their feelings shut off.

CHAPTER 13

What Are the Outcomes of Neuropsychoanalytic Treatment of Addiction?

Ideally, we would have funded studies comparing conventional treatments against our approach. We have not been able to find funding. When I came to Upstate, I began to show our outcomes by publishing cases. The number of cases in the table below varies from 1 to 254. If it is a single case, the patient has had a careful assessment and baseline and serves as her/his own control. Larger case series involve having a volunteer help me accumulate cases. Most commonly, the volunteer has been a medical student or two working with me between the first and second years.

Citation/ Year	Number of Subjects	Problem	Intervention	Outcome
24/2010 Note 1	1	IV heroin	Psychoanalysis	Sober and high functioning on 9-year follow-up
77/2011 Note 2	1	Alcoholism	Psychoanalysis	Sober and high functioning on 9-year follow-up
30/2012 Note 3	1	Fibromyalgia	LDN	Much improved over 6 months, CPT 7 to 60 seconds (s)

33/2012 Note 4	83	Opioid dependence	Detox, LDN, transference-focused psychotherapy (tx)	92 % completion of detox, 60% sober 1 month
29/2014	41	OIH	Detox, LDN, tx	CPT improved from 16 to 55 s
29/2014	20	Fibromyalgia	Detox, LDN, tx	CPT 21 to 42 s
92/2017	117	Pain / OIH	Detox, LDN, tx	66% sober 1 month, pain worse 3%, same as on opioids 46%, better 51%
38/2018	254	Pain / OIH	Demonstrated universal OIH cause by opioids	Initial CPT on opioids 44 s, controls 113 s
89/2020	25	Buprenorphine maintenance / pregnant / preventing NAS	Drug use targeted therapy	20/25 women stayed in tx until delivery, 19 off all addictive drugs, no clinically significant NAS in the 19
31/2021	55	Pain / OIH	Detox, LDN, tx	CPT 24 s to 107 s, LDN effect size 0.82
31/2021	21	Fibromyalgia	Detox, LDN, tx	CPT 14s to 30 s, LDN effect size 0.63
27/2021	1	Autism	High-dose naltrexone, tx	From bizarre and unemployed to good job, high functioning
90/2022	1	Depression and fibromyalgia	LDN, tx	Improvement of fibromyalgia, remission of a previously refractory depression

Papers That Are Out for Review

Between 2012 and the end of 2022, we evaluated 265 nonaddicted chronic pain patients. The average age at the intake was fifty-two years old. Thirty-eight percent were men. We had an average of three years of follow-up from the initial evaluation to the last encounter. Sixty-seven of the patients (25 percent) had only one or two visits, meaning they came for an evaluation and sometimes one more time for a discussion of treatment options. Often, the two visits were separated by months or years. The mortality rate was 2.8 percent per year for this untreated group.

Once they came for at least three visits, there was some treatment involved. Often, the patient began detoxification. With more visits, detoxification was completed, and usually, some LDN was taken. With more visits, we could follow the CPT to the resolution of OIH. The mortality rate for 119 patients who had 3-10 visits was 0.4 percent per year. No deaths were reported for seventy-nine patients who had eleven or more visits. The baseline mortality for persons ages fifty-five to sixty-four is 1.1 percent per year. Gender, race, ethnicity, insurance types, and clinical characteristics (depression, borderline personality, and smoking) had no significant impact on the survival rates.

The mortality for 1,398 patients with opioid use disorder whom we treated during the same period is shown. Among them, 449 were similarly considered untreated (seen with only 1 to 2 visits), 571 were detoxified from opioids and maintained drug-free, and 375 were on buprenorphine maintenance. Given that OUD patients, average age forty, were younger and had more men (49 percent) than those with chronic pain but without addiction, mortality was compared to the same age and gender adjusted CoxPH model for different treatment groups with various follow-up visits: baseline, three to ten visits, eleven or more. Untreated pain and OUD patients had similar survival rates; however, treated pain patients (three or more visits) overall had significantly higher probabilities of survival than treated OUD patients. If drug-free patients came at least eleven times, their mortality was lower than buprenorphine maintenance patients who came at least eleven times.

Here is one way to summarize our approach and MOUD:

Type of treatment / What is addressed	Drug-free treatment of opioid use disorder	Buprenorphine maintenance treatment of opioid use disorder
Treats comorbid psychopathology	Yes	No
Treats comorbid addiction	Yes	No
Endless treatment	No	Yes
Cost	Low	High
Chronic pain improved	Yes	No

Here is an abstract of a paper on opioid dreams:

> The mechanism of drug dreams is that the ventral tegmental dopaminergic SEEKING system, responsible for both drug craving and drug dreams, is changed so that drugs are sought—even while asleep. Both gambling dreams and pain relief involve dopamine. Dopamine release is associated with controllability, unpredictability, and novelty seeking—exactly the traits that are associated with addiction. We used a database of 1,663 patients with substantial exposure to opioids, divided between 1,398 with opioid use disorder ("addicted") and 265 "pain-only" patients. A total of 472 addicted patients reported opioid dreams (34 percent), significantly higher than the pain-only patients, among whom only 2 (<1 percent) reported opioid dreams ($\chi^2_{(1)}$ = 119.1, p<0.001). Having opioid dreams was associated with a more than threefold increase in the likelihood of experiencing dreams of other, non-opioid drugs.

Nicotine use, and a transition from sourcing from doctors to risky alternative opioid providers, were the two strongest contributors to becoming addicted. This suggests that risk-taking behaviors involving drugs mediate the phenomenon of "addiction to painkillers." Dopaminergic changes underlie both addiction to opioids and production of opioid dreams. Opioid dreams are a marker of irreversible addiction. It may be helpful to include their presence as a criterion in future diagnostic manuals.

A case report of Reuben's treatment is out for review: the first ever report of successful treatment of a serial killer. Reuben murdered fifty Chilean drug dealers and thirty-seven American drug dealers. He had 540 hours of transference-based psychotherapy over seven years. He has been sober for two years. Reuben is attending AA.

Here is how he described his experience on and off buprenorphine: Reuben reported feeling "mentally sluggish and emotionally numb." He asked to discontinue buprenorphine maintenance. A major concern about remaining on buprenorphine specifically cited was that he was "unable to feel a connection to or feel love from my fiancé." With detoxification from buprenorphine and LDN, he demonstrated a significantly different behavior with me. He reported improvements in his cognition, restoration of his ability to experience emotions, both positive and negative, and could experience his fiancé's love and affection again. Reuben demonstrated better engagement in the therapeutic discussion, openly shared his thoughts and feelings related to the pain of his prior life experiences, and was receptive to my interpretations of his defense mechanisms and confrontation of cognitive distortions. His affect became brighter and less constricted. Reuben did continue to have some interpersonal difficulties at work but was able to tolerate social interactions with his coworkers.

Several months after his buprenorphine detoxification, Reuben briefly relapsed on alcohol and street fentanyl following a narcissistic injury. But when I offered to restart buprenorphine, he adamantly refused, stating, "On buprenorphine, I couldn't feel anything, I didn't care about anything, and I felt like I was losing my intellect. I need to be able to tolerate my feelings without drugs. I want to feel love from my fiancé."

The alcohol detox paper is out for review.

CHAPTER 14

Conventional Treatment of Addiction

The most important intervention at Upstate Addiction Medicine is psychotherapy. Let's start with a basic question: "What is psychotherapy?"

One way to describe the psychotherapy landscape is that there are only three schools of psychotherapy: psychoanalytic, cognitive-behavioral, and contingency management. In psychoanalytic therapy, the patient is the source of all initiative. We simply give the instruction, "Say whatever comes to mind." As long as there is a therapeutic alliance, the patient does the work.

If we are doing an optimal job, we introduce nothing into the patients' thinking. This concept was beautifully described by Marie Cardinal in *The Words to Say It*.[97] The novel describes her psychoanalysis with one of the former presidents of a Paris psychoanalytic society. Her analyst allegedly said only one thing. At the very beginning of treatment, she had what may have been a psychotic delusion about her uterus. The analyst asked her not to talk about it. After that, he did not say a word.

This is metaphorically true. We try not to introduce anything about our thinking. The treatment is all about the patients. We may give biological facts at the very beginning, such as, "Your drug dreams mean that you will never again be able to drink safely." If we do our job optimally, patients have Marie Cardinal's experience.

Cognitive-behavioral therapy also depends on a good relationship with the psychotherapist. Within this relationship, the therapist wants to train the patient. For example, one wants to teach "refusal skills."

"You are at a party. There is a pile of cocaine on the table. What do you do?"

Over time, CBT has incorporated more flexibility into its approach. For example, acceptance and commitment (ACT), where skills training includes mindfully processing uncomfortable feelings. Dialectical behavioral therapy (DBT) has a set of skills to teach. For example, how to distract oneself when encountering uncomfortable feelings.

Psychotherapies in the current environment must be "branded." This means you label and "test" your psychotherapy, usually against no treatment at all, to show efficacy. There are hundreds of branded psychotherapies. Despite this need to brand in order to do psychotherapy research, most branded therapies either follow the approach of psychoanalysis or CBT.

There are two fundamental differences between psychoanalytic and cognitive-behavioral therapies. The first is, whose agenda is it? The psychoanalyst wants to help the patient be more conscious of their own good thinking. The cognitive-behavioral therapist wants to teach the patient skills.

For example, a drug dream might provoke the psychoanalyst to ask for associations to the dream elements. The same dream might provoke the cognitive-behavioral therapist to focus on refusal skills and distraction techniques, "coping skills," such as, "If you wake up with a drug dream, go for a thirty-minute walk to let the craving go down." One treatment treasures feelings or dreams as meaningful, even if uncomfortable. The other treatment teaches techniques for minimizing the impact of feelings.

What about MI? Isn't that a widely used, unique therapy?

No. The brilliance of William Miller, its inventor, is that he took clarification and confrontation and "branded" them as "reflexive listening" and "double-sided reflections." He then proceeded to write reviews of his "innovative" approach trouncing psychoanalytic treatments in terms of outcomes. He is a successful burglar.[72]

The last kind of treatment, contingency management, means that various kinds of behaviors desired by treaters, perhaps UDS negative for particular drugs, are rewarded. For example, one National Institute of Drug Abuse (NIDA)-sponsored study looked for the cocaine metabolite benzoylecgonine—and opiates—in the urine of buprenorphine or methadone-maintained patients.[98] Unfortunately, this approach set a goal that the UDS for cocaine would be negative, while the other plant-produced insecticide, nicotine, was ignored. Contingency management is a perfect match for opioid-maintained patients because the opioid allows them to march through life never distracted by feelings and adverse relationships. They can focus on rewards such as money.

The goal of any psychotherapy is to improve functioning. There are various measures of outcome, most commonly in conventional outcome studies expressed as drinking/drug use days per month. For example, the COMBINE study, the best-done study of alcoholism, with 1,400 subjects, showed that the highest-rated intervention, 100 mg per day of naltrexone with good compliance, along with nine medical management visits that included urging subjects to attend AA, led to 81 percent of days not drinking over four months of treatment, compared to 75 percent of days not drinking for placebo pills and medical management. At one year follow-up, the naltrexone group had 67 percent not drinking days compared to 64 percent for placebo treated subjects.[99] COMBINE is a main source of the "evidence base" that naltrexone is the best medication for alcohol use disorder.

This kind of study leaves most people cold since we don't care if drinking days per month declined from 67 to 64 percent or that that result is statistically significant. It is not significant in terms of how the person is living their life. The person is still drinking. They are still sick with alcoholism.

Outcome studies are often misleading. For example, Kathleen Carroll published a study of a computer-delivered variant of CBT named CBT4CBT to treat cocaine use among methadone-maintained patients. At this point, you would invoke the quadratic equation inverse U model and say that her claim that CBT depends on a therapeutic relationship makes it inapplicable to methadone maintenance. But the computer delivery makes this a fit for unrelated people. Over eight weeks of treatment, 17/47 CBT4CBT subjects attained at least three weeks of abstinence from cocaine versus 9/54 control subjects who were just on methadone maintenance without any other treatment. Twenty-seven percent of UDS were negative with CBT4CBT versus 12 percent of controls.[100]

In other words, this is the reality of opioid maintenance; methadone is only one of many drugs being used. Do we care if 88 percent or 73 percent of UDS were positive for drugs in addition to the methadone provided by a physician? And as you know, tobacco is not counted as a drug.

The conclusion says, "Results of a 6-month follow-up also indicated significant enduring benefit of CBT4CBT relative to TAU (treatment as usual) over time. Effects on percent of urine specimens negative for all illicit drugs also approached statistical significance." You can see that there is a conflict between these two statements. The first sentence says the result was significant. The second says, in a canny way, that it was not. Since, in terms of deaths from drugs, most Americans die from tobacco and alcohol, Dr. Carroll and colleagues were focusing on some lesser drugs.

And she was discussing statistics, not living life. Patients on methadone maintenance have a ferocious appetite for drugs. Once you put methadone and nicotine in your brain, few people can hold out against craving for every other addictive drug.

In an accompanying editorial, *American Journal of Psychiatry* Editor Freedman called the study a solution to Freud's problem that in psychoanalysis "working through" is so time-consuming. A few computer lessons, and treatment is done. Dr. Freedman cited a movie where, "The protagonist falls in love with his computer's interactive operating system, portrayed only in voice by Scarlett Johansson."[101]

He may have gotten the point unconsciously that methadone makes people so unrelated that they could "fall in love with a computer." We know that feeling love on methadone is impossible. But the message was that Dr. Carroll's treatment was effective. I was so mad that I wrote Dr. Friedman and suggested he had published false results that encourage ineffective treatments. He referred me to Dr. Carroll.

I had a nice conversation with Dr. Carroll. I asked her if the researchers had found no significance to their study and invented the three-week abstinence from cocaine idea to have something positive to report about the fact that most patients on methadone maintenance keep using other drugs no matter what additional treatment is provided.

Dr. Carroll said no, that the three-week abstinence idea came from an addiction research conference where participants were upset about the lack of efficacy of psychotherapy for addiction. "The whole field was so discouraged that we agreed to set the bar for success low," she explained.

This conference is nowhere discussed in the article. I may be one of a few people who knows that this is the origin of the claim of efficacy. But the message to the addiction treatment community was that the computer program, a program one could buy from Dr. Carroll, worked at least as well as psychoanalysis. And computer programs are cheaper than trained staff!

I would say in our seminar, when this paper was presented by our psychiatry resident and discussed by our trainees and senior staff, "Imagine if we claimed that neuropsychoanalytic treatment of addiction was able to keep a few patients off drugs for three out of eight weeks during treatment. Would we be acclaimed as efficacious?"

My point was that the addiction treatment field uses ideology rather than science. Since CBT and computer-administered treatment are on the good list, the conclusion precedes the evidence. Any paper, no matter what is found, is acclaimed as another example of "evidence-based treatment." Since psychoanalysis is on the bad list, it is unlikely that anything we publish will influence how treatment is delivered.

In religion, it is the true believers who get to heaven. In addiction treatment, it is CBT that is acclaimed, and that gets the grant money.

A 2018 follow-up study in the *American Journal of Psychiatry* starts with the claim, "Computerized CBT is . . . safe, effective, durable relative to standard treatment approaches." The follow-up treatment trial showed that with computer treatment, 37 percent of urine drug screens (UDS) were negative for all drugs, 34 percent for treatment as usual (TAU) (no added treatment), and 33 percent for psychotherapist-delivered CBT during an eight-week trial. The unspoken truth is that most of the participants were injecting opioids, smoking crack, using methamphetamine, etc. The accurate statement is "No treatments were effective."

The text says, "In sum, this study provides strong support for CBT4CBT as an efficacious treatment for substance use, even when offered with limited clinical contact."[102]

To give one more example, there was an article published in the *American Journal of Psychiatry* about adding clonidine to buprenorphine to reduce relapse to illicit opioid use.[103] Some of our patients try to get us to prescribe clonidine to "boost" intoxication caused by buprenorphine. The idea that subject satisfaction with clonidine could be because it "boosts" intoxication was not mentioned in the article. The article simply said that subjects liked clonidine. It is not clear whether any of the authors talk to patients. This study explained that the clonidine was intended to reduce "stress."

What stress is is unclear to me. One of our patients explained that his "stress" was generated by sitting on his parents' couch after he had dropped out of high school, playing video games and watching TV.

The animal model of stress is often the "forced swim test," where the rat is put in a glass bowl of water that the rat can't escape from because of the smooth glass walls. The researcher times how long it is until the rat gives up swimming and drowns.

I can't imagine how either of these stresses could be helped by clonidine.

While I did not speak to the authors, they defined "lapse" as the first opioid positive UDS and "relapse" as two consecutive UDS positives. Although they were unable to find any evidence of efficacy of clonidine regarding relapse, they reported a "significant" extension of opioid-free days when providing clonidine, thirty-five days to lapse versus twenty-six days with placebo. Remember that the goal of buprenorphine maintenance is to have the patient rely on a physician to provide their opioid drug rather than a drug dealer. One way to summarize the finding is "Gee, we hoped that the patients would only use our buprenorphine, but we found that they want drug dealer opioids too."

An accompanying editorial[104] said, "The study by Kowalczyk et al. is an exemplary instance of rigorous data collection techniques applied in a natural setting to maximize ecological validity and advance our understanding of the pervasive and costly problems of addiction."

This seems to be another example that any paper, no matter what it found, is acclaimed as "evidence-based treatment." But the treatment needs to respect the status quo, in this case that opioid maintenance is the only valid treatment for opioid use disorder. When I submitted an article to the *American Journal of Psychiatry*, along with Lance Dodes, about psychoanalytic treatment of alcoholism, it was rejected. The *American Journal of Psychiatry* may have more in common with the Spanish Inquisition than science that is tied to empirical findings. True believers receive blessings. Heretics are burned at the stake.

The best outcome study of opioid maintenance treatment ever done was by a UCLA team headed by Walter Ling, a leading researcher in addiction.[56] This study started with 1,080 participants and was able to interview 795 buprenorphine and methadone maintenance patients at five academic treatment centers over an average of 4.5 years. Patients cycled in and out of treatment. Buprenorphine patients spent, on average, 52 percent of the 4.5 years in treatment. Methadone maintenance patients spent 63 percent of the time in treatment. For those who remained in treatment, monthly heroin use dropped from eleven days per month to seven days per month. In the last month, after 4.5 years on average, heroin use was 51 percent of buprenorphine maintenance patients, 41 percent of methadone maintenance patients, UDS 43 percent positive for other opioids on buprenorphine maintenance, and 32 percent positive on methadone maintenance. It is true that mortality was reduced to about 1 percent per year—"harm reduction." With no treatment, mortality is about 2 percent per year. The conclusion was that "each medication is associated with a strong reduction in opioid use."

Here is a graph from the National Institute of Drug Abuse website, sourced 3/15/23. Three of their chosen studies showed that about 45 percent of patients on methadone maintenance were using opioids bought on the street. What do you think? Does this mean that the treatment "works"?

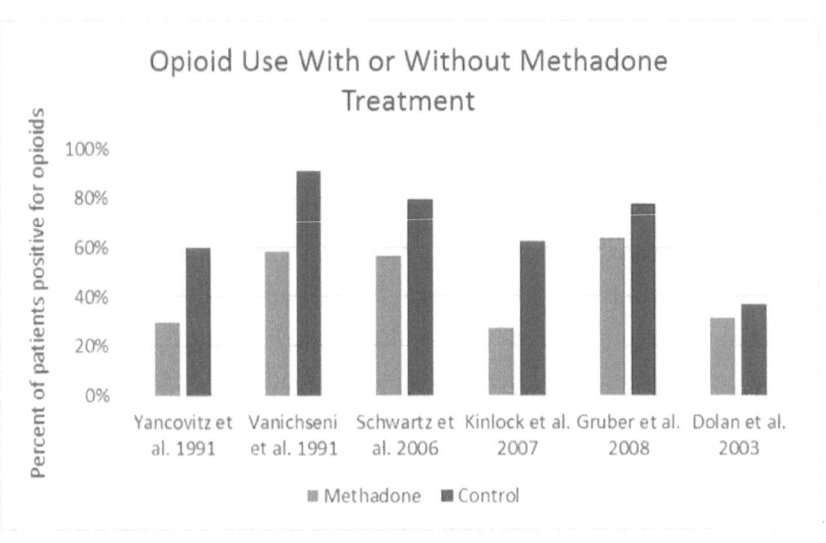

The headline in academic publications and in the press trumpets that this is proof that opioid maintenance is the gold standard for opioid use disorder. "If only there were more treatment beds and more providers prescribed buprenorphine."

What we hear reported is that patients take prescribed opioids and continue with other drugs. If we took patients who were drinking a quart of vodka per day and "prescribed" twelve "less dangerous" beers per day, would we say with authority that our less dangerous form of alcohol had successfully reduced vodka use to a pint per day? There is no mention in these papers that overall opioid use may be the same. Would it be a surprise if methadone-maintained patients use less illicit opioids than persons who are not in treatment?

We hear that the pattern of use is different. While on methadone, one doesn't have to inject heroin three times a day. You can wait for your support check to arrive and inject an amount of heroin/fentanyl that has an effect despite the "blocking dose" of methadone. The reason I say "support check" is that it is unusual for methadone-maintained patients to have a job.[105] At Crouse Chemical Dependency, patients leaving after dosing either smoke cigarettes in the parking lot or go out for coffee and nod.

The mortality is lower. Undiscussed is the emotional impact on the staff providing methadone or buprenorphine under these conditions. I would think that an honest and forthright discussion would help practitioners tolerate how difficult it is to provide methadone when you know that almost all of your patients are using other drugs and that a substantial minority continue to inject heroin/fentanyl, no matter what you do.

The fact that many providers avoid giving buprenorphine is addressed only with condemnations from academics. Maybe admitting that the patients are unrelated and have a motive to be dishonest because of not wanting you to stop prescribing buprenorphine would help more practitioners hang in there. But this would require saying publicly that there are liabilities as well as advantages to buprenorphine maintenance, in conflict with the current status of opioid maintenance as "the gold standard."

Endogenous opioids regulate human relationships. Being on methadone or buprenorphine makes one unrelated. What does it do to the children of all the parents on maintenance? What is it like to have a parent who can make your lunch for school but who doesn't feel comfortable giving you a hug? Has anyone looked into this? Not that I am aware of.

When I worked in methadone maintenance, I advocated for an informed consent at the outset of care, explaining that methadone was lifelong treatment, and it had potential harms, such as death, if combined with sedating drugs such as benzodiazepines, would compromise sexual functioning, would make depression more likely by shutting off human contact, create severe constipation, increase pain, and make falls and fractures more likely. This suggestion was regarded as undercutting treatment.

In summary, conventional treatment of addiction, allegedly "evidence-based," is built on studies that are not valid and are sometimes dishonest. The headlines and hype suggest that we addiction specialists have it going on! The reality is that little is new. Addiction continues to kill people no matter what treatments are offered.

CHAPTER 15

One Physician's Experience of Attempting to Provide Principled Leadership

If you want to skip a lot of complaining, use this summary—"Principled leadership in medicine results in being fired all the time," and "Ideology trumps human welfare in grant applications"— and go to chapter 16.

One of my Columbia Engineering professors suspended me from my physical chemistry class in 1971. My experience was simply turning around in class because the friend sitting behind me had asked to borrow a pencil. My mentor at the time, Elmer Gaden, PhD, said that the professor told him that the infraction was "Fomenting revolution at the engineering school." Dr. Gaden helped me get back to class so I wouldn't suffer academically. This was the period right after student protests had shut down Columbia.

My department chair at the Cambridge Health Alliance spent an hour screaming at me that I had dishonestly claimed a psychiatry department Harvard appointment. I had my Harvard appointment through the medicine department at Cambridge at the time. I had left psychiatry for medicine exactly because I feared this department chair's belligerent narcissism.

What I learned subsequently was that the feminist leadership of our alcohol detox had, at the last minute, stuck my old curriculum vitae into a grant application we had submitted—the one I used when I had been recruited from psychiatry to the internal medicine department. I had been hired at this academic detox because they needed a doctor, and I had a reputation for knowing medicine.

The grant application for a women's service at our detox received the highest score in the state of Massachusetts, but no funds were issued because the psychiatry department chair informed the state that he did not back the application. The underlying issue was a feud about state positions. The grant would have resulted in the medicine department getting some positions that psychiatry preserved by scuttling the grant.

Wanting to get even farther away from this department chair, I responded to an invitation to shift over to Beth Israel Hospital. A hospital merger created Beth Israel Deaconess Medical Center (BIDMC). I was asked to make an alliance with the Dimock Health Center in Roxbury. Almost every staff member on the addiction service at Dimock was African American, including the leadership. I was able to get grant funding to support my work and my Harvard residents in psychiatry, who came full time for training in addiction. This grant was initially supported by the Massachusetts Department of Public Health (DPH).

With great effort, I secured a five-year grant from the Department of Mental Health by demonstrating how much mental illness we found at the inpatient detox/rehab in which we worked. At that point, a new team of administrators at Dimock fired me and all the leadership on the addiction service. They felt that they could use the five-year grant and hire some psychiatrist who had less power.

Unfortunately, Dimock was regarded as such a dangerous place to work that they could not hire anyone competent. The residents reported that the conditions and teaching were so dismal that they were pulled, and most of the grant money was never used.

I have already described my experience of being fired at Harvard Medical School after trying to get a letter certifying that my patients could be seen at BIDMC. I didn't care. I secured a letter that in an emergency, my patients could be seen at Boston Medical Center. This was one of many requirements to obtain a license to do outpatient detox from DPH.

I spent $50,000 to outfit my office to meet DPH regulations. The DPH field inspector found four minor issues and told me that I would be certified at the next central office meeting. I did not hear for two months. Finally, I was told that the central office had found fifty new infractions. When I fixed all fifty, the central office notified me that they had found seventeen more infractions. When I asked for an in-person meeting, I was told that it was impossible to schedule over the next two months.

I decided that the issue was that I was advocating for 100 percent outpatient detox and that this was regarded as undercutting the financial viability of all the DPH clients who were charging the state of Massachusetts for inpatient detox. Although this cost the taxpayers much more money to provide an inferior detox, it preserved power relationships. DPH employees often retired with a state pension and then were hired by the services they had just stopped regulating.

I accepted an offer from Upstate Medical Center to join the faculty as the main teacher of addiction medicine. Robert Gregory, MD, the former Harvard resident who I had supervised for three years, worked with Mantosh Dewan, MD, to recruit me. Mantosh offered me the backing to be creative. I was fired twice more in Syracuse, for advocating outpatient detox when Crouse was making thousands of dollars for each inpatient detox and when Mantosh was fired as department chair over a struggle with the university president.

These kinds of experiences are not mine alone. Physicians all over the medical community experience that differences and dissent are not allowed.

At the Boston Psychoanalytic, I was regarded as too outspoken. I applied for the faculty eight times. I taught in the extension division and submitted student evaluations with high ratings. At one point, I met with the head of the committee to ask why I was not put on the faculty.

I said, "Look how much I am publishing in psychoanalysis!"

The smugly delivered response was "Publishing has nothing to do with being on the faculty." I took this to mean one had to be liked, well liked.

I treasure my last big meeting there. The topic was "healing" after Eliot Schildkraut, a training analyst, had started living with one of his analysands. I was already upset that two of my three supervisors in analytic training had been fired from the faculty for having sexual relationships with patients. Psychoanalyzing a trainee came across to me as a form of "grooming" a potential victim. Eliot's wife, Barbara, was in my neuroscience and psychoanalysis study group. Barbara is an outstanding person.

The leadership had protected Dr. Schildkraut from medical license sanctions by allowing him to resign. I said in front of a hundred colleagues that I disagreed with this maneuver: "You have all been fucked by Eliot Schildkraut." As with AAAP, colleagues came to me privately, saying that I spoke for them. But no one wanted to join me publicly since this was guaranteed suicide in terms of future leadership positions.

Same at the American Psychoanalytic Association. When I was cochair of the Addiction Discussion Group, the chair called and asked me to write a rebuttal to Dr. Richard Friedman, who had panned his book in the *New York Times*. When my answer was "It's complicated, and I am not able to do what you ask," he responded by firing me as cochair. (I agreed with much that Dr. Friedman had to say.)

I appealed to the head of the discussion group committee. The temporary solution was three chairs, including me. But the other two chairs told me that as soon as I said anything about neuroscience, what I was doing was "not psychoanalysis," and I would never again be allowed to present to the discussion group.

When I reported this, the group was disbanded. My repeated applications to restart it have been rejected. When 22 percent of Americans die from addiction, ending the previously well-attended discussion group undercuts the social mission of a wonderful organization.

When I shifted to Upstate, I had already started applying for grant funding to prove that the concepts of neuropsychoanalytic addiction treatment work. My first try was a K23 training grant submitted with my mentor from the Cambridge Health Alliance, Ed Khantzian, MD. He was a Harvard professor. He had been president of AAAP. He had received two R-01 grants from NIH/NIDA.

The application failed. My project officer at NIH, Harold Gordon, said that I was too old at fifty to apply for a training grant, that NIH didn't like Dr. Khantzian, and that they did not like psychoanalysts, but that I should continue to apply for NIH grants.

My first try while at Upstate was a SAMHSA application in 2009 to educate Syracuse high school students and local physicians about addiction. It failed.

I have allied with Steve Faraone, PhD, our director of research in psychiatry. Steve has received many millions of dollars in NIH grants, has published a paper a week over his seventeen years since Mantosh recruited him from Harvard, was ranked in 2023 as the #80 scientific researcher in the world, and has been closely involved in most of my grant submissions—about twenty—sent to various government funding agencies, drug companies, and private foundations.

Our first attempt in 2012 was an NIH transformational application that suggested we use our insight into the confluence of fibromyalgia, autism, and opioid use disorder to understand better how to treat these three. We would measure C-terminal beta endorphin as a guide to how to dose naltrexone to move opioid tone up or down. Like almost every application, this one was rejected unscored, with little comment.

A memorable rejection was from the Patient-Centered Outcomes Research Institute (PCORI). I wanted to show how easy, cheap, and humane doing outpatient detox from alcohol and opioids is. For PCORI, one has to build a board of patients, stakeholders, and colleagues to oversee the application and, if funded, the project.

I was proud of our board's diversity. It included a gay welder, a local Native American, a businessman—who had all been patients—and the mother of a teenager who had a wonderful, successful treatment for injecting heroin, only to die from an accidental overdose when his father got out of prison, told him to stop the bupropion he was taking for ADHD, and had him move in with him—leaving his mother's attentive care. Adding a board to writing the application made it especially time-consuming.

The PCORI feedback was that the board was too enthusiastic about our approach and that we would be killing research subjects. I assume this meant that alcohol detox is not safely done outside the hospital and that the treatment for opioid use disorder is uniformly insisting that patients take prescribed opioids like methadone or buprenorphine. The feedback that we would be killing research participants made resubmitting pointless.

As I have explained, we had the case series showing that we could use our neuropsychoanalytic approach to build a contingency management treatment that effectively eliminated NAS, and we had discovered that what had been called by Hendree Jones "neonatal opioid abstinence syndrome" is actually combined drug withdrawal, probably combined opioid-tobacco withdrawal. I thought we had a can't-lose potential grant proposal. The amount of suffering to children and their parents from NAS, the amount of damage to unborn children from tobacco, and the billions of dollars in medical costs—how could a potential solution not be investigated?

Steve felt strongly that anything that sounded like psychoanalysis would result in vituperative rejection. Steve told me *not* to put anything about psychoanalysis into the application. We branded the approach DUST: drug use treatment.

I sent him a draft application, explaining that I could not figure out how to leave out the concept of defense, that pregnant women who use drugs use defenses: rationalization, "I am under too much stress to stop now," minimization, "I've had three babies while I smoked cigarettes, and they are fine," and denial, "Drugs don't affect the developing child."

Steve rewrote the application so these defenses were explained without using any words that implied we were using psychoanalytic concepts. We supplied pilot data that are in our 2020 publication.[89]

The responses included a reviewer being aghast that we allowed medical students to deliver some of the treatment, despite the fact that in conventional treatment, almost no one talks to pregnant buprenorphine-maintained women about using other drugs. The application was rejected and unscored.

Opioid withdrawal is frowned on unless injected naltrexone 380 mg monthly is recommended. Most patients relapse before they have cleared the week needed to transition from illicit opioids to naltrexone injection. In 2019, Steve and I submitted a grant application to Alkermes, the company that makes injected naltrexone. We proposed to use daily psychotherapy and LDN to increase the rate of retention until the naltrexone could be injected. Our control group would have stayed on LDN for six months.

We suspected this group would have better outcomes. We don't know if Alkermes worried about the same thing. They rejected the application.

As we have seen, methadone and buprenorphine maintenance and injected naltrexone are the only endorsed "client-centered" treatments. I wrote a 2019/2020 Health Resources and Services (HRSA) training grant application. I had assembled huge community support—the mayor of Syracuse, the superintendent of schools, the president of the Syracuse Common Council, leaders in rural medical centers, Mantosh as president of Upstate Medical University—to create an increase in training of physicians to provide addiction treatment. There would be an adolescent track based in Syracuse's inner-city schools and a rural track in the vast, thinly populated area of Central New York.

My error was probably to write that not only did we provide buprenorphine and naltrexone for opioid use disorder, we have an innovative, drug-free, LDN, holistic, psychotherapy option. This was not the "client-centered" answer the government is looking for. Five out of six sections had only "no merit" written as the reviewer's response.

Do administrators of NIH divisions know that innovation is not allowed? Being me, I have emailed my two favorite NIH directors: Thomas Insel, at the time head of NIMH, and Nora Volkow, head of NIDA. Both are wonderful researchers and administrators. Dr. Volkow, from the New York Psychoanalytic Institute, had received the Pfeffer Prize for her spectacular work/discoveries in neuroscience.

Dr. Insel was sympathetic and suggested I try the National Center for Complementary and Alternative Medicine, using psychoanalysis as an "alternative medicine" approach. I corresponded with the director, who said that if she ever accepted psychoanalysis as an "alternative" treatment, she would be defunded by Congress. Dr. Volkow, in person and years later by email, blandly said that if my grant applications were good, they would be funded.

There is an American myth that "research" is iconoclastic, welcoming new ideas. If addiction kills 22 percent of Americans and endorsed treatments like opioid maintenance have a 1 percent per year mortality, government organizations like the National Institute of Drug Abuse should be wide open to new ideas. My experience is that they are not.

I have had to be careful in submitting papers for the same reason, careful to avoid what I call "vituperative rejection." For example, when my text said, "We were able to get pregnant women off all addictive drugs except buprenorphine," the AAAP journal reviewer's rejection note said, "Buprenorphine is not an addictive drug! It is a prescribed medication."

I have had limited success publishing with my American colleagues. Europeans in my field are much more open to novel ideas. After a submission of the NAS report to the American Society of Addiction (ASAM) journal was also rejected, that paper was accepted in European *Frontiers in Psychiatry*, and it received 1,000 views within a month.

Some journals are open to innovative ideas.

PART 4

PUBLIC HEALTH SOLUTIONS

In a 2018 paper, I estimated the income of the addictive drug industry to be $858,000,000 per year, 5 percent of the gross domestic product of the United States. The drugs were tobacco, alcohol, opioids, benzodiazepines, marijuana, and drug cartel income. For comparison, the auto industry income was $70,000,000.[106]

How are we doing in curbing deaths from addictive drugs? I was able to find reliable numbers for 1990 and 2021.[107-9]

Year / drug	1990	2021
Tobacco	400,000	480,000
Alcohol	100,000	140,000
Overdose deaths—mostly due to opioids	4,506	107,622
Illicit drugs, cocaine, methamphetamine	20,000	45,000
benzodiazepines	Could not find	12,000—benzo numbers were not used in totals
US population	248,922,111	332,031,554
Drug deaths / population change	**1.57 larger**	784,622 deaths 1.33 larger

We are losing the war on drugs. These numbers are congruent with the thesis that the addictive drug industry is using its power to expand their market while all the research at NIH, medications such as naltrexone for alcoholism and MOUD, and all the government regulators such as the FDA have little impact. Time to try something new.

Using our concepts about how drugs take over the brain, turn on craving, and shut off awful feelings, with idealization as a constant part of all denial systems, we will cover two categories of addiction: alcohol and drugs. Alcohol has a distribution system that could be left intact. For alcohol, we need public health input to alert our citizens about what to do if one becomes addicted and to protect those who need our protection because they have become zombified by alcohol. Other drugs require a different approach.

CHAPTER 16

Alcohol Purchase License[110]

Alcohol has been rated by experts as the most dangerous addictive drug.[110] When I go to my local grocery store and pull out my driver's license to prove I am old enough to buy beer, I am embarrassed. What does my driver's education course and my road test with a state trooper have to do with buying beer? Alcohol is dangerous, but we don't treat it as dangerous.

If I was a bad driver, if I got three speeding tickets in a month, New York would make my license to drive a car invalid. But I could still use the picture ID driver's license to buy beer.

My alcoholic patients drink with terrible consequences. They are hospitalized with alcoholic pancreatitis, alcohol withdrawal seizures, alcoholic myopathy where hip girdle muscle deterioration makes them too weak to walk, upper GI bleeds created by a combination of bone marrow suppression of platelet formation, and rupture of dilated esophageal veins created by alcoholic cirrhosis and vomiting during alcohol withdrawal. They are hospitalized for intoxicated falls and accidents. Our current cultural denial system is that despite severe progression of alcoholism, they are free agents who could stop drinking if they wanted to.

Alcoholism is a nightmare! One drinks, one awful thing after another happens, and the longer the illness goes on, the less likely one will ever recover. Morning withdrawal and beer for breakfast fuel the nightmare. Sometimes they have such bad alcohol-induced cognitive damage that they are certain to leave the hospital and drink immediately because craving and alcohol drinking dreams are so intense.

The definition of when someone becomes a hopeless alcoholic is when they have sustained such severe brain injuries that they can no longer use people to help them stay sober. At that stage of cognitive impairment, people frighten them because they have lost practice relating and the ability to think, both that are necessary to negotiate human relationships. After being treated for hepatic coma caused by ascites and liver failure, with terrible cognitive functioning, patients are discharged home, usually without aftercare for alcoholism.

Even having a zero prognosis for doing anything except incur huge expenses for treatment of medical consequences that do nothing to address alcoholism, these persons can still use their driver's license to buy beer. The medical costs of setting up our society this way are enormous. The overall cost of alcoholism in the United States is $1/4 trillion/year.[111]

We don't have to put up with this.

Forty-three thousand Americans lost their lives in automobile accidents in 2022. Driving is a privilege. No one has a right to drive. You have a right to life and liberty. You have a right to free speech. No one can take those away from you. But unsafe drivers threaten your life. That is the reason unsafe drivers lose their license. Driving requires a license combined with a record of good driving behavior.

Everyone remembers drivers' ed, the ritual we go through as teenagers, ending with an anxiety-filled road test. The trooper sits next to you in the car. She or he decides whether you are skillful enough to safely operate your vehicle, safe for yourself and safe for others.

One hundred seventy-eight thousand Americans lost their lives to alcohol in 2022. Is buying alcohol a right or a privilege? Has it ever crossed your mind that we treat buying alcohol as a right? No one can take it away from you, even though four times as many people die from alcoholism as driving.

What do we do now to limit death from alcohol? We tax it. Since half of all alcohol sold in the United States is sold to alcoholics, public health experts note that increasing the price slightly reduces harm. Poor people are most affected. They can't afford to buy oceans of alcohol. Above a certain income, everyone with alcoholism can afford to drink themselves to death.

Try to get elected on a platform of raising taxes on alcohol. It is a disincentive for politicians. Half of Americans drink. That is a big voting block. We do other things like limit sales on Sundays in some states. Nothing works as well as raising taxes. We punish drunk drivers. But if you lose your license to drive because of drunk driving, that falls under driving laws.

Why not have a state policy that treats buying alcohol as a privilege? It would be easy. All adults could automatically be grandfathered in as licensees.

For teenagers who want a license, let's have a course that teaches that, while most people can drink without consequences, there is a substantial minority of users who lose control of intake, drink compulsively, and injure themselves and others because of addiction to alcohol.

Teenagers should be taught that if this happens to them, it is not their fault, but it is their responsibility to get help. Teenagers should be taught about Alcoholics Anonymous.

Teenagers who want to obtain their alcohol purchase license at twenty-one would have to take a brief course with questions like the following:

A 130-pound woman is out on a date at a restaurant with a 180-pound man. How many drinks can she have over a two-hour period and still fall below 80 mg/dl, or 0.08 g/liter, above which it is illegal to drive?"

    A. 1
    B. 2
    C. **3**
    D. 4
    E. 5

How many drinks can her date have over that two hours and still drive legally?
   A. 1
   B. 2
   C. 3
   D. 4
   E. 5

"How big is one drink?"
   A. 5 ounces of wine
   B. 12 ounces of beer
   C. 1.5 ounces of liquor
   D. All of the above

Which is the definition of alcoholism?
   A. Drinking every day
   B. Drinking more than five drinks on any occasion
   C. Repeated harm from drinking
   D. Moving from beer to hard liquor

What is it that gives alcoholics a bad name?
   A. Not getting help because you want to stop drinking on your own
   B. Going to Alcoholics Anonymous
   C. Going to psychotherapy to find out why you keep drinking dangerously, despite the fact that alcoholism is fatal
   D. Telling your friends that you have decided to stop drinking

You can take the test online, as many times as it takes to get all the answers right.

Instead of a state trooper, a counselor would spend an hour doing a motivational interview that uses clarification and confrontation. The counselor has no interest in the interviewee's responses, so long as the answers represent careful thinking. The counselor helps the alcohol purchase license applicant sort through their own values to decide what is right for them. The counselor doesn't want to stir up trouble, to contradict, or to offer their own opinions. The only way to fail the "road test" is to not show sincerity about knowing that drinking alcohol has potential bad consequences.

"You plan to drink? What is your thinking about how to be careful that you don't develop alcoholism?"

"What would you do if you were convicted of drunk driving? Would you continue to drink? What is your thinking about it? What about developing an alcohol-related disease such as alcoholic hepatitis? Would you continue to drink then?"

"You know that you can't have more than three drinks over two hours at a restaurant or you will be driving home drunk. What would you do if you had four drinks?"

"Have you ever gotten into a car with someone who had been drinking enough that it scared you? What did you do? If you haven't, or if you had to do it over again, what would you do?"

"What would you do if you started to feel out of control by your drinking? If you woke up after drinking and couldn't remember how you got there? If you woke up after drinking and felt someone had had sex with you without your consent?"

These questions address issues of safety that are important for a lot of Americans. If it is not an issue for any one individual, it might help someone help a friend. Coming up with carefully considered answers will sensitize everyone to the fact that drinking can be dangerous. It will alert potential victims to danger before they are in a bad spot. Thinking about it ahead of time will allow them to respond to danger more effectively. A motivational interview will spread conscious awareness about these common events to vulnerable young people.

We are living out the alternative now—these things happen because people are not prepared for the potential for harm.

How will we check that a patron at a grocery store, liquor store, or restaurant has a valid alcohol purchase license? A simple electronic scanner that is connected to the state-banned-drinker registry.

Unrestricted

Restricted

What will we do in New York if someone flies in from Arizona or Australia? This will be a state law. The out-of-towner can purchase alcohol as long as they are twenty-one. They just have to show their driver's license or passport.

Okay, all adults will be grandfathered in, and gradually, more and more of the population will have to take a licensing exam that increases awareness of the nature of drinking. What do you have to do to lose your license?

Be a bad drunk. This, then, will not affect half the population. Three percent of Americans are the target population.

How long do you lose your license for? Five years. After five years, you can apply for a new license. It has the same requirement as getting a new alcohol purchase license at twenty-one: an online course and a motivational interview. "You had two driving-under-the-influence convictions five years ago. How are you going to be sure that you can drink safely now?"

Medical complications of alcoholism that are irreversible could be reported by medical personnel, the same way that hospitals, doctors, and nurses are mandated reporters about child abuse. Who wouldn't want to report a patient who is admitted for alcohol withdrawal seizures, alcoholic pancreatitis, liver failure, alcohol-induced dementia, or alcoholic myopathy that results in falls when drunk?

Reporting such a patient to the banned-drinker registry would address the primary reason for hospital or emergency department admission. Reporting a patient would remove the helplessness that is currently endured by hospital personnel, condemned to knowing that all the good they have done for a patient is likely to be undone by renewed drinking on discharge.

Legal reporting would be for crimes committed when drunk. Being intoxicated is recorded now by arresting officers. Requiring a license to purchase alcohol would reduce crime.

Alcoholism is horrible for family members. Abuse of partners and children would cause a report to the banned-drinker registry. Police called because of a drunk and violent partner or parent would be the reporters. Not only would families be protected, but police would also be less likely to be exposed to drunken, violent behavior because the first report would result in a loss of the alcohol purchase license, whereas now, police are called to the same homes over and over.

Many nonalcoholic drinkers drive over the legal limit and get convicted of driving while intoxicated (DWI) once. Getting convicted of a second DWI would put you on the banned-drinker list. This sanction would address drivers who know they shouldn't drive while intoxicated but who urgently want to drink because they have alcoholism.

You could give up your license to buy alcohol voluntarily. What a nice question to ask on any addiction service intake—"Would you like to give up your alcohol purchase license? We can help you with the paperwork." Whatever the answer, the discussion will help with treatment. What a nice topic in group therapy. "Have you given up your alcohol purchase license? Why or why not?"

Once one of these offenses was reported, it would trigger a legal proceeding. If not contested, the hearing would be with a counselor. The counselor would review the event in a MI style. Or the person could hire a lawyer and have a hearing before a judge.

The loss of license is not a punishment. It is an opportunity to think about whether you have alcoholism, and if so, what to do about it. It would give the drinker a "time-out."

The alcohol purchase license would not prevent alcoholic drinking any more than loss of a driver's license abolishes dangerous driving. One can drive without a driver's license. If a person with alcoholism was hospitalized for withdrawal seizures, they would not be able to stop at the liquor store for a quart of vodka on the way home—"Because doctors do such a shitty job treating withdrawal."

This was said to me by a patient we would not steadily engage in treatment. He would come back after each detox at the hospital, tell us AA was a worthless place where people complain about their lives, and after a few visits, drop out for a while because he had resumed drinking.

Without a license to purchase alcohol, our patient would have had to stop at home and ask, "Mom, would you buy me a quart of vodka? Those doctors do such a bad job of detox. I am still shaking."

The main value of the alcohol purchase license would be public awareness that recreational drinking is always fun, while alcoholic drinking is a nightmare. Thinking of public health, we would keep it simple: "Is your drinking recreational or alcoholic?" If you drink, you fit into one of those two categories.

CHAPTER 17

Government Distribution of Drugs: SAD Centers

State governments are an ideal incubator for new ideas about how to sell drugs. Stores might all be called "State Addictive Drug Centers" or "SAD Centers." The goal here is to undercut the ubiquitous idealization that goes with drug use. It would be hard to imagine marijuana as the most chill drug or that only the coolest people inject opioids if one had to take the course, engage one's thinking at the motivational interview, and buy one's drug from a counselor at a SAD Center. I have fantasized being the public voice of New York's advertisements.

"Citizens of New York. We would like to control your brain so that we can harvest your money. PLEASE buy New York's private (sic) brand of diacetylmorphine, SuperHeroin. We will even do your detox at our SAD Centers if you can't keep buying SuperHeroin because of all the money you have already given us!"

"Citizens of New York. Please buy our New York State tobacco/cocaine. This natural insecticide will cause gradual cognitive deterioration since it is made by the plant to kill the brains of insects that would eat its leaves. Us making you stupid will ensure that you will keep buying this drug until you lose too much brain function to bring us more money. It's great!"

What a refreshing change from having psychopaths with guns sell bad drugs in neighborhoods where they terrify others and sometimes shoot or rob them. One of our patients went to the drug-infested section of Syracuse with money for drugs. A man got into his car on either side, and they shot him in the chest seven times. He had no idea why. With incredible presence of mind, he drove two blocks to a firehouse and collapsed getting out of his car. His life was saved.

With SAD Centers, this would never happen.

Accidental overdoses occur constantly with criminal drug sales. SAD Centers would supply measured doses of known drugs and clean needles.

One of our problems is that opioid use disorder progresses until addicted persons give their whole life over to buying drugs They give up jobs, family, and housing. This is what leads to experiences such as opening the door to a bathroom at a fast-food restaurant and finding a dead person inside with a needle in their arm. All available money went to the drug dealer. A bathroom to inject in for free had to be found. SAD Centers could offer observed injection facilities for those who had given all their available money to the state. We could use these centers in advertising.

"Citizens of New York. Please come to our SAD Centers. We have some high-donor citizens who have given up everything to supply us with money. For these generous patrons, we offer observed injection sites staffed by nurses trained to save your life if you accidentally overdose. They also watch for all the infections caused by injecting drugs!"

Sales would fall through the floor. The state would not care since the medical, occupational, and social costs of addiction would be balanced by income from drug sales. The bizarre social contract we currently employ is that private enterprise collects the money while the taxpayers/state bears most of the costs of the industry.

Will legal drug dealers agree to turn over their businesses to this kind of state control just because they feel guilty about all the people they have killed? Of course not. Sellers of illicit drugs (who I have spoken to) claim to be "American entrepreneurs." I am sure those who sell tobacco and marijuana legally feel the same. One owner of a chain of convenience stores told me he was eager to sell marijuana but that he would do UDS for employees because he didn't want impaired personnel working for him.

The captains of the legal addictive drug industry have many elected collaborators. They will find a way to combat the resistance to their killing by claiming that their freedom to enslave with mind control drugs is as American as their progenitors, who first enslaved Africans.

PART 5

MASS PSYCHOLOGY

CHAPTER 18

The Awful Reality of Addiction

What have we learned by this long exposition about addictive drugs?

Drug addiction kills more Americans than any other disease. This fact is hidden. If you Google *What disease kills the most Americans?*, the CDC will tell you it is heart disease.

Addiction to tobacco and alcohol kills most of the Americans who die from drugs. These drugs were widely sold in 1789 and have been legal since then—except for the failed experiment of Prohibition. Members of our government, starting with the president and Congress, collaborate in the killing. Without tobacco and alcohol money to win reelection among a complacent, ignorant set of voters, politicians would be vulnerable to losing their jobs.

The persons employed in the tobacco industry knowingly kill. Everyone knows how lethal the drug is. Having killed 100 million people in the twentieth century, they are on course to kill ten times that many people this century.

Tobacco is a key gateway drug. It sensitizes the SEEKING system. Children who start using the drug are eighty times more likely to use illicit drugs. Tobacco is the keystone of addiction.

The ideal drug causes insane craving, cognitive impairment, and continued ability to obtain money—better a leech than a tiger.

A drug cannot be an addictive drug unless it takes over the SEEKING pathway. Drugs take over the will.

Idealization is a ubiquitous defense, turning fear about the danger of the drug into admiration for the drug.

"Denial" is a summary of the psychological defenses employed by all of us to ignore killing with drugs. If mass denial were not used, we would feel an awful reality.

Child abuse is common in our culture. The study showing that 25 percent of Americans meet the criteria for adult antisocial personality helps us understand why this would be. Children who feel trapped in families where they are constantly under attack use drugs to shut off the signal that something is wrong. This is like turning off the fire alarm when one's house is on fire. By starting to use drugs as teenagers, these children put themselves under the bootheel of drug dealers. As the child abuse devolves into a vicious cycle of drug use to shut off feelings, and further abuse, addicted persons are stigmatized and called "drug abusers." They are regarded as subhuman by many people in our culture.

The abusive regard of persons with addiction extends to some physicians. Denial allows physicians who treat addicted patients to focus on the medical complications of the drug without addressing the underlying disease. By not addressing addiction, the physician often repeats parental neglect.

Our approach to opioids is codependent. Persons without addiction feel superior and behave in ways that ensure that addiction persists. Boundaries are blurred—"It is their problem, not ours"—when the reality is that we all suffer because of addiction.

Physicians are instructed that helping patients off opioids is dangerous. Ninety-one percent of persons sober from opioids are drug-free (Meadon R, Zhang-James Y, Aslam S, Johnson B. Recovery from opioid use on a neuropsychoanalytic service. Front Psychiatry. 2024).

Our approach to opioids is further undercut by the insistence of many physicians and treatment services that opioid maintenance, usually accompanied by tobacco addiction, means that you are "sober."

Most patients who go to opioid maintenance programs are actively addicted to multiple drugs. Most have disabling comorbid psychiatric disorders. "Treatment" consists of providing opioids. Usually, comorbid disorders are disregarded.

A therapeutic alliance is not possible when the patient has an incentive to be dishonest so as to procure the drug that they urgently, for both psychological reasons and because of SEEKING pathway drug craving, want to add to other drugs they are using. Opioid maintenance services set up a cops-and-robbers relationship where patients bring in someone else's drug-free urine to submit for the UDS or find other ways to avoid the treatment service, knowing that they are using other drugs. Patients report that one methadone maintenance program in Syracuse has a "urine lady" who sells "clean" urine in the parking lot.

The entire nation has been instructed that "medication-assisted treatment" is the only treatment that has legitimacy. The startling doublethink phrase "client-centered treatment" of opioid use disorder simply means that most horribly and complexly ill persons arrive once a month to get medication.

Academic medicine seems to be overtly dishonest. One negative study after another is proclaimed as a "breakthrough."

Psychological trauma cannot be addressed when opioids render the person unrelated.

One honest review by Kathleen Carroll and Roger Weiss, giants in the addiction treatment field, showed that psychotherapy that requires a therapeutic alliance, "feeling" the psychotherapist, does nothing for patients on buprenorphine maintenance. From the neuropsychoanalytic perspective, this makes perfect sense. Opioids make people unrelated. The foundation of any psychotherapy is the therapeutic alliance. Why the NIH has funded many studies of psychotherapy outcomes that never had a chance to work is a mystery.

Funded research in addiction is ideology-driven. I know that because when we come up with discoveries on SUNY Upstate Addiction Medicine, they are disregarded. Several government grant applications have been rejected, all but one unscored. Our discoveries contradict the current conviction, based on poor evidence, that medication-assisted treatment is the only legitimate treatment for opioid addiction. This, along with our use of psychoanalysis, seems to be the reason we are not funded.

The poor opioid-maintained chronic pain patients! Their treatment occurs in a culture where OIH is not recognized. A survey of pain specialists who use the subjective FPS, published in 2020, found that they estimated OIH to occur in one in ten thousand patients, so rare as to be insignificant.[112] Using the more reliable CPT, valid because it is an empirical test, not an opinion, shows OIH to be a universal response to providing drugs like oxycodone. If doctors called oxycodone a hormone, patients like Toby would be less likely to be put on hormone replacement. Therefore, chronic pain patients and their physicians only know the "a" part of the opponent process. Every opioid pill helps. The "b" part of the opponent process shows up on the CPT. Despite our publications, it is not used in patient care, to my knowledge, outside of Upstate Pain and Addiction Medicine in Syracuse, New York.

Almost no one can tolerate an opioid taper after years of opioid medications. If the patient can tolerate a taper, they may have long-lasting centrally mediated pain from opioid exposure. This means the "pain treatment" has made the pain worse.

Despite our publications, the easy opioid detox with a single dose of buprenorphine, LDN, and nonaddicting medications for minor subsequent withdrawal symptoms is not used. We can detox nearly 100 percent of patients from alcohol and benzodiazepines in a safer, more humane, and cheaper way than what is done on inpatient facilities.

Physicians have created an epidemic of chronic pain without being aware that they have been doing that. No one else knows. For example, the baseline CPT in a large case series of addicted patients was 35 seconds for women and 56 seconds for men, with a normal control time of 113 seconds. Despite our publications, the use of LDN to fix OIH is not practiced. Does OIH go away without LDN?

No one knows.

Physicians approach their patients with a sense of duty and responsibility that is a dysfunctional countertransference. The patient asks, "Doctor, what will you do for my pain?" Instead of recognizing that this question involves a projection of responsibility from the patient, who needs to engage with active treatments, to the physician, the physician accepts the projection and gives pills, creating a vicious cycle of increased hyperalgesic pain and opioid prescribing, sometimes killing their patients.

In our culture, opioid pills are "pain pills." This reflects idealization of an addictive drug. Nonsteroidal anti-inflammatory (NSAID) drugs are slightly better for pain than opioids, carry no addiction risk, and have dramatically fewer side effects. But NSAIDs are not idealized.

Part of the marketing of addictive drugs is the way physicians are recruited into sales. Many of the "right to pain treatment" advocates were paid by opioid manufacturers.

The way we make the most addictive drugs legal, then demonize illicit drugs that cause less harm, makes no sense. If you look back at American deaths from drugs, the illicit ones kill about 1/10 as many Americans as the legal drugs. The mass delusion becomes that these drugs are our enemy. Mass denial protects most drug dealers since they legally sell tobacco, alcohol, stimulants, opioids, benzodiazepines, and in most states, "medical marijuana."

We are watching the use of physicians to help legitimize and market cannabinoids, just as physicians were used to help legitimize and market tobacco and opioids. In many states, doctors grant licenses for "medical marijuana." The most common use is for chronic pain. We have shown that daily marijuana users had significantly shorter CPTs, compared with a control group of patients who inhaled nicotine daily but had no opioid exposure.

While myself and many colleagues cringe in terror at the consequences of marijuana marketing, other physicians are cashing in. This potential $45 billion market is for a drug that increases schizophrenia, creates transient psychosis, vascular changes that result in strokes, and myocardial infarctions in young people, hospital admissions for hyperemesis . . . and who knows what it is doing to the fetuses of women who inhale it while pregnant? Fear of harm is a disincentive to use. Physicians are degrading that barrier.

It is up to us to recognize the horrible and awesome denial that infects our culture. The solutions are in this book. Alcohol buying should require a purchase license. All drugs should be sold cheaply and with as much safety as possible at State Addictive Drug Centers by counselors who make referral to treatment easy. Advertising should say, "Citizens of [state], please buy our addictive drugs! We will take over your brain and extract money from you until you die! You are welcome to buy our cocaine or diacetylmorphine/heroin, but nicotine builds our state income the best because you contribute to state finances for decades before our drug kills you!"

The mass psychology of addiction is that the defenses are used to make most Americans codependent. The realistic view is that selling drugs is a huge economic force. People who get addicted are victims. The realistic approach to this tragedy is to fight the addictive drug industry.

Blaming victims is an attack on vulnerable people. Going back to the discussion of May's alcoholism in the introduction, let's answer the questions:

If you were connected to May and learned of her addiction, what would you think?

Shame on us for not having instituted the alcohol purchase license. If we had that legal sanction, the first question we could ask when May entered treatment could be "Would you like to give up your license? Why or why not?"

What would your first reaction to her alcoholism be?

OMG, what is wrong? May needed to find out what was driving her difficulty with recovery. Alcoholism is a nightmare. May must have been afraid of something that she felt was even worse than dying.

Would you assume she lacked moral fortitude?

Morality has to do with following one's own values. There must have been something in the way for May. May is a professor who works with students and colleagues. She has good morals in general. Something was wrong. It had nothing to do with May's good morals.

Would you think she was weak, had no self-control, or was disgusting?

It takes huge self-discipline to succeed in academia. The drinking had nothing to do with self-control. May is an admirable person.

Would you shame her?

Shame about drinking is an everyday reaction to having been helpless because of living with hostile adults as a child. As uncomfortable as feeling shame is, feeling helpless is more uncomfortable. Shaming anyone would be a hostile behavior on our part. The unconscious thought is *I am better than you.*

Even if you consider yourself evolved enough to understand that alcoholism is a disease and expressed compassion for May, would some of your negative associations with her drinking also be lurking around in your unconscious?

Yes. Alcoholic drinking is hostile. May needed to become conscious about the driver of her self-destructive behavior but eventually apologize to the people she hurt with her drinking.

Our cultural norm is to shame people with addiction issues, to judge them harshly, to believe those who don't have these issues are somehow superior.

We are all in this together. We have been watching people be killed by the addictive drug industry our whole lives. Whether we have addiction or not, once we know this is going on, it is our responsibility to do something about it. Feeling superior is one aspect of codependence. Anyone who feels superior should get a clue: an emotional problem is causing their narcissism.

Let's answer another question that was raised but not answered, the one about why cigarette lung has received the euphemism COPD in medical practice. Why do doctors talk about packs instead of quantity of cigarettes, adding to denial?

This is codependent denial by the medical community, denial that can be reversed. We are constantly modifying our language with concern for stigma, saying, for example, "persons with addiction" rather than drug addicts.

Modifying language would allow doctors to say, "You are inhaling ten cigarettes per day, and it has led to cigarette lung. I am going to put in a prescription for varenicline. Any time you feel the urge for a cigarette, take a pill and go for a walk. You will see that in twenty minutes, the craving is gone. Don't let the bastards who changed your brain when you were a child kill you!"

While stigmatizing the mass killers who sell cigarettes, the physician destigmatized their patient. It is no one's fault that you have an addiction, but it is your responsibility to get help, to do something about having a disease.

If the patient was not able to get off cigarettes by using varenicline, it sets the doctor up to say, "Using cigarettes is about something. You and I don't know what the something is. Let's have you talk to someone who can help you connect this lethal behavior with something."

What about the 890,000 people per year worldwide who are killed by secondhand smoke? Is this secondhand smoke killing done consciously? Does it matter?

This is part of our mass denial that addiction involves hostile behavior. Addiction is a form of compulsion where the hostile intent is not undone, say, by checking and rechecking the knobs on the stove. The hostile intent is displaced into an act that continues the wish to harm.

As a society, we need to acknowledge that addiction contains hostility and advertise that secondhand smoke kills. I have never seen an ad with this warning, and many who die from secondhand smoke were not aware that relatives smoking around them was potentially lethal.

I did not understand why pregnant buprenorphine-maintained

patients convincingly stated that they were off tobacco, with positive UDS tests for cotinine. Listening to "My boyfriend drove me to this appointment and smoked in the truck," or "I live with my grandma, who won't stop smoking in the house," I understood secondhand smoke the way I do now.

If you inhale tobacco, you inhale a lot of carbon monoxide. Once we bought a carbon monoxide meter and found that these women would blow carbon monoxide zero, I really understood that nicotine and tobacco components are inhaled by friends and families of smokers. The nicotine was shared, but of course, carbon monoxide immediately diffuses in the air.

Before you read it here, were you aware that we are likely to see a billion deaths from tobacco in this century worldwide? Does it matter if you are aware of it or not?

This is the clincher. We are watching mass killing. Yes, it is up to us to know about it—and do something about it.

CHAPTER 19

Choosing a Different Path

What is it about Brian Johnson that leads to him saying things that no one else says? One way to understand it is that this is the classic American attitude of individualism. I know what I know, others be damned. I hope that many readers have this same attitude.

I was fortunate from birth. My mother was in another state with my father, who had a near-fatal roadway accident. I was passed around to relatives from ages seven to nine months. I don't think I ever bonded with my parents. This kept me from identifying with them.

I can remember a lot, in part thanks to starting my first psychoanalysis at twenty. I remember nearly drowning before I was a year old. The phone rang. My mother left me alone in the bathtub. I remember how smooth my bottom was as I slid helplessly under the water. Is this real? Constant dreams of drowning suddenly stopped when I recovered this memory.

I remember meeting my father. His injuries included a lost leg and a hypoxic brain injury. He smelled like the hospital. I remember my mother telling me to walk over to him, two feet away, and how I was afraid I would fall down because I had just learned to walk.

I remember watching my parents have sex through the bars of my crib. My first psychoanalyst challenged this, calling it an oedipal fantasy. I called my mother and asked if she used to keep her diaphragm in the second drawer of the rosewood chest next to her bed.

"Yes."

My morbidly obese mother had a psychotic system against me. I was the evil child who ruined her life. She would come up behind me and smack my head. I felt embarrassed that I flinched when she was near. It was involuntary.

My father would go to the Eagle Bar and Grill for hours every afternoon, then drive back home at five miles per hour. I can't believe that he never got arrested for drunk driving. Once home, he would sit in his chair and drink a fifth of Johnnie Walker Red Label scotch. When I got up in the morning, I would find him passed out in front of the TV.

I learned that my sin was doing well at school and separating from my mother, which my younger siblings did not. At first, I had terrifying separation anxiety at school. But my teachers filled in for my parents. I remember Margaret Britain taking wonderful care of me, as both my first and fifth grade teacher.

I did something I have not heard others do. In junior high, I asked in fantasy, "What spaceship dropped me with these people?" By not identifying with my parents, I escaped.

The other teacher I remember most is Barbara Miller, my eleventh grade English teacher. At the end of the first quarter, she asked me why I was in her slow English class. I hadn't known who comprised the students I was with. She said, "I'm going to put you in my enriched class."

At the end of eleventh grade, Ms. Miller read out the names of the kids going into advanced placement English. I went to her after class to ask why I wasn't on the list. She looked at me and said, "I didn't think of you. Of course you should go into advanced placement." It took me a few years of psychoanalysis to realize that the look we shared meant that each of us, me not consciously, realized that all the kids who went into advanced placement came from the rich side of town, that this was an expression of poor kids expected not to do well in school.

The summer I was eighteen, I worked for the "Urban Corps," a summer jobs program where I was one of the few European Americans who qualified based on income. I had the highest income in my family because I also mowed lawns all summer. My family lived on a modest settlement from the bus company, given as compensation for my father's accident.

The morning of my father's death, I left at 7 a.m. to ride my bike an hour to Elmhurst Hospital, where I was a clerk in the blood bank. When I got home at 6 p.m., my mother said, "Your father died." At 11 a.m., my seven-year-old sister had found him dead in his favorite chair in front of the TV.

I said, "Why didn't you call me?"

"I didn't want to bother you at work."

I tried to get my younger brother to go into drug treatment when he was a teenager. He refused. By forty, he was so sick, he threatened he would come up to Boston and cut my throat—which I thought he could do, so I disengaged. My father died at fifty, my brother at sixty-five.

My teachers saved me emotionally, but their help did not pay my tuition. I skipped a year of college expenses by passing advanced placement courses. By junior year, I was living in a roach-infested apartment on the Lower East Side. I could not afford the rent on my own, $44 per month, so I shared the two-room apartment with a friend.

Junior year, I had no money to pay my spring tuition at the Columbia School of Engineering. Feeling hopeless, I temporized by taking a week's job registering other students. I realized that the woman I worked under used a "payment deferred" stamp. At the end of the last day, I offered to carry the "heavy" stamp back to the safe for her, stopped at the bathroom to stamp all my registration cards with payment deferred, and went to class that spring. The day exams ended, I started making a lot of money at an engineering firm that wanted to recruit me after graduation. The "deferred" bill arrived in August, and by working until the day classes began again, I was able to pay the rest of my Columbia tuition.

Senior year, I lived with eighteen students near Columbia. Everyone else went to Columbia College. One night at dinner, someone said, "Let's talk about our shrinks." Fourteen were in psychotherapy. I thought, *Oh, this is interesting.*

I went to Columbia's counseling service until, at the end of the fifth session, the psychologist told me that I was "too sick" to be treated there. He recommended the St. Luke's Hospital psychiatric clinic across the street from Columbia. I could not afford the bottom of the sliding scale.

I learned from my girlfriend, who was in psychoanalysis, that the fee at the New York Psychoanalytic Institute for patients who worked with student analysts who needed training cases started at $1 per session. I paid $1 five days per week for my first four years of psychoanalysis.

When my aunt, Sister Muriel Angela, bought me a year's subscription to *Reader's Digest* for my birthday, I bought her a subscription to the weekly *The Militant* newspaper of the Socialist Workers Party for her birthday and had it delivered to the convent.

Medical school is nearly impossible to get into with a "C" average. However, when I walked into my New York Medical College interview with activist Anthony Clemendor, MD, I immediately said, "You must get a lot of shit being a Black doctor."

He responded, "You're not kidding. When I walk in the front door of Metropolitan Hospital, they treat me like I'm here to rob the place!"

We talked politics for an hour, at the end of which, he said, "You know your grades suck."

I replied, "Yeah, but you've talked to me. You know I can do the work."

I applied to many and got into one medical school.

I had a storied career at New York Medical College as the champion sleeper of the class. I would wake up at 5:30 a.m., drive to psychoanalysis at 6, get back by 9, get some rest during lectures, and work as the organizer of the Young Socialist Alliance at night. The Columbia professor who kicked me out of physical chemistry class for fomenting revolution had probably seen me selling *The Militant* at the Columbia gates.

An interview for medicine residency with Gerald Thomson, MD, of Harlem Hospital, similar to that with Dr. Clemendor, got me in as a medicine resident. Harlem is a Columbia teaching hospital. At the time, it had almost all African American internal medicine residents from Ivy League medical schools. The key to getting along with anyone who has been hurt socially is to use your own experience to identify with them. Once you can do that, everyone's the same. This has been a key to my success.

After my first psychoanalysis, I tried to maintain contact with my mother. I called her every week or two. At one point, she said, "You are the disgrace of the family."

I said, "Oh, what did I do?"

"You didn't go to your aunt's funeral."

I said, "Oh, my aunt died?"

She said, "Yes, and you killed her!"

I said, "How'd I do that?"

"She sent you a birthday card, and it was returned 'addressee unknown.' She got that from you and dropped dead with a heart attack."

During my second psychoanalysis, I decided to ask my mother why she took my drunk father home from the Long Island Jewish Hospital when the doctors wanted him admitted to the ICU for a dangerous cardiac arrhythmia. I asked her why she didn't just leave my drunk, disabled father there. He had no other way to get home. I asked why she drove him home to die. That was the last time she spoke to me.

Her dying wish was that I not be told about her death. My sister told me a month later, saying that except for my sister and her husband, there was only one other person, a neighbor, at the funeral. What killed her? Lung cancer from smoking cigarettes.

We work constantly to help our patients recognize identification or "introjection," the result of pulling away from abusive parents. The result can be envy, based on feeling the same as one's parents, and responding by undermining treatment to try to feel somewhat better despite the conviction that "people like us" are inferior. If you can't identify with your analyst, you can show her or him that they suck, just like you.

My advantage that I did not identify with my parents may have saved me from envy, allowing identification with teachers. No wonder I feel so strongly that teaching is a core value of Upstate Addiction Medicine.

I grew up with a feeling, as many abused and neglected children do, that some people in authority are not worth respecting. If I am attacked for principled leadership, that is an expression of distress that my attackers suffer from—even if they use that power to fire me.

Most people in our society qualify for "inferior" status one way or another. I had a get together with three friends at my house, all men. We laughed at the discrimination we had suffered. One guest was an Indian immigrant physician, one was a gay physician, and one was a Jewish American physician. Almost anyone can find themselves treated as "inferior."

One aspect of success in life is making one's human environment as salubrious as possible. A key decision was to leave Boston for the protection of Mantosh Dewan and other principled members of Upstate Psychiatry. When Dr. Dewan was faced with supporting my substantial salary after I was fired at Crouse Chemical Dependency, it was just a problem to be solved. He and I did not take it as any reflection on me as a person.

At my first demonstration, in 1969, there were two dozen police with sniper rifles on a rooftop overlooking the protesters. The question that their presence invoked in me was this: is it worth risking your life to protest killing? Our government was killing Americans and people in Vietnam at that time. I decided then, *You can shoot me if you want. I'm still going to say what I think when lives are at stake.* But I notice that academic medicine is full of practitioners who keep their mouths shut and their heads down.

From Me to You

I am not the only one who feels an identification with people who have been mistreated and abandoned. I hear from my friends and colleagues that it is most of us. The way to use these feelings is to be aware of them and channel them into actions.

Can one join cultural denial and work without impairment? What about seeing one patient after another for buprenorphine maintenance for a few minutes each month and never recognizing or understanding why the patient started using drugs in the first place? It is a question for each practitioner to ask themselves.

What about issuing transdermal nicotine patches routinely to inpatient rehab patients addicted to inhaling burning tobacco leaves? The patches just help rehab patients stay addicted to nicotine until inhaling the drug again is permitted. Would offering varenicline as an alternative get the doctor in trouble with an administration worried that this might lead to fewer admissions? Would some doctors take a chance and advocate for this, or is it better to go along and get along?

What do we do about the mass killing with drugs? One response is to have a denial system. Americans as a group don't acknowledge tobacco and alcohol as addictive drugs. Diverting attention to the other 3 percent of drug deaths is a mechanism of denial.

Governments blame the victims. For example, South Carolina had a law from 1989-1994 that prosecuted pregnant women for using cocaine sold to them by illegal drug dealers. Tennessee passed a law in 2014 to charge a pregnant woman for assault if there was a pregnancy complication from using opioids illegally. This is despite the fact that nicotine and alcohol cause more fetal damage than any other addictive drugs.[113] The government is taking on the victims of drug dealers. This seems pusillanimous and ignorant.

This book is an attempt to undermine denial so that we can use conscious information to guide behavior—the psychoanalytic way. Where do we start?

Will my addiction treatment colleagues start refusing to allow articles about addiction that are completely misleading to be published? Or will they continue to deceive? The truth about opioid use disorder is that no treatments are satisfactory. We are ignorant about what to do. Will anyone admit that this is true?

What about leaders at the NIH? What if Dr. Volkow publicly said, "There is mass killing with drugs. We need to admit it, and we need to take public health measures to stop it!" Sellers of tobacco and alcohol would call the politicians they support and immediately demand she be fired.

Will the government take some of the common sense suggestions in this book? What about an alcohol purchase license? What about selling addictive drugs in SAD Centers and collecting all the revenue to pay some of the much larger cost of health care for the victims of addiction? In New York, I have been able to ask, "Who gets the revenue from marijuana?" to Governor Cuomo's chief of legalization (in 2018). The choices were

Leave the money with the drug dealers who violate the law.

Change the law so that selling marijuana is legal and leave the money with other drug dealers.

Sell marijuana as a monopoly of the state of New York. Sell it cheap to undercut illicit dealers. Advertise it to make citizens aware of potential harm. Keep all the money to offset the medical costs.

Governor Cuomo's chief of legalization said that he was sympathetic to the third choice. But the universal answer for marijuana in the US has been either the first or the second.

What about nonprofessional readers who are now aware that many of those around you are being killed? Let me make an analogy from psychoanalytic thinking about bullying. If there is a ring of children watching a big bully hurt a smaller child, can one say, "Not my business"?

Our answer is that there is no neutral stance. A passive attitude is siding with the bully. Either you do something, or you are part of the attack. To put it another way, it is our responsibility to help helpless persons in need.

What are you going to do? If the answer is only to talk to nice friends about the ideas in this book, then you are part of the mass killing. The term for people who only talk about social problems is "political hobbyism."

Every person who is aware of mass killing needs to find their own answer as a political action, not only as a thought or an ineffective complaint to a friend. The most common and effective political response for medical professionals is often working through their county, state, or national professional organization.

Being Aware that "Research" in Addiction Is Part of Mass Denial

My experience has also demonstrated something that I have not seen described elsewhere regarding medical science and discoveries in addiction:

We have solved a problem regarding how to integrate brain science into psychiatry. It is the neuropsychoanalysis approach. Neuroscience discoveries are abstracted to models that provide a platform for patient care.

We have invented an ideographic research approach that modifies the psychoanalytic concept that every treatment is research. We have taken a research tool, the CPT, and shown that it is an objective, if not perfect, measure of pain tolerance. By adding neuroscience concepts and nomothetic procedures such as the CPT, we have discovered one novel concept after another.

We have used a biological reality—that endogenous opioids are a hormone that circulates through the blood with diverse receptor sites and systematic observations combined with CPT—to discover that autism, fibromyalgia, and opioid use disorder are all hormonal disorders. We have shown that the CPT can be followed, along with reports from patients, to understand and treat the three opioid hormonal disorders. Treatment uses manipulating opioid tone, the combination of hormone and receptor response, so that too much or too little tone is corrected to optimize CPT/pain/human relatedness. The prevalence of these diseases is large: autism 2 percent, fibromyalgia 3 percent, and opioid use disorder 1 percent of the American population.

We have discovered that after blocking down the high opioid tone of autism, the patient is related and functional but suffers from feelings they had never before experienced. Use of naltrexone is only the first step in treatment. Psychotherapy is needed to help the autistic person tolerate their altered experience.

We have shown, using the CPT, that OIH is a near-universal and expectable outcome of chronic opioid treatment for pain. Exogenous hormone administration causes receptor downregulation. The pain is centrally mediated. It is experienced in the periphery despite being brain-mediated. For example, practitioners give "trigger point injections" for fibromyalgia, as if there were something wrong with muscles. We don't know why the fat pad on the inside of the knee becomes painful as a result of fibromyalgia's centrally mediated pain, but injecting it is a bizarre treatment.

We have used our quadratic equation model that human contact hurts when pregnant women are on buprenorphine maintenance to create a contingency management psychotherapy that successfully gets most pregnant women off all other addictive drugs. We discovered through the case series approach that what has been called "neonatal opioid abstinence syndrome" is probably combined opioid/tobacco withdrawal. By using *DUST*, we were able to eliminate the horrible suffering and cost of neonatal drug withdrawal.

We have created a model of opioid use disorder that gives three reasons for relapse: renewal of PANIC, RAGE, and FEAR that had been ameliorated by exogenous hormone administration, intensification of drug craving by use of nicotine, cannabis, stimulants, or other drugs that share the SEEKING pathway, and long-lasting or permanent downregulation of the receptor system by exogenous hormone administration. We have demonstrated the power/effect size of LDN to correct the receptor problem. PANIC, RAGE, and FEAR may be turned on by comorbid psychiatric disorders or cause psychiatric disorders such as depression, ADHD, and borderline personality.

ADHD is worth mentioning specifically because it was 55 percent of our opioid-addicted patients in a case series versus zero of the pain patients who had an opioid detox in the same case series. Bupropion, desipramine, and atomoxetine make such a huge difference in functioning for the patients. They can finally take in and use treatment. ADHD is identified by the elegant and simple DIVA interview.

We have created a novel treatment delivery model that relies on leadership from neuroscience-oriented psychoanalytic practitioners. These practitioners use transference-focused psychotherapy delivered by students. In nonacademic environments, students could be replaced by CASAC counselors. Formal psychoanalytic training is not needed, although psychoanalytic treatment for the leadership may be helpful.

We have created an explanation for why persons cling to drug use. Psychological addiction has to do with PANIC, RAGE, and FEAR being intolerable. Comorbid psychiatric disorders are the rule, not the exception. Teenagers growing up in settings where PANIC, RAGE, and FEAR are frequently turned on find that they can turn off distressing signals with drugs. This worsens the distress because SEEKING is changed, from constantly responding to drives such as wanting sleep or relationships to urgently wanting drugs.

Addictive drugs take over the will. The person with addiction does not identify that the person(s) who provide the drugs are in control of their brain. The newly addicted teenager assumes that they themselves want drugs. The physical addiction involves conflating wanting and liking. The internal explanation is "I like using drugs." Unpleasant experiences such as inhaling burning leaf smoke are described as "I like smoking cigarettes."

Huge economic forces entrain this phenomenon. The government and the cigarette industry use this misunderstanding of who is in control of addictive behaviors to team up to kill citizens, blaming the victims of addiction for their deaths. The discovery, "Drugs take over the will," helps us ally with victims of the addictive drug industry.

We have used our approach of learning from our patients to perfect outpatient detox. Conventional treatment uses expert guidelines while psychoanalysts consider every treatment an experimental journey of discovery. Outpatient detox keeps patients in their supportive environments, facilitates engagement by loving, supportive others, such as families, and allows psychotherapy to begin the next day. The psychotherapy is intense, at least twice a week, and often more frequent. This makes detox safer, more available, and cheap. If there is relapse, the reason can be taken up in psychotherapy, and the detox can be repeated. Imagine the difference between going to a hospital for an alcohol detox, sweating and shaking alone in a bed, having nurses come by twice a shift to administer inadequate doses of benzodiazepines, and leaving in a fog, versus having medical professionals see you every hour, administer large doses of valproic acid and chlordiazepoxide, and leaving loaded on disulfiram that your loving support person gives you every day for your first year sober!

We have identified a potential cause for autism that also explains the increase in prevalence over the last half century. Baseline opioid tone is set by the pain of childbirth. Modifying pain and opioid tone by opioid administration during childbirth sets the tone too high. Human contact hurts. The infant begins avoiding the pain, initially by gaze avoidance. A simple randomized study using virtual reality for analgesia as the control would be able to test the hypothesis that opioids given during childbirth cause autism. Gaze avoidance is apparent by six months of age.

We have used our observations to create a hierarchy of brain-based motivation:

SEEKING is always turned on and is the most powerful, but it is nonspecific. It is the "goad without a goal." A drug cannot be addictive unless it is capable of changing SEEKING. If the drug changes SEEKING, it now becomes a more important goal than anything else. Drug craving may or may not be conscious, but it is a powerful motivator. At night, the SEEKING pathway produces drug dreams. Once the SEEKING pathway is changed by a drug, the change is irreversible.

Drives require a hormone to lodge in the lateral hypothalamus to turn SEEKING toward a specific goal. The current list of drives is food, water, sex, sleep, and relationships. The list of hormones is ghrelin, angiotensin 2, estradiol/testosterone, adenosine, and oxytocin.

Unpleasure is the experience of having the target of SEEKING not reached. Whether it is not being able to drink alcoholically or not being able to go to sleep, it is unpleasant. If one is attracted to one's partner, and they don't want to have sex, it is unpleasant.

Instincts are a response to the environment: PLAY, CARE, LUST, PANIC, RAGE, and FEAR.

Pleasure has to do with being in proximity to loving, known persons for the right amount of time, according to the goldilocks or inverse U/quadratic equation model. Pleasure is created by other choices. But it is not related to drug addiction.

SEEKING is the strongest and pleasure the weakest motivator of human behavior. This explains why addiction is so intractable. SEEKING, unpleasure, and PANIC, RAGE, FEAR militate toward continued use, no matter how awful. This also helps us understand why the concept of "reward," so commonly used in academic papers on addiction, blames the victim of addiction, as if they choose a drug hedonistically.

None of these discoveries can be investigated/proven/extended without funded research. The reason is that research grant applications are evaluated by ideology. Every discovery on the list would compromise the system.

Testing the neuropsychoanalytic paradigm against CBT would contradict what every addiction practitioner "knows": CBT is the best treatment.

The tone of self-congratulation in publications is beyond belief. Smug declarations that we have yet another "evidence-based" treatment need to be replaced by humble admissions that, once again, our intervention didn't work.

Accepting the CPT would let people see that opioid-induced hyperalgesia is a universal response to COT, disrupting the most lucrative market for opioid sales. People who use opioids four times a day for years buy a lot more pills than someone who uses a few pills for acute pain.

Calling opioids a hormone that makes people autistic, while reality, would disrupt opioid sales. It would undercut MOUD.

Either potentially opposing CBT as the gold standard of psychotherapy or potentially disrupting opioid sales makes many of the innovations we have made: DUST, treating autism, benign detoxes from opioids with LDN used to repair the opioid receptor system, use of the CPT, a disruptive force.

Research on psychoanalytic treatments for detoxed patients with OUD would undercut the shared conviction that detox kills and that MOUD is the only legitimate treatment. It would require the entire field to shift from a supercilious attitude that "We are experts who know what we are doing" to "We are like cancer researchers. Many of our patients die, and if we don't humbly admit that we are up against a disease that is expanding its lethality, more people will die."

Funding studies to show that alcohol, benzodiazepine, and opioid detox do not require inpatient admission would undercut the way many treatment facilities receive funding. Acknowledging that nicotine patches do nothing for tobacco addiction and that tobacco use makes relapse to other drugs far more likely would similarly threaten businesses. The idea that everyone wants to cut the high cost of medical care is not my experience.

Public health solutions would require us to admit that we have been blaming addicted persons for diseases that they are not responsible for having. The major unsolved problems for addiction as a disease are not inside the sick but outside in our culture.

There are very real consequences for individuals who don't submit to the ideology of the field.

CHAPTER 20

Up Against the System That Sells Drugs

Let's define what "the system" is for drug addiction. The government oversees the sale of drugs. The legality of selling tobacco has a huge impact. Most people don't count tobacco as an addictive drug because it is legal. No one learns in school that slavery and racism started on Virginia tobacco farms. No one is warned in school that addictive drugs are used to lessen the emotional impact of childhood abuse and neglect or that addictive drugs change your brain forever. Ignorance is essential to protecting drug sellers' income.

You can look up which elected government officials receive contributions from tobacco companies on Google. But their work for tobacco companies remains invisible to almost all who voted for them. Although ignorance is perpetuated by government agencies, I have never seen any elected official complain that the CDC, the FDA, or NIH mislead and misinform.

If you Google "Most common cause of death in the United States," the answer from the CDC is "heart disease." The correct answer is "drug addiction." The CDC doesn't tell the truth.

The job of the FDA is to be sure that food and drugs are provided in a safe way. The FDA regulates all tobacco products. They seem to be doing "something" to regulate the drug nicotine, but the number of deaths from tobacco has gone up since 1990. The FDA gives cover to an industry that kills with drugs.

NIH agencies the NIDA and the National Institute of Alcohol Abuse and Alcoholism (NIAAA) do research into how to understand

and address drug addiction. Use of the term "reward system" spreads stigma that not only damages addicted persons but also misleads researchers. NIDA and NIAAA funded Dr. Carroll's work on computer-delivered CBT4CBT treatment for $8.5 million over twenty-four grants.[114] If any reader can see that there is no functional effect of CBT4CBT addiction treatment, the reviewers of grant applications and the institute directors Dr. Volkow and Dr. Koob can see that also.

Members of our medical community control the flow of misinformation. Journal editors and reviewers of papers about addiction treatment can see the lack of results that are proclaimed as "breakthroughs." Leaders of addiction treatment organizations like AAAP enforce ignorance while proclaiming interventions such as CBT4CBT during methadone maintenance as "effective." I have given evidence about what happens when someone speaks the truth.

Medicine in general is codependent. Medical practitioners spread addiction by prescribing stimulants, benzodiazepines, and opioids. Physicians are addicting their patients and then blaming them for being addicted. Proprietary drugs are advertised to patients, students, and colleagues by ignoring generic names. Physicians who use reaction formation rather than appreciating that addicted patients are hostile both give too much and avoid.

Physicians buy into behaviors that extend the reach of the addictive drug industry. They use terms that hide danger such as COPD and counting packs of cigarettes. Racism is continued by identifying patients by race, such as "African American," using the "one drop of blood" system that started during slavery to mark people as property.

Profits power the sale of addictive drugs. Money drives the killing, and removing money from drug sales is the weapon that any interested party would use to protect our citizens. There are solutions to take the money out of the industry: the alcohol purchase license and SAD Centers.

EPILOGUE

Recovering from Denial Requires Courage

From Internal Change to Action

Two themes have been that awful aspects of reality are made unconscious and the difference between inside and outside problems. The constant killing of the addictive drug industry is an outside problem. By being a nation in denial, we make it an inside problem.

Psychoanalysts have no power over reality. But none of us can change unless we are conscious of a problem. I hope I have helped you be conscious. My message is to get this problem out of your unconscious and back outside where it can be acted on.

Sigmund Freud died from his use of tobacco. He needed psychological help that he never got. I suspect that, like May before her treatment, he harbored a sense of superiority that allowed him to refuse offers of help. If you are addicted to tobacco, the first thing you can do is to get help with your addiction.

Many of the rest of us are codependent. Feeling superior is a pillar of codependence. Our cultural norm is to shame people with addiction issues, to judge them harshly, to believe those of us who don't have these issues are morally superior. Notice the projection: they have the problem; we do not. Codependence is an illness.

The defense involved in blaming the victims of the addictive drug industry for what has been done to them is identification with the aggressor. Drug dealers are scary, both when they carry guns and when they work with government leaders. Addicted persons are helpless. The mass use of identification with the aggressor means that we take our unconscious fear of drug dealers and, using blame and shame, attack helpless addicted persons.

There are other aspects to our denial. We appreciate the government, the police, for going after dealers of cocaine and methamphetamine and putting them in prison. This is also a displacement of our concern from mass killing with tobacco and alcohol to more minor drugs. Putting people in prison has nothing to do with addressing the problem that 22 percent of Americans die from addiction. Mass incarceration is another problem generated by ignoring what is being done by the addictive drug industry.

"We are addicted to the coffee we drink, to the TV shows we watch." This defense is another displacement, from a real problem that demands action to pleasurable activities that we have no intention of changing.

There are no consequences for us using these defenses. It makes us safer. It is like watching the bully hurt a smaller child. As long as you just watch, you are safe.

The Matrix could be a metaphor for what happens if one gives up cultural denial. When Neo took the red pill, he went from comfortably passive to frighteningly embattled. He became aware of the reality that he and his friends were in danger. The punishments involved in standing up for people who are being killed fill this book. Giving up being codependent requires courage.

I can't tell someone what to do any more than they can tell me that Japanese restaurants are great, and I should try eating seaweed. Each of us is in a unique place in life and has a unique life that we lead. If addiction is all around us, potential actions are all around us too. Your efforts need to be actions, not just thinking, not just talking with friends.

Let's get going.

REFERENCES

1. Kelly JF, Humphreys K, Ferri M. Alcoholics Anonymous and other 12-step programs for alcohol use disorder. Cochrane Database Syst Rev. 2020 Mar 11;3(3):CD012880. doi: 10.1002/14651858.CD012880.pub2. PMID: 32159228; PMCID: PMC7065341.
2. https://www.cdc.gov/alcohol/features/excessive-alcohol-deaths.html
3. War and Drugs: The Role of Military Conflict in the Development of Substance Abuse. Dessa K. Bergen-Cico. New York:Routledge 2012. DOIhttps://doi.org/10.4324/9781315631226
4. Brandt, A. M. (2007). The Cigarette Century: The rise, fall, and deadly persistence of the product that defined America. Basic Books.
5. .Kulikoff A. (1986) Tobacco and Slaves. Chapel Hill:University of North Carolina Press.
6. https://iiwisdom.com/mo-2017/wp-content/uploads/sites/172/2017/04/Altria-Group-Inc.-2016-Annual-Report.pdf
7. Panksepp, J. (2004). Affective neuroscience: The foundations of human and animal emotions. Oxford university press.
8. Johnson B, Brand D, Zimmerman E, Kirsch M. Drive, instinct, reflex-Applications to treatment of anxiety, depressive and addictive disorders. Front Psychol. 2022 Sep 26;13:870415. doi: 10.3389/fpsyg.2022.870415. PMID: 36225690; PMCID: PMC9549915.
9. Johnson, B. Drug dreams: a neuropsychoanalytic hypothesis. Journal of the American Psychoanalytic Association 2001;49:75-96.
10. Stuyt EB. Recovery rates after treatment for alcohol/drug dependence. Tobacco users vs. non-tobacco users. Am J Addict. 1997 Spring;6(2):159-67. PMID: 9134078.
11. LaiS, LaiH, PageJB., McCoyCB. (2000). The association between cigarette smoking and drug abuse in the United States.*Journal of Addictive Diseases* 19:11–24.
12. Johnson B. Addiction and will. *Frontiers in Human Neuroscience* 2013;7:545. Doi 10.3389/fnhum
13. Gentzke AS, Wang TW, Jamal A, et al. Tobacco Product Use Among Middle and High School Students — United States, 2020. MMWR Morb Mortal Wkly Rep 2020;69:1881–1888. DOI: http://dx.doi.org/10.15585/mmwr.mm6950a1

14. MorganD, GrantKA, GageHD, MachRH, KaplanJR, PrioleauO, NaderSH, BechheimerN, EhrenkauferRL, NaderMA. Social dominance in monkeys: dopamine D2 receptors and cocaine self-administration. Nature Neuroscience 2002;5:169-74
15. https://www.caffeineinformer.com/7-good-reasons-to-drink-coffee accessed 2/25/23
16. Johnson, B. A developmental model of addiction, and its relationship to the Twelve Step Program of Alcoholics Anonymous. J.Substance Abuse Treatment 1993;10:23-32.
17. Dodes LM. Compulsion and addiction. J Am Psychoanal Assoc. 1996;44(3):815-35. doi: 10.1177/000306519604400307. PMID: 8892189.
18. Freud, Sigmund. (1909d). Notes upon a case of obsessional neurosis. SE, 10: 151-318.
19. Robert Wälder (1936) The Principle of Multiple Function: Observations on Over-Determination, The Psychoanalytic Quarterly, 5:1, 45-62, DOI: 10.1080/21674086.1936.11925272
20. Erreich A. Unconscious Fantasy and The Priming Phenomenon. J Am Psychoanal Assoc. 2017 Apr;65(2):195-219. doi: 10.1177/0003065117702105. Epub 2017 Mar 21. PMID: 28899121.
21. Fonagy P. A genuinely developmental theory of sexual enjoyment and its implications for psychoanalytic technique. J Am Psychoanal Assoc. 2008 Mar;56(1):11-36. doi: 10.1177/0003065107313025. PMID: 18430700.
22. GoldsteinRB. Et. al. The epidemiology of antisocial behavioral syndromes in adulthood. JClinPsychiatry 78;2017:90-8
23. Poland WS. The analyst's witnessing and otherness. J Am Psychoanal Assoc. 2000 Winter;48(1):16-35; discussion 35-93. doi: 10.1177/00030651000480011301. PMID: 10808473.
24. Johnson, B. The Psychoanalysis of a Man With Heroin Dependence; Implications for Neurobiological Theories of Attachment and Drug Craving. Neuropsychoanalysis 2010;12:207-15.
25. Panksepp J, Bishop P. An autoradiographic map of (3H)diprenorphine binding in rat brain: effects of social interaction. Brain Res Bull. 1981 Oct;7(4):405-10. doi: 10.1016/0361-9230(81)90038-1. PMID: 6271349.
26. Brown N, Panksepp J. Low-dose naltrexone for disease prevention and quality of life. Med Hypotheses. 2009 Mar;72(3):333-7. doi: 10.1016/j.

mehy.2008.06.048. Epub 2008 Nov 28. PMID: 19041189.
27. AnuguV, RinghisenJ, JohnsonB. CASE REPORT: CAUSE AND TREATMENT OF "HIGH OPIOID TONE" AUTISM", Frontiers in Psychology 2021. DOI: 10.3389/fpsyg.2021.657952
28. Steven Strogatz Infinite Powers: How Calculus Reveals the Secrets of the Universe Houghton Mifflin Harcourt, 2019
29. Johnson B. Ulberg S, Shivale S, Donalson J, Milczarsky B, Faraone SV. Fibromyalgia, autism, and opioid addiction as natural and induced disorders of the endogenous opioid hormonal system. Discovery Medicine 2014; 18:209-20.
30. Ramanathan, S., Panksepp, J., Johnson, B. Is fibromyalgia an endocrine/endorphin deficit disorder?—Is low dose naltrexone a new treatment option? Psychosomatics 2012;53:591-4.
31. JacksonD, SinghS, Zhang-JamesY, FaraoneS, JohnsonB. The effects of low dose naltrexone on opioid induced hyperalgesia and fibromyalgia. Frontiers in Psychiatry 2021; doi: 10.3389/psyt.2021.593842
32. The Safety and Efficacy of Low-Dose Naltrexone in Patients with Fibromyalgia: A Systematic Review Juan Yang 1 , Kyung-Min Shin2 , Alex Do JPainRsch 2023
33. Johnson B., Faraone SV. Outpatient detoxification completion and one month outcomes for opioid dependence: A preliminary open label study of a neuropsychoanalytic treatment in pain patients and addicted patients, Neuropsychoanalysis 2013;15:145-60.
34. Yovell Y, Bar G, Mashiah M, Baruch Y, Briskman I, Asherov J, Lotan A, Rigbi A, Panksepp J. Ultra-Low-Dose Buprenorphine as a Time-Limited Treatment for Severe Suicidal Ideation: A Randomized Controlled Trial. Am J Psychiatry. 2016 May 1;173(5):491-8. doi: 10.1176/appi.ajp.2015.15040535
35. Chou R, Fanciullo GJ, Fine PG, Adler JA, Ballantyne JC, Davies P, Donovan MI, Fishbain DA, Foley KM, Fudin J, Gilson AM, Kelter A, Mauskop A, O'Connor PG, Passik SD, Pasternak GW, Portenoy RK, Rich BA, Roberts RG, Todd KH, Miaskowski C; American Pain Society-American Academy of Pain Medicine Opioids Guidelines Panel. Clinical guidelines for the use of chronic opioid therapy in chronic noncancer pain. J Pain. 2009 Feb;10(2):113-30. doi: 10.1016/j.jpain.2008.10.008. PMID: 19187889; PMCID: PMC4043401.
36. https://www.aafp.org/pubs/fpm/issues/1999/0100/p40.html accessed 2/2/23

37. https://www.cdc.gov/mmwr/volumes/65/rr/rr6501e1.htm accessed 2/2/23
38. OaksZ, StageA, MiddletonB, FaraoneS, JohnsonB. Clinical utility of the cold pressor test: evaluation of pain patients, treatment of opioid-induced hyperalgesia and fibromyalgia with low dose naltrexone. Discovery Medicine 2018;26:197-206.
39. Koob GF, Le Moal M. Drug addiction, dysregulation of reward, and allostasis. Neuropsychopharmacology. 2001 Feb;24(2):97-129. doi: 10.1016/S0893-133X(00)00195-0. PMID: 11120394.
40. Vargas-Schaffer G, Paquet S, Neron A, Cogan J. Opioid Induced Hyperalgesia, a Research Phenomenon or a Clinical Reality? Results of a Canadian Survey. J Pers Med. 2020 Apr 21;10(2):27. doi: 10.3390/jpm10020027. PMID: 32326188; PMCID: PMC7354508.
41. NunesEV, ShulmanM. Commentary on Stein et al.: Whither detoxification in the face of the opioid epidemic? Addiction. 2020;115(1):95-96. doi: 10.1111/add.14834
42. Providers Clinical Support System (PCSS) 2021—https://pcssnow.org/resource/detoxification-from-opioids/ accessed 2/2/23
43. Santo T Jr, Clark B, Hickman M, Grebely J, Campbell G, Sordo L, Chen A, Tran LT, Bharat C, Padmanathan P, Cousins G, Dupouy J, Kelty E, Muga R, Nosyk B, Min J, Pavarin R, Farrell M, Degenhardt L. Association of Opioid Agonist Treatment With All-Cause Mortality and Specific Causes of Death Among People With Opioid Dependence: A Systematic Review and Meta-analysis. JAMA Psychiatry. 2021 Sep 1;78(9):979-993. doi: 10.1001/jamapsychiatry.2021.0976.
44. American Society of Addiction Medicine (ASAM) National Practice Guideline 2020 Focused Update accessed 2/2/23
45. Dhanda A, Salsitz EA. The duration dilemma in opioid agonist therapy. J Opioid Manag. 2021 Jul-Aug;17(4):353-358. doi: 10.5055/jom.2021.0668. PMID: 34533830
46. Sivils A, Lyell P, Wang JQ, Chu XP. Suboxone: History, controversy, and open questions. Front Psychiatry. 2022 Oct 28;13:1046648. doi: 10.3389/fpsyt.2022.1046648. PMID: 36386988; PMCID: PMC9664560
47. Pergolizzi JV Jr, Raffa RB, Rosenblatt MH. Opioid withdrawal symptoms, a consequence of chronic opioid use and opioid use disorder: Current understanding and approaches to management. J Clin Pharm Ther. 2020 Oct;45(5):892-903. doi: 10.1111/jcpt.13114. Epub 2020

Jan 27. PMID: 31986228.

48. Agnoli A, Xing G, Tancredi DJ, Magnan E, Jerant A, Fenton JJ. Association of Dose Tapering With Overdose or Mental Health Crisis Among Patients Prescribed Long-term Opioids. JAMA. 2021 Aug 3;326(5):411-419. doi: 10.1001/jama.2021.11013.

49. Barnett PG. Cost effectiveness of methadone maintenance. Addiction. 1999;94.479-88

50. Lynch, F.L., McCarty, D., Mertens, J. et al. Costs of care for persons with opioid dependence in commercial integrated health systems. Addict Sci Clin Pract 9, 16 (2014). https://doi.org/10.1186/1940-0640-9-16

51. Fairley M, Humphreys K, Joyce VR, et al. Cost-effectiveness of Treatments for Opioid Use Disorder. JAMA Psychiatry. 2021;78(7):767–777. doi:10.1001/jamapsychiatry.2021.0247

52. Rosic T, Naji L, Bawor M, Dennis BB, Plater C, Marsh DC, Thabane L, Samaan Z. The impact of comorbid psychiatric disorders on methadone maintenance treatment in opioid use disorder: a prospective cohort study. Neuropsychiatr Dis Treat. 2017 May 24;13:1399-1408. doi: 10.2147/NDT.S129480. PMID: 28579787; PMCID: PMC5449137

53. Van L. King, Robert K. Brooner, Jessica Peirce, Ken Kolodner & Michael Kidorf (2014) Challenges and Outcomes of Parallel Care for Patients With Co-Occurring Psychiatric Disorder in Methadone Maintenance Treatment, Journal of Dual Diagnosis, 10:2, 60-67, DOI: 10.1080/15504263.2014.906132

54. Patient Termination as the Ultimate Failure of Addiction Treatment: Reframing Administrative Discharge as Clinical Abandonment Izaak L. Williams, CSAC University of Hawaii System izaakw@hawaii.edu Edward Bonner, Ph.D. Psychotherapist Private Practice/Independent Scholar beyondnerd@gmail.com Journal of Social Work Values and Ethics, Volume 17, Number 1 (2020)

55. Claudio Colace (2004) Dreaming in Addiction: A Study on the Motivational Bases of Dreaming Processes, Neuropsychoanalysis, 6:2, 165-179, DOI: 10.1080/15294145.2004.10773458

56. Hser YI, Evans E, Huang D, Weiss R, Saxon A, Carroll KM, Woody G, Liu D, Wakim P, Matthews AG, Hatch-Maillette M, Jelstrom E, Wiest K, McLaughlin P, Ling W. Long-term outcomes after randomization to buprenorphine/naloxone versus methadone in a multi-site trial. Addiction. 2016 Apr;111(4):695-705. doi: 10.1111/add.13238. Epub 2016 Jan 13. PMID: 26599131; PMCID: PMC4801718.

57. Hser YI, Huang D, Saxon AJ, Woody G, Moskowitz AL, Matthews AG, Ling W. Distinctive Trajectories of Opioid Use Over an Extended Follow-up of Patients in a Multisite Trial on Buprenorphine+Naloxone and Methadone. J Addict Med. 2017 Jan/Feb;11(1):63-69. doi: 10.1097/ADM.0000000000000274. PMID: 27898496; PMCID: PMC5291756.

58. Rice D, Corace K, Wolfe D, Esmaeilisaraji L, Michaud A, Grima A, Austin B, Douma R, Barbeau P, Butler C, Willows M, Poulin PA, Sproule BA, Porath A, Garber G, Taha S, Garner G, Skidmore B, Moher D, Thavorn K, Hutton B. Evaluating comparative effectiveness of psychosocial interventions adjunctive to opioid agonist therapy for opioid use disorder: A systematic review with network meta-analyses. PLoS One. 2020 Dec 28;15(12):e0244401. doi: 10.1371/journal.pone.0244401. PMID: 33370393; PMCID: PMC7769275.

59. SolmsM. BJPsych Int. 2018;15(1): 5–8.doi: 10.1192/bji.2017.4

60. This paper is out for review.

61. Modell J. G., Katholi C. R., Modell J. D., DePalma R. L. (1997). Comparative sexual side effects of bupropion, fluoxetine, paroxetine and sertraline. Clin. Pharmacol. Therapeut. 61 476–487.

62. Clayton A, Keller A, McGarvey EL. Burden of phase-specific sexual dysfunction with SSRIs. J Affect Disord. 2006 Mar;91(1):27-32. doi: 10.1016/j.jad.2005.12.007. Epub 2006 Jan 20. PMID: 16430968.

63. Angell M. Is academic medicine for sale? N Engl J Med. 2000 May 18;342(20):1516-8. doi: 10.1056/NEJM200005183422009. PMID: 10816191.56

64. . DaviesJ, ReadJ. A systematic review into the incidence, severity, and duration of antidepressant withdrawal effects: Are guidelines evidence-based? Addictive Behaviors. 97;2019.111-21

65. Bill W How We Learned To Recover 1955 St. Louis International Convention of Alcoholics Anonymous in Celebration of AA's 20th Anniversary

66. Bion WR. Experiences in Groups. 1961

67. Johnson B, Mosri D. The Neuropsychoanalytic approach: using neuroscience as the basic science of psychoanalysis. Frontiers in Psychology 2016;7. doi: 10.3389/fpsyg.2016.01459

68. Solms, M., & Turnbull, O. (2002). The Brain and the Inner World: An Introduction to the Neuroscience of Subjective Experience (1st ed.). Routledge. https://doi.org/10.4324/9780429481239

69. https://www.youtube.com/watch?v=SWBUwPoKz5Q
70. Johnson, B. A 'neuropsychoanalytic' treatment of a patient with cocaine dependence. Neuropsychoanalysis 2009;11:151-67.
71. Kernberg OF. New developments in transference focused psychotherapy. Int J Psychoanal. 2016 Apr;97(2):385-407. doi: 10.1111/1745-8315.12289. PMID: 27112823.
72. St. Fleur, D., Johnson, B. "Integrating Psychotherapy and Medication for Addicted Patients" in I. R. de Olivera,, T. Schwartz, S. M. Stahl, eds. Integrating Psychotherapy and Psychopharmacology NY: Routledge Press 2014
73. Johnson, B. A Neuropsychoanalytic approach to addiction. Neuropsychoanalysis 2003;5:29-34.
74. DodesL, DodesZ. The Sober Truth. NY:Beacon Press 2015
75. Paper out for review.
76. WilkersonD. Caste, the origin of our discontents. NY:Random House 2020
77. Johnson, B. Psychoanalytic treatment of psychological addiction to alcohol (alcohol abuse). Frontiers in Psychology 2011;2:article 362
78. Vaillant GE. A 60-year follow-up of alcoholic men. Addiction. 2003 Aug;98(8):1043-51. doi: 10.1046/j.1360-0443.2003.00422.x. PMID: 12873238.
79. Carroll KM, Fenton LR, Ball SA, Nich C, Frankforter TL, Shi J, Rounsaville BJ. Efficacy of disulfiram and cognitive behavior therapy in cocaine-dependent outpatients: a randomized placebo-controlled trial. Arch Gen Psychiatry. 2004 Mar;61(3):264-72. doi: 10.1001/archpsyc.61.3.264. PMID: 14993114; PMCID: PMC3675448.
80. Papakostas GI, Trivedi MH, Alpert JE, Seifert CA, Krishen A, Goodale EP, Tucker VL. Efficacy of bupropion and the selective serotonin reuptake inhibitors in the treatment of anxiety symptoms in major depressive disorder: a meta-analysis of individual patient data from 10 double-blind, randomized clinical trials. J Psychiatr Res. 2008 Jan;42(2):134-40. doi: 10.1016/j.jpsychires.2007.05.012. Epub 2007 Jul 12. PMID: 17631898.
81. Cortese S, Adamo N, Del Giovane C, Mohr-Jensen C, Hayes AJ, Carucci S, Atkinson LZ, Tessari L, Banaschewski T, Coghill D, Hollis C, Simonoff E, Zuddas A, Barbui C, Purgato M, Steinhausen HC, Shokraneh F, Xia J, Cipriani A. Comparative efficacy and tolerability of medications for attention-deficit hyperactivity disorder in children,

adolescents, and adults: a systematic review and network meta-analysis. Lancet Psychiatry. 2018 Sep;5(9):727-738. doi: 10.1016/S2215-0366(18)30269-4. Epub 2018 Aug 7. PMID: 30097390; PMCID: PMC6109107.

82. Garnier LM, Arria AM, Caldeira KM, Vincent KB, O'Grady KE, Wish ED. Sharing and selling of prescription medications in a college student sample. J Clin Psychiatry. 2010 Mar;71(3):262-9. doi: 10.4088/JCP.09m05189ecr. PMID: 20331930; PMCID: PMC2845992.

83. Johnson, B. The mechanism of codependence in the prescription of benzodiazepines to patients with addiction. Psychiatric Annals 1998;28:166-71.

84. Barker MJ, Greenwood KM, Jackson M, Crowe SF. Persistence of cognitive effects after withdrawal from long-term benzodiazepine use: a meta-analysis. Arch Clin Neuropsychol. 2004 Apr;19(3):437-54. doi: 10.1016/S0887-6177(03)00096-9. PMID: 15033227.

85. Johnson, B. The psychoanalysis of a man with active alcoholism. J.Substance Abuse Treatment 1992;9:111-23.

86. Neonatal abstinence syndrome after buprenorphine or methadone exposure, H. Jones et al. N Engl J Med 2010; 363:2320-2331

87. DOI: 10.1056/NEJMoa1005359

88. Devlin LA, Young LW, Kraft WK, Wachman EM, Czynski A, Merhar SL, Winhusen T, Jones HE, Poindexter BB, Wakschlag LS, Salisbury AL, Matthews AG, Davis JM. Neonatal opioid withdrawal syndrome: a review of the science and a look toward the use of buprenorphine for affected infants. J Perinatol. 2022 Mar;42(3):300-306. doi: 10.1038/s41372-021-01206-3. Epub 2021 Sep 23. PMID: 34556799; PMCID: PMC8459143.

89. Carroll KM, Weiss RD. The Role of Behavioral Interventions in Buprenorphine Maintenance Treatment: A Review. Am J Psychiatry. 2017 Aug 1;174(8):738-747. doi: 10.1176/appi.ajp.2016.16070792. Epub 2016 Dec 16. PMID: 27978771; PMCID: PMC5474206.

90. Tabi S, Heitner SA, Shivale S, Minchenberg S, Faraone SV, Johnson B. Opioid Addiction/Pregnancy and Neonatal Abstinence Syndrome (NAS): A Preliminary Open-Label Study of Buprenorphine Maintenance and Drug Use Targeted Psychotherapy (DUST) on Cessation of Addictive Drug Use. Front Psychiatry. 2020 Sep 23;11:563409. doi: 10.3389/fpsyt.2020.563409. PMID: 33173512; PMCID: PMC7538830.

91. Siembida J, Johnson B. Depression in Fibromyalgia Patients May

	Require Low-Dose Naltrexone to Respond: A Case Report. Cureus. 2022 Feb 28;14(2):e22677. doi: 10.7759/cureus.22677. PMID: 35386139; PMCID: PMC8967077.
92.	Volkow ND, McLellan AT. Opioid Abuse in Chronic Pain--Misconceptions and Mitigation Strategies. N Engl J Med. 2016 Mar 31;374(13):1253-63. doi: 10.1056/NEJMra1507771. PMID: 27028915.
93.	Belkin M, Reinheimer S, Levy J, Johnson B. Ameliorative response to detoxification, psychotherapy, and medical management in patients maintained on opioids for pain. *American Journal on Addictions*. 2017 Aug 11. doi: 10.1111/ajad.12605
94.	Campbell G, Hall WD, Peacock A, Lintzeris N, Bruno R, Larance B, Nielsen S, Cohen M, Chan G, Mattick RP, Blyth F, Shanahan M, Dobbins T, Farrell M, Degenhardt L. Effect of cannabis use in people with chronic non-cancer pain prescribed opioids: findings from a 4-year prospective cohort study. Lancet Public Health. 2018 Jul;3(7):e341-e350. doi: 10.1016/S2468-2667(18)30110-5. PMID: 29976328; PMCID: PMC6684473.
95.	Olfson M, Wall MM, Liu SM, Blanco C. Cannabis Use and Risk of Prescription Opioid Use Disorder in the United States. Am J Psychiatry. 2018 Jan 1;175(1):47-53. doi: 10.1176/appi.ajp.2017.17040413. Epub 2017 Sep 26. PMID: 28946762; PMCID: PMC5756122.
96.	AntonSD, HidaA, HeekinK, SowalskyK, KarabetianC, MuctchieH, LeeuwenburghtC, ManiniTM, FarnettTE. Effects of popular diets without specific calorie targets on weight loss outcomes: systematic review of findings from clinical trials. Nutrients 2017;9: doi: 10.3390/nu9080822
97.	https://www.robertsapolskyrocks.com/advanced-neurology-and-endocrinology.html Accessed 2/23/23
98.	CardinalM. The words to say it. Cambridge, Ma:VanVactor and Goodheart 1984
99.	Toegel F, Holtyn AF, Subramaniam S, Silverman K. Effects of time-based administration of abstinence reinforcement targeting opiate and cocaine use. J Appl Behav Anal. 2020 Jul;53(3):1726-1741. doi: 10.1002/jaba.702. Epub 2020 Apr 6. PMID: 32249414; PMCID: PMC7387179.
100.	Anton RF, O'Malley SS, Ciraulo DA, et al. Combined Pharmacotherapies and Behavioral Interventions for Alcohol Dependence: The COMBINE

Study: A Randomized Controlled Trial. JAMA. 2006;295(17):2003–2017. doi:10.1001/jama.295.17.2003

101. Carroll KM, Kiluk BD, Nich C, Gordon MA, Portnoy GA, Marino DR, Ball SA. Computer-assisted delivery of cognitive-behavioral therapy: efficacy and durability of CBT4CBT among cocaine-dependent individuals maintained on methadone. Am J Psychiatry. 2014 Apr;171(4):436-44. doi: 10.1176/appi.ajp.2013.13070987. PMID: 24577287; PMCID: PMC4042674.

102. Freedman R. Computerization of the therapeutic task of working through. Am J Psychiatry. 2014 Apr;171(4):388-90. doi: 10.1176/appi.ajp.2014.14020168. PMID: 24687192.

103. Kiluk BD, Nich C, Buck MB, Devore KA, Frankforter TL, LaPaglia DM, Muvvala SB, Carroll KM. Randomized Clinical Trial of Computerized and Clinician-Delivered CBT in Comparison With Standard Outpatient Treatment for Substance Use Disorders: Primary Within-Treatment and Follow-Up Outcomes. Am J Psychiatry. 2018 Sep 1;175(9):853-863. doi: 10.1176/appi.ajp.2018.17090978. Epub 2018 May 24. PMID: 29792052; PMCID: PMC6120780.

104. Kowalczyk WJ, Phillips KA, Jobes ML, Kennedy AP, Ghitza UE, Agage DA, Schmittner JP, Epstein DH, Preston KL. Clonidine Maintenance Prolongs Opioid Abstinence and Decouples Stress From Craving in Daily Life: A Randomized Controlled Trial With Ecological Momentary Assessment. Am J Psychiatry. 2015 Aug 1;172(8):760-7. doi: 10.1176/appi.ajp.2014.14081014. Epub 2015 Mar 17. PMID: 25783757; PMCID: PMC6233893

105. deWit H. A New Role for Clonidine in Addictions: Catching Relapses Before They Happen. Am J Psychiatry. 2015 Aug 1;172(8):700-1. doi: 10.1176/appi.ajp.2015.15040426. PMID: 26234590

106. Erling Segest, Ole Mygind & Hans Bay (1990) The Influence of Prolonged Stable Methadone Maintenance Treatment on Mortality and Employment: An 8-Year Follow-up, International Journal of the Addictions, 25:1, 53-63, DOI: 10.3109/10826089009056200

107. Johnson B. Engineering Neurobiological Systems: Addiction. Psychiatr Clin North Am. 2018 Jun;41(2):331-339. doi: 10.1016/j.psc.2018.01.011. PMID: 29739530.

108. McGinnis JM, Foege WH. Actual causes of death in the United States. JAMA. 1993 Nov 10;270(18):2207-12. PMID: 8411605.

109. accessed 2/5/23 https://en.wikipedia.org/wiki/United_States_drug_

overdose_death_rates_and_totals_over_time
110. https://www.cdc.gov/nchs/pressroom/nchs_press_releases/2022/202205.htm accessed 2/5/23
111. Merrell E., Johnson B. (2022) Using New Technology and Concepts on the Oldest Addiction on Earth, Alcoholism. In: Patel V.B., Preedy V.R. (eds) Handbook of Substance Misuse and Addictions. Springer, Cham. https://doi.org/10.1007/978-3-030-67928-6_57-1
112. https://www.cdc.gov/alcohol/onlinemedia/infographics/cost-excessive-alcohol-use.html
113. Vargas-Schaffer G, Paquet S, Neron A, Cogan J. Opioid Induced Hyperalgesia, a Research Phenomenon or a Clinical Reality? Results of a Canadian Survey. J Pers Med. 2020 Apr 21;10(2):27. doi: 10.3390/jpm10020027. PMID: 32326188; PMCID: PMC7354508.
114. Ross EJ, Graham DL, Money KM, Stanwood GD. Developmental consequences of fetal exposure to drugs: what we know and what we still must learn. Neuropsychopharmacology. 2015 Jan;40(1):61-87. doi: 10.1038/npp.2014.147. Epub 2014 Jun 18. PMID: 24938210; PMCID: PMC4262892.
115. rePORT of NIH

NOTES FOR CHAPTER 13:

1. Conventional treatment would be opioid maintenance for life.
2. Childhood trauma had to be addressed.
3. First article ever suggesting fibromyalgia is an autoimmune disease that strikes the mu opioid receptor.
4. National Institute of Drug Abuse (NIDA) sponsored opioid detox trial comparison: 14 percent, 4 percent, 0 completion of opioid detox. These NIDA studies are what led to the "wisdom" that the only viable treatment for opioid use disorder is maintenance on opioids or eternal blockade of the opioid receptors with high-dose naltrexone.